Muslim American Women on Campus

SHABANA MIR

Muslim American Women on Campus

Undergraduate Social Life and Identity

THE UNIVERSITY OF NORTH CAROLINA PRESS *Chapel Hill*

This volume was published with the assistance of the Greensboro Women's Fund of the University of North Carolina Press.

FOUNDING CONTRIBUTORS Linda Arnold Carlisle, Sally Schindel Cone, Anne Faircloth, Bonnie McElveen Hunter, Linda Bullard Jennings, Janice J. Kerley (in honor of Margaret Supplee Smith), Nancy Rouzer May, and Betty Hughes Nichols.

The paper in this book meets the guidelines for permanence and durability of the Committee on Production Guidelines for Book Longevity of the Council on Library Resources. The University of North Carolina Press has been a member of the Green Press Initiative since 2003.

Library of Congress Cataloging-in-Publication Data

Mir, Shabana.
Muslim American women on campus : undergraduate social life and identity / Shabana Mir.
pages cm
Includes bibliographical references and index.
ISBN 978-1-4696-1078-8 (cloth: alk. paper)
ISBN 978-1-4696-2996-4 (pbk.: alk. paper)
1. Muslim women—United States—Social life and customs. 2. Women college students—United States—Conduct of life. 3. Women college students—United States—Social life and customs. 4. Muslim women—Conduct of life. 5. Muslims—United States—Ethnic identity. I. Title.
HQ1170.M567 2014
305.6'97—dc23
2013025581

A portion of the text was previously published, in different form, as "'Where You Stand on Dating Defines You': American Muslim Women Students and Cross-gender Interaction on Campus," *American Journal of Islamic Social Sciences* 24 (3): 69–91. Used with permission of the journal.

Finally there are the tribal stigma of race, nation, and religion. . . . In all of these various instances of stigma, . . . the same sociological features are found: an individual who might have been received easily in ordinary social intercourse possesses a trait that can obtrude itself upon attention and turn those of us whom he meets away from him, breaking the claim that his other attributes have on us. He possesses a stigma, an undesired differentness from what we had anticipated. We and those who do not depart negatively from the particular expectations at issue I shall call the *normals*.

—Erving Goffman, *Stigma: Notes on the Management of Spoiled Identity*

Imperialism consolidated the mixture of cultures and identities on a global scale. But its worst and most paradoxical gift was to allow people to believe that they were only, mainly, exclusively, white, or Black, or Western, or Oriental.

—Edward Said, *Culture and Imperialism*

Contents

Acknowledgments ix

1 Introduction 1

2 Muslim American Women in Campus Culture 30

3 I Didn't Want to Have That Outcast Belief about Alcohol
Walking the Tightrope of Alcohol in Campus Culture 47

4 You Can't Really Look Normal and Dress Modestly
Muslim Women and Their Clothes on Campus 87

5 Let Them Be Normal and Date
*Muslim American Undergraduate Women
in Sexualized Campus Culture* 126

6 Conclusion 173

Glossary 185
Appendix The Research Participants 187
References 189
Index 201

Acknowledgments

I take this opportunity to thank my research participants who made this book possible and who have given me some of my fondest memories. These young people spent precious time in their busy schedules answering my tiresome questions, and they generously included me in their social lives. I made many genuine friends during my fieldwork and am honored to be part of their lives. I only regret that I cannot name them in this book. Chief among these aforementioned are my primary research participants at Georgetown and George Washington Universities, whose voices are incorporated into my narrative. I could not have completed the task without other members of the campus communities, men and women who volunteered their considerable networking abilities and their assistance to enable my data collection. I extend my gratitude also to the students I interviewed during follow-up fieldwork, especially in 2009 and 2010, and to others who shared their thoughts on the issues since I never left off plaguing those around me with my questions.

For their affectionate and patient support and their intellectual mentorship, I am grateful to Prof. Bradley A. Levinson, Prof. Robert F. Arnove, and Dr. Jasmin Zine. I subjected you to endless angst-ridden outpourings about my data and theoretical frameworks, yet you were always for me as my dear friends.

I thank my professional colleagues and friends in anthropology, education, and religious studies for their searching questions that enriched my work. An incomplete list would include Emily Regan Wills, Omid Safi, Doug Foley, Sally Campbell Galman, Wesley Shumar, Carol Brandt, Teresa McCarty, Carol Greenhouse, Heidi Ross, Prof. Peter Mandaville, Prof. Marcia Hermansen, Prof. Zafar Ishaq Ansari, Prof. Mumtaz Ahmad, Prof. Farid Esack, and Lesley Bartlett.

I thank Elaine Maisner, my editor at the University of North Carolina Press, and her colleagues Caitlin Bell-Butterfield, Paul Betz, Ellen

Bush, Regina Mahalek, and Dino Batista whose excellent work has been invaluable to the success of this book.

I thank the administrators, faculty, and staff at Georgetown and George Washington Universities for granting me access and college IDs. Special appreciation goes to Prof. John Voll, Dr. Hibba Abugideri, Prof. John Esposito, Prof. Amira Sonbol, Imam Yahya Hendi, and Prof. Yvonne Haddad. I offer deep gratitude to the Center for Muslim-Christian Understanding (CMCU) at Georgetown University for appointing me Visiting Researcher there during my fieldwork. I also thank members of the institutional review boards at Indiana University and Oklahoma State University.

For their support in enabling me to conduct and present my work at various venues, I thank the Council on Anthropology and Education, the American Anthropological Association, the Comparative and International Education Society, the International Institute of Islamic Thought (IIIT), the Aga Khan University in London, the Association of Muslim Social Scientists, and Michigan State University's Muslim Studies program. I offer my deep gratitude to Layla Sein at the IIIT for her loving and loyal support.

Those who supported and helped me in a multitude of ways as I successfully battled breast cancer and worked on this book are far too many to name, but they are in my heart always. Karen Altendorf, Tonia Sharlach, Jonathan Nash, Raquel Payne, Laura Emerson, Suzii Parsons, Denni Blum, Holly Hartman, the staff at the Presbyterian Preschool of Stillwater, and many others—gratitude is an insignificant word for my feelings for you.

For their love and support in both good times and bad, I thank my friends Jasmin Zine, Ayesha Ahmad and Usman Sarwar, Robert Lawrence, Anas Malik, Hassan and Rabiah Ahmad, Najeeba Syeed-Miller and Jonathan Miller, Junaid S. Ahmad, Abeer Tebawi, Nidal Tebawi, Hina Azam, Safoi Babana-Hampton and Mark Hampton, Maliha Chishti, Nuha Elkhiamy, Michael Thomas, Shahed Amanullah, Ayesha Tuabin, Sevim and Aydan Kalyoncu, Rasheda Amin, Itrath Syed, Uzma and Bushra Rehman, Kamran and Silvy Mir, Uncle Wahaj, Shams and Yunus Wesley, Shafiqa Ahmadi, and many, many more people who are inscribed on my heart forever. To my beloved Sufi sisters and brothers—Auntie Tehzeeb, Nazlee Ahmed, Sophia Chaudhry, and many others—I love you.

For their sacrifice and boundless love, I thank my parents, Zarina and Dr. Saleem Mir, in words that are inadequate to the task. I thank my brother Dr. Imran Mir, my sister Imrana Mir, my sister-in-law Dr. Tayyba Imran, and my nephews and nieces, Umar, Asaad, Zahra, Taha, and Izza, my cousins, my aunts and uncles. What a blessing to have a loving family.

Through all my self-doubt and my struggles, he of the unwavering faith my husband, Svend White, has not only supported and encouraged me but has found my work endlessly fascinating. I owe him for hours and hours of parenting while I was holed away working on my manuscript. To him I say: ready for the next book, honey?

Last and *definitely* not least, for her loving hugs, her watchful impatience, and her demands that I turn my laptop *off*, I thank my daughter Raihana. And I thank her for her reminders that the most important things are not theory and analysis, but hugs and bedtime cuddles.

Muslim American Women on Campus

1

Introduction

INTISAR: [People say,] "How do you handle the
differences [as a Muslim woman]?" Yeah, it's not an agenda,
you know: every day in the morning you wake up and say, OK,
now I'm *going* to pray and I'm *going* to go play basketball! It's
contradictory, but it's just life, we just go through it. We don't
have a journal; we don't have a schedule every day.

Intisar: Muslim Women in the Spotlight

I met Intisar at one of the informal Muslim gatherings on the fourth
floor of the student union at the George Washington University
campus. Affectionate and dryly witty, Intisar quickly became a good
friend despite the fourteen-year age difference between us. She had
a ready reserve of self-deprecating immigrant jokes, as did I, but
we had arrived in this country under very different circumstances.
I traveled from Pakistan to the United States in the early 1990s as a
cash-strapped doctoral student. Intisar, along with her large family
headed by a widowed mother, had fled war-torn Somalia as a young
child.

When she was in elementary school in the United States, Intisar
was acutely aware of the multilayered stigma attached to her as a
poor black African refugee and Somali Muslim. But there was one
thing she enjoyed at school: she loved basketball—and she played
well. This gave her immediate entry into the mainly African American basketball youth culture at school. Suddenly, the poor Somali
refugee was a cool kid. She successfully performed being an "integrated" American youth—except that she was acutely *aware* of her
performance.

Intisar's life changed as she approached puberty. Like the Sikh mother in *Bend It Like Beckham*, Intisar's mother disapproved of girls playing contact sports. It exposed sexual attributes to the public eye, and Intisar was, as she said meaningfully, "a *big* girl." Intisar and her mother maintained an uneasy compromise for a while. Intisar started wearing *hijab* and continued to play basketball. This was not easy. From her hijab and her physiognomy, non-Muslim peers at first deduced that she could not play basketball, rolling their eyes as they passed her over during team selection. Then they gawked when she played: She played basketball so well! They hadn't seen that coming! How could a Muslim woman combine hijab and sports?

As for her Muslim girlfriends, some privately gossiped about how immodest it was to play a fast-paced contact sport like basketball—with *boys!*—while others admired her for being a "cool *hijabi*" (see glossary). The woman who blocked and dribbled the ball also labored to shatter stereotypes about weak, timid, secluded, and immobile Muslim women. Intisar wilted under Muslim *and* non-Muslim peers' scrutiny and "amazement," and wearied of shattering the mold set for Muslim women by both groups.

Eventually, Intisar's mother lost patience and forbade basketball altogether. Long afterwards Intisar continued to play in secret from her family. While other teenagers hid condoms and pot from their parents, Intisar guarded *her* big secret—sports. Her doubts grew and she questioned herself. Was she absolutely *sure* it was Islamically permissible to play a contact sport with boys? If it was not, she could be serving as a bad example to other Muslims, legitimating a religiously problematic act and destabilizing the besieged community, during the War on Terror no less. The intensity of surveillance on and by Muslims, especially of Muslim female bodies, magnified the implications of Intisar's athletic activity. Intisar stopped playing basketball. She missed it. Sometimes, she shot hoops when she was by herself.

This book unpacks the ways that people like Intisar are not free to *be*. Intisar wanted to play basketball and to be a religious Muslim woman. The questions poured in from all directions: Surely Muslim femaleness and basketball were opposed to each other. Surely the very *American* qualities we see in the sportswoman—mobility, flexibility, and freedom—are not qualities the immigrant and Muslim woman can or should share. Intisar's experience shows us that, though identity options on U.S. campuses are becoming almost cliché in their multiplicity and people identify with diverse, multiple, and changing identity backgrounds, these options are not freely available to all. Nor are these "options" chosen lightly: for Muslims, whose backgrounds and lifestyles span a dizzying range, identity choices can be explosive. For minoritized people in a racist social order, these are not really choices at all (Waters 1990).

This book is an ethnographic study of Muslim American undergraduate women on U.S. college campuses. Most of the women in my research study were members of what is commonly called the first generation of Muslim Americans raised in the United States after the 1964 immigration laws were liberalized. Muslim Americans are, overall, highly educated, with 40 percent holding a college degree or higher, compared to 29 percent among the general American public (Gallup 2009: 22). In this book, I investigate the relationship between the reality of religious pluralism as it occurs on college campuses and the processes by which undergraduate women construct their identities during one of the most formative times in their lives. Contextualizing my study in religious and ethnic minority experiences generally, I find that while the women experience double scrutiny—from their own communities and from the dominant ones—they find and create spaces within both communities to grow and assert themselves as individuals. They encounter numerous conflicting expectations, and the process of becoming individuals for them is a tangled story of resistance, triumph, compromise, and surrender.

What This Book Does

This book is based on a research study of Muslim American women undergraduates at Georgetown and George Washington Universities in Washington, D.C. In it, I examine the following:

» Muslim American women's struggles on university campuses to pursue religious authenticity while being "normal" Americans/women/youth;
» majority Americans' Orientalist stereotyping of Muslims;
» how Orientalist images constitute a pervasive presence in Muslim American women's own identity constructions;

» campus social and leisure culture via a new window, the perspective of marginal students, demonstrating specifically how campus culture marginalizes some Muslim undergraduates;

» the flawed pluralism in America and American campus culture.

My work is interdisciplinary, but grounded in the discipline of anthropology. Anthropological studies of immigrants within first world contexts explore a variety of minority identity strategies, such as assimilation into majority behavior patterns, selective "accommodation" of such majority norms as are perceived as positive or beneficial by minority persons, and rejection of majority practices (Gibson 1998). I examine all these types of cultural strategies among Muslim American women. This study, situated in the field of critical ethnography, uses the case of Muslim American women as a vehicle by which to examine the cultural strategies of minority and religious undergraduates.

My most important finding is that Muslim women have multidimensional identities—with religious, ethnic, racial, and gendered aspects—that fly in the face of the identities expected of them both by many within Muslim communities (such as fellow Muslim students and families) and by those outside their communities (non-Muslim peers, college administrators, etc.). Second, in exploring how they manage to "become themselves" within and against this context, I find that Muslim women undergraduates face a great deal of scrutiny and pressure during years crucial to the construction of self-identity. Third, as we see how liberal pluralism in U.S. higher education both falters and succeeds, my book contributes to understanding how dominant discourses are inscribed on marginalized people. In doing so, I also celebrate the agency and strategies of the marginalized.

American Muslim Women

AMBER: [I wish faculty and peers understood] the basics about what we believe, and to separate culture from the religion, that American Muslims are a lot different from Muslims [elsewhere]. . . . But that being American isn't contrary. . . . Because I think a lot of people think Islam is such a monolith; that every Muslim's like every single other person, and it's not really like that. I mean, I guess ideally it would be like that to some people. But it's not like that. . . . Nowadays, typical stereotypes. Threatening, the whole clash of civilizations thing, especially with what's going on.

I still wince at the memory of the above conversation I had with Amber, a Pakistani American senior and an officer in the Muslim campus organization. Beneath a taciturn surface, as she battled her way through words, I sensed that anxious tears threatened to silence Amber just a heartbeat away. This was a common occurrence in my research interviews. I struggled to record and convey the "imperial feeling" of post-9/11 America (Maira 2009: 24) as I encountered it in my youthful research participants' stress, fear, and inner struggles, but as I did so, I was often faced with a wry, set, unhappy smile and diffident, fragmentary remarks. I struggled to draw Amber out, but with every utterance, she seemed to shut down in despondent fatigue. Still, while Amber despaired of campus community members' inability to see *particular* Muslim Americans, instead of the undifferentiated monolithic world of Islam, she also hinted at the *Muslim* imagined homogeneous community ("I guess ideally it would be like that to some people") of good, devout Muslims united on religious doctrine and practice.

Amber and I both reject monolithic notions of Muslim identity. Yet I am also interested in the social processes that make some identities hypervisible while others become invisible. Among Muslim American women's various legacies, which ones "crowd out" others? Why do we even speak of "Muslim American women" when we do not usually speak of, say, "white American Christian women?" While I recognize the religious affiliation of Muslim American women, I also wish to subvert the notion that this descriptor is enough, or even that it conveys *anything* beyond the kaleidoscopic term "Muslim" itself. Although "Muslim women" implies a primarily religious identity—and I certainly focus on their religious identities to the extent that my research subjects did—these Muslim women are also *women*, and the construction of gendered selves is extremely significant to this book, to their religiosity—however they construct it—and to their ethnic-cultural identities.

And then they are *Americans*. How brash and radical it seems to make that claim about Muslim women! How sensational it still is for many Americans to see a brown-skinned woman in a silk headscarf and blue jeans open her mouth and speak "perfect" American

English. Why are Muslims and especially Muslim women so palpably *foreign*, so deeply other? I suggest that a significant portion of the explanation lies in the peculiar relationship between Islam and the West, in the Orientalist lenses many (Muslims and non-Muslims) wear to examine Islam and Muslims. This book wrestles with that troubled Islam-West relationship, but unlike other scholarship, not as it is manifested in "big" cultural spaces of national policy, military action, and popular cultural products. I investigate that Islam-West relationship as it is situated in the "small" moments of Muslim women's campus experiences. My research participants are also racially and ethnically defined, but all, even indigenous white and black Americans, become racialized, de-Americanized, and "religionized" by their association with Islam.

The many varied Muslim women in the pages of this book may furnish some readers with an unsettling confusion about which one is a *typical* Muslim woman—because none of them is. Neither Intisar (devout hijabi *and* part-time sportswoman) nor Yasmin (avid clubber *and* introspective interrogator of religious absolutes) was a "norm" for all Muslim American female undergraduates. The super-identity of Islam often drowned their voices and overpowered their narratives, yet these women's identities shattered the theologocentrism (Rodinson 2006: 104) that equates all *Muslims* with *Islam*. These women's identities remind us that they are young, female, American, ethnically distinct (for the most part), and in college, all at the same time, and that they, in a variety of ways, create third spaces of identity. These women are sometimes emphatically different and sometimes indistinguishable from their majority American peers, as they do what Intisar called "just life" and they "just go through it"—all of it.

The Research Moment

From 1996 to the present day (2013), I have keenly observed Muslim American youth and gender identities. I collected data at my research sites, George Washington University and Georgetown University, between August 2002 and May 2003. I continued to follow up with my participants long after that date. In 2009, I interviewed Muslim undergraduates at the University of Texas at Austin for the triangulation of findings. In 2010, I visited Georgetown and George Washington Universities, logged observation time, and collected fresh interview data on Muslim American students' identity construction. This updated data, while not the primary focus of this book, corroborates the conclusions of my earlier fieldwork, albeit in a climate somewhat less charged than that of a year after the events of September 11, 2001. My findings throughout this decade confirm my conviction that racist Orientalist stereotyping and the consequently "spoiled" Muslim American identities are an enduring feature of American culture and higher education, not primarily a consequence of the September 2001 attacks.

It was painfully awkward to be a researcher examining my Muslim community in the post-9/11 climate. Muslim Americans experienced the War on Terror directly, through intelligence agencies, law enforcement, physical and psychological attacks, and indirectly, through military campaigns replete with human rights violations of Muslim populations abroad (Maira 2009). Hundreds were secretly arrested, incarcerated, and held without the presumption of innocence in the investigation. Muslims in the United States often had little recourse to fundamental legal rights. Political authorities, law enforcement, and security agencies have targeted Muslim Americans on a large scale since 9/11, and civil rights cases of harassment, violence, and discrimination, as well as incidents of anti-Muslim hate crimes have increased since 2001 (CAIR 2005). Anti-Muslim hate crimes shot up by 1600 percent in 2001, with a 10 percent increase between 2005 and 2006 (Read 2008: 40).

I have often agonized over the nature of my research in the political climate after September 11, 2001, and the War on Terror. Many have observed that my topic was timely, even professionally expedient, but scrutinizing fellow Muslims in the post-9/11 atmosphere was unspeakably uncomfortable, both ethically and emotionally. I did not wish to become an unwitting pawn for the use of Islamophobic pundits trawling my articles for evidence of Muslim sexism and extremism (this fear was not unfounded; see Dowd-Galley 2004). An ethnographer can try to present a community "as it is," warts and all. But over a decade after 9/11, the Muslim community is not allowed the luxury of warts. I feared that my data collection could endanger vulnerable youth and terrified immigrant families, who witnessed the fruit of their labors rot and stink before them.

And Muslim women were in the spotlight again. Hijab (the Muslim headscarf) being the second-highest "trigger" of discrimination

(CAIR 2005, Ghumman and Jackson 2010), hijabis were the first to be recognized as Muslim and treated accordingly. Muslim women have historically been objects of both pity and fear because they are associated with Islam and because are hyperfeminized as victims of the stereotypically brutal Muslim man. More likely than men to be recognized as Muslim because of their distinctive clothing, but less likely to be deported than their male counterparts, Muslim women were at the forefront of efforts to represent and defend their coreligionists. "We are not terrorists," they said ad nauseam. "We are not oppressed. Don't pity us, but don't fear us either. We are good people. We are just like you. Islam means peace. Muslims are also Americans"—but the unsaid part was: "We are very tired right now."

This was the community I was investigating—tense, tired, and under several layers of surveillance.

By the summer of 2002, I had been a fixture in the D.C. Muslim community for a year, having moved from Bloomington, Indiana. I had also, for some years, been a public speaker and writer on Western Muslims' identity and religiosity, Muslim women, progressive Islam, and Sufism.

I was an "insider" anthropologist in many ways, but in many ways, my age, my immigrant status, my discipline (anthropology), and my undertaking (scholarly research) distanced me from my participants. Born in the United Kingdom, I grew up mostly in Lahore, Pakistan, where I graduated from college, obtained a graduate degree, and did a stint teaching English. Then I moved to Britain to do a graduate degree at Cambridge University. My religious journey had taken me through conservative, neo-fundamentalist, orthodox, and progressive Islam, and for some years I had been, spiritually and intellectually, an orthodox Sufi as well as a progressive Muslim. By 2002, I was a kind of moderate Muslim par excellence, almost as if I were crafted to suit a diverse Muslim research sample. During fieldwork, I tried to drown many of my other roles in the researcher's persona, muting my voice so as to be a good interviewer for a variety of people.

Muslims in America

From an anthropological perspective, *who* we are is possible because of *where* we are and *when* we are. While I am not of the opinion that we are purely creatures of circumstance devoid of agency, I believe that the specific possibilities of our agency—as well as the potential to stretch our agency—are structured by our given circumstances.

For my second-generation Muslim American youth, these circumstances include the growing physical presence of immigrant populations in the United States. Their very presence (we hope) brings about a cultural sea change that shifts the balance of the broader population against xenophobia and toward acceptance. When the composition of "us" is transformed, surely our perceptions of "them" will shift too?

Unfortunately, sometimes perceptions change for the worse.

I like to illustrate this by telling an immigrant story set in the 1950s, before the Islamic revolution in Iran and the Soviet invasion of Afghanistan. My uncle, then in his late teens, arrived amid farms in the Deep South, the only foreigner in the area. Wherever he went, he was recognized and greeted as "Mo" (for Mohammad) since his face was splashed all over the newspapers as the exotic foreigner, the attractive and debonair Pakistani student with a sports scholarship at the local university. Soon enough, Mo showed up to introduce himself to the mother of a young woman. Nancy's mother wanted to know where the young suitor was from, but, being more familiar with the Bible than with the world map, she heard "Palestine" rather than "Pakistan." Most 1950s Americans didn't know Pakistan existed, after all. Young Mo adapted to being from Palestine for the moment since it was the only category available to him. When the subject turned to religion, the youth tried to explain what Islam was, but being fairly unlettered in such matters (religion was not very popular among modern, Western-educated Pakistanis in those days), he did not get far. "Is that like being Catholic?" the mother inquired suspiciously. "Oh no," Mo said. "Then," Nancy's mother announced, "you can date her!"

Mo assimilated steadily, raising a devoutly Baptist family with Nancy, and granting he was never especially immersed in Islam, he became a designated church speaker on the evils of Islam. In time, Mo's nephew immigrated during the 1970s and stayed with Mo and Nancy while he attended college. The nephew was destined to become cofounder of a Dallas mosque and of networks that enabled his children to live rich and full *Muslim* and Pakistani American lives. In 1996, Mo's niece emigrated from Pakistan and became an anthropologist aspiring to study Muslim American patterns of cultural adaptation.

While Euro-American Christendom is not new to horrid fascination with Islam, Muslims became known to the United States in a new light after the Cold War. With the Iranian Revolution and the collapse of the Communist bloc, the specter of Muslim power and protest became the primary threat to U.S. global supremacy. Times have changed. Today, Mo would have a better chance with Nancy's mother if he was a Palestinian Catholic. Mo's neighbors in South Carolina did not know what Pakistani Muslims were. Today Americans think they do.

The 1960s were an eventful period globally, with the Algerian and Iranian Revolutions and the rise of Islamist organizations. The Muslim Brotherhood (in the Arab world) and the Jamaat-e-Islami (in South Asia), ideological cousins in the Islamist movement, commanded a significant following among diasporic Muslims until the 1990s. Muslim students had created the Muslim Students Association (MSA) in 1963, and in 1981, the founders created a community organization, the Islamic Society of North America (ISNA), for the Muslims who were no longer college students. When I arrived in the 1990s, Islamist and Salafi-oriented South Asians and Arabs were gatekeepers and activists within many predominantly immigrant Muslim American religious organizations. To openly subscribe to Sufism, feminism, or progressive Islam was to invite a good deal of trouble in many religious contexts (as I learned!). The immigrant and outwardly Islamist identity of these organizations remained quite solid until the mid-1990s, when Sufi orders began to attract the younger generation with the promise of deeper spirituality, the appeal to greater universalism, and (in many cases) roots in medieval Islamic interpretive sources. At the same time, the seeds of reformist critique sown by postcolonial intellectuals started to bear fruit as Salafism and Islamism began to lose their numerical majority.

Most of my participants were raised in the United States by parents who had arrived in the 1970s or early 1980s. A small number of them were more recent arrivals, and a few were converts. There was a variety of types and levels of religious ideology, belief, and practice among my research participants, yet all self-identified as Muslim. On most metropolitan American campuses today, the MSA is solidly second generation, and the predominantly international (and male) MSA is a thing of the past. An accurate count of Muslim Americans is impossible to find, and estimates vary widely, depending on the source, between 2.6 million and 6 million (depending on how much you like or fear Muslims). Some say almost half of Muslim

Americans are indigenous (mostly African American), while the remainder are immigrants from more than eighty countries (Read 2008, Cesari 2004: 10–11). Not only can Muslim Americans be racially and ethnically identified in a multitude of ways, but their religious beliefs and practices are also legion.

Muslim Americans are situated at a nexus of political, religious, racial, ethnic, cultural, and transnational identities. This nexus can be most helpfully described as a "third space"—an in-between space awkwardly straddling recognized categories, fitting into none. Muslim Americans' identities do not fall into singular theoretical and census categories. Moreover, conversion among African Americans (though, in addition to new converts, there are a few generations of African American Muslims), whites, Hispanics, and Native Americans means that Islam is not just an immigrant religion in the United States. Muslim Americans' identity construction follows the trends of earlier immigrants in many ways, but is complicated by the lens of Orientalism (Said 1978). This makes Muslims much less easily accommodated (Moore 1995: xi) and allows them to be preemptively stamped with the stigma of being "not ordinary" (Sacks 1984). The terrorist attacks of September 11, 2001, and the fallout thereafter have threatened to further jeopardize the integrity of Muslim identity (Steinback 2011). U.S. identity shifted when, on that date, the United States experienced not only a rare challenge from a foreign source but also a direct attack on its soil. The attacks gave birth to a new identity that combined the fragility and hypermasculinity of a threatened superpower. For the United States to find itself in the shadow of real physical threat was a relatively new and overwhelming experience. No longer buttressed by its Cold War mission, America constructed itself in relation to "Muslim terrorism." Because the specific attackers were Muslim, a broad swath of Americans decided that Muslims in general were fanatical terrorists. The terrorists' hatred and violence could be simplified, defined, and explained briefly by "Islam." Images of men glaring through dark eyebrows (a throwback to Ayatollah Khomeini's omnipresent image after the Iranian Revolution) and of figures enveloped in blue burqas flooded our screens. A modern-day Uncle Mo would be welcomed with suspicious glares and NSEER (National Security Exit-Entry Registration) queues, rather than with young white women eager to settle down with a handsome foreigner. As we learned in the case of the Oklahoma City bombing, and years later in the case of the mass killings in Oslo and on a nearby island, almost no terrorism could take place in the world without the immediate assumption that the perpetrators were Muslim. In the Norwegian Anders Breivik's video and written manifestos, he gives "frank, graphic expression to the very opposite of pluralism," to "fear of diversity, anger at immigration and multiculturalism, and a contempt for dialogue," but we should be painfully aware that a "muted articulation of this same fear and anger can be heard in mainstream debates across Europe and in the United States around issues of immigration" (Diana Eck, e-mail communication, August 8, 2011). Recently, the Boston marathon bombing has reignited the flames of this hatred.

In the wake of 9/11, information about Islam and Muslims has been a hot commodity. Yet much of this so-called information is based on little but opinion (at best) or xenophobia (at worst): much of the content, like the *Princess* books about the Saudi royals, addresses readers' thirst to "know" the Muslim Other but serves merely to strengthen Westerners' sense of superiority to Muslims (FAIR 2008). On the other hand, in their effort to provide a counterweight to the demonization of Muslims, Muslim writers and spokespersons sometimes commit the common error of apologetics by idealizing Muslims as ahistorical and religious (Kandiyoti 1991: 1). Based on empirical data gathered by an insider, the present book attempts to correct this imbalance and more by avoiding errors of both apology and prejudice. I critique Orientalist stereotypes of sexist Muslims, but I also investigate gender inequity among Muslim Americans and examine the tendency of many of them to idealize their religious community as a timeless, unchanging monolith.

America and Muslims

ZEINAB: I don't think that being Muslim conflicts with being American. . . . I'm not going to go out in shorts and a tank top because I'm American. I'm going to go out in pants and a shirt because I'm an American and I'm a Muslim. . . . I know so many Americans who are feminists who hate short skirts, would never wear it because it goes against their beliefs. There are so many Jews who wear the yarmulke or when they get married they put hats on or wigs on, but they do that not because they're un-American, but that's what their beliefs are. A nun, or a monk, they have a certain life in America: it doesn't conflict with them. Similarly, I can be Muslim and live in America.

If a nun, a monk, or an Orthodox Jew can be an American and live by his or her religious precepts, should it not be natural to be able to live an Islamic life and be an American? Muslim identity or religiosity is not inherently opposed to being American. But to many Americans, the moniker "Muslim American" is an oxymoron rather than a demographic group, and in many academic circles such notions as universal human rights and gender equality are perceived as inherently in conflict with "Islam," while Christian or Jewish theology need not be on the defensive. Islamophobia is neither fringe nor unusual and is often intimately linked with such positive values as patriotism in a nation where the president needs to emphatically clarify that he is not a Muslim; where some FBI trainees have been taught that "mainstream" Muslims (and not just extremists) are radical and violent, and that being devout is an indicator of radicalization (Ackerman 2011); where military trainees have discussed the use of "Hiroshima tactics" for "total war" against Islam (Shachtman and Ackerman 2012); and where the New York Police Department has conducted surveillance on Muslim neighborhoods and Muslim college students across the Northeast (Associated Press 2012).

A vocal segment of the American population believes that Muslim Americans are, and *should be*, seen as enduringly different, as un-Western and anti-Western. Campaigners against the TLC reality show *All-American Muslim* were angered by the depiction of Muslim Americans as utterly normal Americans. The bland, unremarkable depiction of the Muslim characters was perceived as a momentous threat—an attempt "to manipulate Americans into ignoring the threat of jihad" (the Florida Family Association). For such people, the normal Americanness of *All-American Muslim* characters only serves as a warning of how the hidden enemy only *pretends* to combine the qualities of clashing worlds (Nussbaum 2012).

But surely, some may say, these stereotypes belong in rural red-state communities, and among those with no access to social scientific analysis. Surely, in elite liberal college cultures, for example, where professors deconstruct myths, where freshmen live together in dorms, where students get credit for engaging in diversity-related activities, Islamophobic stereotypes might seem outlandishly strange. Many Americans assume that university campuses are bastions of open, liberal, accommodating, and diversity-loving cultures where difference flourishes and is nurtured. If we are to believe the moral panic of the Right, the academy is the domain of "guilt-ridden" Muslim-lovers, leftists, atheists, and socialists (they are apparently interchangeable) (Spencer 2008: 228). Yet by examining how Muslim American women's subjectivities interact with campus culture, I show that despite the fantasy (both liberal and conservative) of college as a hotbed of tolerance, minority students are still subject to majoritarian pressures to conform to Anglo culture. While I do not see the post-9/11 era as fundamentally new in terms of Islamophobic racism, this period offers rich and fresh possibilities for the scrutiny of Orientalist Islamophobia in our everyday American lives. While this book is about Muslim American undergraduates, it is also about America. I am equally interested in America, in who America is, and in who "America" thinks she is, via a study of Muslim Americans, as I am interested in Muslim Americans and who *they* think they are.

Muslims in College

To study America and Muslim Americans, I chose American university campuses. At liberal university campuses "America" is arguably at its most liberal and self-consciously inclusive. Since before 9/11, the neoliberal backlash and the campus adventures of the intelligence community and of law enforcement cast dark shadows on the ivory tower. The action of this book is set in the (mostly) social leisure spaces on campus and to a lesser degree, in the academic spaces. Often the distinction between academic and social spaces is an artificial one. Social spaces are "primal scenes of sociology" and of crucial importance to social scientists since it is in the sustained social encounter between "normals" and those who possess stigmatized identities that "the causes and effects of stigma must be directly confronted by both sides" (Goffman 1963: 13). As informal social networks are profoundly powerful in the constitution of youth identity (Willis 1981), I focus on these in a variety of spaces—classrooms, the extracurricular spaces of student clubs, and leisure spaces such as parties, nightclubs, and bars.

In the fall of 2001, all across America, thousands of young Muslim Americans, along with their college classmates, entered or returned to college. A few weeks later, three planes flew into the World Trade Center in New York City and the Pentagon in Washington, D.C. Now these young Muslim Americans would have to prove continually that they were not potential terrorists. Long before they entered the classrooms and opened their mouths, they were known: they were Muslim. In the newly under-attack country where they were born and/or raised, they suddenly became xenophobic potential hijackers, inflamed by a timeless hatred; and if they were "good Muslims, they were attempting to exorcise that hatred." The shadow of those planes, once it had fallen on these young people's paths, remained. The dark shadow over higher education was lengthened when Dzhokhar Tsarnaev, a student at the University of Massachusetts, Dartmouth, and his brother Tamerlan, a part-time student at Bunker Hill Community College, were identified as suspects in the Boston Marathon bombing.

This is a book about that long shadow. It is about how young Muslim Americans come up with a rejoinder to the identity stamped on them, how they snap back and explain and teach in many tones of voice that they are American and Muslim and not violent, barbaric, or foreign. It is also about how they often *cover* those telltale signs of Muslim identity and sometimes *pass* as non-Muslim (Goffman 1963). This book is about stereotyping, double consciousness, self-surveillance, and essentialism visited on Muslim Americans by both dominant majority Americans and other Muslim Americans. It is also about those among them who tire of the projects of cultural assimilation and social integration, who embrace the only identity category available and stick out their chins to assert that they *are* indeed different, religious, traditional, and weird. Their brows are already stamped with this identity: they embrace it and accept the representative burden—because to refuse it would be cowardly, incomprehensible to the interlocutor, and/or exhaustingly complicated.

Muslims at Georgetown and George Washington Universities

AMBER: I think it's *soooo* stressful [being Muslim post-9/11]. . . . Things happen, that remind me, constantly. Like today I got a call from a good friend; she's a very strong person, and she's sobbing on the phone. She's like, "I can't take it anymore. I'm so stressed out." . . . She's very active [as an activist], and she's been on spring break so it's been a week and she hasn't done anything. I guess she feels bad. She was sobbing for ten minutes on the phone, and she never cries, I never heard her cry, so I didn't know what to say. And that reminded me of what's going on. . . . Emotionally she's just breaking down right now. I asked her, she's like, "No, I don't know what it is. I'm being stupid, I'm being stupid." . . . And I can only attribute that to what's going on. Like our friend's house was raided [by the FBI]. . . . All these things remind you: no matter how much you try to live in this moment, we have to think about what's happened in the broader context. Yeah, we should try to have our own personal goals but—.

In the summer of 2001, I had just moved from my campus in Bloomington, Indiana, to live in Washington, D.C., with Svend, whom I married in March of 2001. When I took the yellow Metro line past the Pentagon on September 12, 2001, I felt a sick sense of shameful relief that I did not wear hijab and that I had with me a white husband who did not look obviously Muslim.

In the late summer of 2002, the memories of raids by FBI, customs, immigration, and law enforcement agents at local Muslim homes and offices were still fresh among prospective research participants when I visited the two campuses for fieldwork. In the large Muslim American community of Greater Washington, D.C., Muslims like Amber, whom I quote above, recalled friends being criminalized, harassed, and humiliated in the post-9/11 raids (styled Operation Green Quest). These sweeps affected my friends and acquaintances, as well as prominent community leaders with a solid track record of working within the system to facilitate Muslim American academic and charitable pursuits. The efforts of these community activists to engage with American democratic institutions were now tarred as fronts for terrorism. Two of my research participants, Heather and Sharmila, told me of one case, in which the northern Virginia home of their girlfriend was attacked by law enforcement officers: a man broke down the door, handcuffed the mother and adolescent daughter, ignored their protests, and photographed them without their headscarves, only later troubling himself to inform them that he was an officer with a search warrant. Such incidents could not fail to have the desired effect on other Muslims—including myself—instilling fear and a sense of perpetual surveillance.

Muslim student groups *were* under surveillance (Skolnik et al. 2002), and suspicion was so palpable that my most religiously skeptical Muslim research participant once commented on her certainty of campus Muslims being monitored. Both Georgetown and George Washington Universities have local MSA chapters, and these figure prominently in my fieldwork. Local campus MSAs are relatively independent of the MSA of the United States and Canada (known as MSA National). Like all predominantly undergraduate organizations, with their diverse membership and high turnover, local MSAs cannot be described in static terms. Demographic factors such as significant Gulf Arab student populations and the presence of influential ex officio members—long-standing graduate students, for instance—can bring longevity to a specific collective style and in an MSA's public character. The collective practices and identities of the Muslim campus group at my alma mater, Indiana University, for example, shifted in the 1990s, with a significant rise in the number of second-generation Muslim Americans and Muslims from Southeast Asia and Turkey to rival the numbers of Gulf Arab students, ousting them from their gatekeeping position in the mosque and MSA.

In the summer of 2002, I commenced feverishly negotiating access with Georgetown and George Washington authorities. I also solicited permission and intermediary assistance from the MSAs as local gatekeepers and cultural spaces of resistance for many campus Muslims (hooks 1990b). My initial recruitment of participants relied on sign-up sheets at MSA meetings and included MSA members and student officers. As I became more integrated into the communities, I identified and recruited participants who did not belong to the MSA, some who had never attended an MSA event, and a few who did not know that there was a Muslim club on campus.

Both the Georgetown MSA and the George Washington MSA had earned university awards for service and activism. Each had strong membership networks and held regular events such as lectures, ice cream socials, coffee nights, Eid banquets, and prayer vigils. Ramadan was the most active time of the year, when MSAs organized fastathons (collective interfaith fasting) and congregational *suhoor* and *iftar* meals and prayers. The Ramadan meals of suhoor and iftar were popular among a variety of Muslim students who gathered to alleviate some of the increased homesickness during this month. (Imagine, for example, Christian students attending college during the Christmas season).

In class and cultural style, the George Washington University (GWU) and Georgetown University (Georgetown) Muslim students were fairly similar with some subtle differences. Due to geographic proximity, shared nightlife venues, and similar academic foci, the two student communities also overlapped rather often at social venues and local events. It was not uncommon to see Georgetown Muslim students at GWU events and vice versa. Class and academic rivalries between the two universities have been highlighted in such formats as a student-produced video, GWU MSA vs. Georgetown MSA. In the highly exaggerated caricature, stocky GWU MSA men in bulky navy hoodies and sweatpants were mocked as the poorer, ghetto, macho "Georgetown waitlist" by their slim, supercilious, bohemian Georgetown counterparts in khakis and colorful polo collars.

As affluent, private universities with substantial numbers of Muslim students, Georgetown and GWU are quite comparable for my purposes. Both universities have majority white undergraduate populations and a large international student body. Georgetown, a Jesuit university and a "hot big city school" (Mathews 2007: 53), is popularly believed to be "hotter," wealthier, more bohemian, more liberal, and more laid back than its secular counterpart, GWU. The physical and architectural layout of the campuses generate distinct styles of community: the urban campus of GWU tends to bleed into the urban off-campus world of Northwest D.C. more easily than does Georgetown, and GWU lacks Georgetown's green and cobblestoned open public spaces that allow students to mill about within campus limits. The upscale, off-campus commercial world adjacent to Georgetown seems to become absorbed within the Georgetown student population. There thus exists a more youth-centric, exclusive yet bohemian climate at Georgetown and a somewhat less bohemian and more urban and worldly feel within the GWU community, yet both campus cultures exude wealth and are characterized by a combination of hard partying and hard studying.

Most existing studies of Muslim American students tend to focus on minors who live with their families and attend grade school. My book focuses on what happens when adolescents grow up, go to college, and move away from parental supervision. Most of my participants were residential students, but a few had families within commutable distance. My Georgetown sample was overwhelmingly residential, while my GWU sample was about one-third commuters. A few of my participants lived in a cluster of apartments designated as the Muslim Interest Living Community (MILC or "Muslim Housing"): in these apartments, residents were not permitted to consume alcohol, nor could a man and a woman be alone together at any time. Muslim housing, open to students of all faiths with an "interest" in "Muslim lifestyle," was particularly beneficial for those who preferred an atmosphere free from the hedonistic excesses of campus leisure culture.

Although Georgetown and GWU enroll undergraduates who possess a combination of strong class and academic capital and my research participants all occupied elite spaces, these participants were not exclusively upper class. A few were solidly wealthy. However, many benefited from the universities' student aid packages, and some relied almost entirely on student aid. To classify them roughly by socioeconomic background, the South Asian participants were all middle to upper class; the Arab participants were middle class; the black and white participants were upper-middle to lower-middle class; and my Somali participant of refugee background was now a frugal member on the margins of the middle class. As a left-leaning scholar, I wish I could speak more about the women's class backgrounds than I do in this book, but in the elite spaces of these universities, socioeconomic status was a sensitive matter and I did not want to pain (or lose) my research participants. I examine social class broadly, in terms of how social class (often treated as the primary form of social advantage in anthropological studies of difference) can be trumped by the stigma of religious identity, how being a religious Muslim can reduce socioeconomic privilege. My participants' sense of belonging in campus culture fluctuated according to how visible their Muslim identities were.

Georgetown and GWU both have fairly well equipped and well designed *musallas* (Muslim prayer rooms). The Georgetown musalla, in a residence hall basement, is decorated with Islamic art and a prayer carpet. The GWU musalla is located in the student union and has custom carpeting, conveniently low steel sinks for ablutions, and separate doors for men and women. The presence of the musalla attracted GWU Muslim students to socialize in the nearby lounge area on the fourth floor; so many of my interviews took place in the surrounding classrooms. During my fieldwork the GWU musalla was also spatially (but flexibly) divided into male and female prayer spaces by a six-foot-high folding screen. When I visited the campus six years later, the screen had been set aside and I interviewed a male MSA member in the musalla (he and I sat together alone, something I had never seen happen in that musalla before). Neither musalla was large enough to accommodate the entire Muslim campus community for Jumʿah prayer. A church basement in Foggy Bottom was rented for the GWU Jumʿah prayer; this bare but convenient urban location brought local professionals and employees to the campus community. Typically, when students are obliged to fall back on the non-campus community for resources, the influence of outsiders is bound to increase (Hermansen 2003). I heard more conservative discourse at the GWU Jumʿah, due mainly to the presence of non-students and graduate students. The Georgetown MSA held its Friday service in an activity room at the center of campus, which attracted far fewer non-campus attendees than the GWU Jumʿah service.

Many Georgetown Muslims proudly described their MSA as more inclusive than others. Conservative Muslims at other local universities (the MSAS at George Mason University and the University of Maryland at College Park were reputed to be very conservative during that time) disapprovingly described Georgetown Muslims as "too liberal" in their gender norms, measuring by the porosity of the Muslim community and the degree of gender "mixing." Liberal Muslims at both GWU and Georgetown shuddered at the notion of separate Muslim organizations for women (extant at some universities), preferring their own intertwined styles of religiosity, class, and gendered behavior.

A variety of ideological backgrounds were represented in both MSAS. The MSA could be roughly divided into the relatively conservative, "official" gatekeepers (this was in itself a diverse group) and large groups of more "liberal" individuals. As I examined their roles on campus, I realized that all of these various Muslim "types" were engaged in the construction of Muslim American youth culture, albeit in different ways. Power shifted across and between these parties in different spaces and at different times. Mainstream American observers tend to identify the "liberal" Muslims as "oppressed" by the conservative "gatekeepers." Yet I found the Georgetown gatekeepers pitted against a hegemonic liberal secularity both within the Muslim community and in the broader campus culture.

While GWU had a short-lived part-time chaplaincy, Georgetown was the first American Catholic university to hire a full-time Muslim chaplain, Imam Yahya Hendi, who served as a liaison between Muslim students and the university administration. Both institutions had strong academic programs focusing on Islam and the Middle East: Georgetown had the Center for Contemporary Arab Studies and the Center for Muslim-Christian Understanding (where I was a visiting researcher), while GWU had the renowned Sufi expert Seyyed Hossein Nasr.

Ethnographic Methods

In researching young Muslim American women who were engaged in constructing identities that were also being constructed for them, ethnographic methods were the only possible choice. I conducted participant observation at two private university campuses, as well as informal conversational interviews with twenty-six undergraduate Muslim women, thirteen at each campus. I spent over one year shuttling between these two Muslim college communities on and off campus, participating directly and indirectly in everyday campus events and non-events, immersed in my participants' "interpretations of their world" (Miles and Huberman 1994: 8).

On a typical day of fieldwork, I would type up field notes and head out to one of the campuses. I would wait for a prearranged interview in a university lounge while I transcribed interviews and watched students study, lounge, socialize, and vegetate. After two or three interviews, I would accompany a research participant to an MSA lecture or an iftar meal, and we would proceed together to the Ramadan *tarawih* prayer. As night fell, I would take the subway back to my apartment in Arlington. On other days, I would have one long interview at the local café, and then my participant and I would walk over to the Metro station together. Or I would arrive on campus just in time to lie down on the ground in the Red Square "die-in" sponsored by campus activists to protest the war in Iraq. Then I would proceed to a classroom observation and afterward hang out in Red Square at Georgetown or on the fourth floor of the student union building at GWU, where I socialized and had valuable impromptu conversations with Muslim undergraduate men and women. I watched bulletin boards and the campus newspapers and kept myself abreast of major campus events. Along with participants, I attended lectures, day conferences, political demonstrations, music concerts, student performances, interfaith dinners, Nowruz celebrations, birthday parties, congregational prayers, class lectures, and even a bridal shower and a wedding.

Over the course of the academic year, I had 126 interviews with my participants (which, in addition to field notes, I personally transcribed, being too poor to hire someone). I held interviews in library study rooms, student lounges, apartments, and cafés. During initial interviews, I introduced my fieldwork as being about university life and identity, and only asked "basic" and non-probing questions about participants' majors, hometowns, interests, preoccupations, and the like. After this, I started asking open-ended questions like "How have you been?"; "What's been happening lately?" My questions during later interviews were a cross between my research questions and each participant's particular interview content. This approach worked remarkably well *most* of the time. My participants would give me the latest news—academic anxieties, budding romances, travel, and so forth. In an early interview, Amber expressed relief that she would be finished with MSA work on graduation, so we fell to chatting about the different types of people involved in the MSA, without my having to probe her on Muslim identities. When I told Elizabeth how difficult it had been to identify African American Muslim participants, she explained why the African American students were "undercover," and marginal in the predominantly immigrant MSA. When I pressed Intisar for details about the social difficulties of sophomore year, she told me of her sense of emotional-cultural isolation, and her desire to create a Somali student club. We discussed religious, ethnic, cultural, youth, and gender identities, being Muslim American in that historical moment, but particularly experiences on and off campus that shed light on being Muslim American female college students.

As my participants and I shared many of the same cultural and social fields, they accepted me as an insider with relative ease. Observant Muslims accepted me as a Muslim who observed obligatory rituals and important practices. Less religiously observant Muslims

confided in me as a critical Islamic feminist with progressive lean-
ings in religion. I shared something important with all of them.

Alcohol, Clothes, and Dating

If you have eyed the titles of my chapters with curiosity, you may
want to hear why alcohol, clothes, and dating are the themes that organize a book about Muslim American undergraduate women. Some
readers have wondered if the choice of these tropes illustrates a lam-
entable Orientalist tendency to focus on the image, both desexual-
ized and hypersexualized, of the Muslim woman.

Muslim American undergraduate women function within majority social and leisure culture, even as many of them wrestle with
it. As peer culture is the most powerful stuff in the construction of
youth identities, it was no surprise when the prominent motifs of
alcohol, clothes, and dating emerged from the data during analysis.
After completing data collection and the grueling task of transcrip-
tion, I searched through my data and played with it, arranging and
rearranging, reading and rereading observation notes and interview
transcripts, inserting parenthetical comments, profoundly overwhelmed by the quantity of data, issues, and tropes. I started trying to identify patterns and themes to represent my findings. While
patterns aplenty arose from the data, I agonized over identifying the
right patterns, the ones real anthropologists would construct. I did
not pull findings out of the void. To use a more painful metaphor, I
pushed them out after the data had gestated for a time, half encountering and co-creating the findings within data.

Initially, I established several categories of data analysis—
pluralism, integration, identity, gender, Muslim student groups, and
parents/families—but these categories unsettled me: as a qualitative researcher I, of course, acknowledge my role in constructing
findings, but these were entirely *my* own categories—nerdy, meta-
analytic themes that could have emerged from keywords in JSTOR. I
contemplated structuring chapters around large themes such as the
relationship between being American and being Muslim. But as I rehearsed organizing a document around cerebral "big themes" (found
in my research questions and the literature), I noticed that doing so
distanced my analysis from the data and broke up the connecting
issues in an artificial manner. One of my main goals was to show

how being American, being Muslim, being youthful, being students, and being women happened seamlessly in these women's lives. How could I make sense of their lives if I chopped them up, like body parts in horror films, into "chapters"? Added to this discomfort were the scholarly trepidation of being one of the first researchers to treat the subject and the anticipated guilt of "doing it all wrong" and establishing a pattern for others thereafter.

As I plowed through the data, I grew increasingly appreciative of how my participants had expressed their engagement with identities not in abstract terms but through particular, concrete experiences, such as the pervasive presence of alcohol on campus. In fact, they talked about drinking *a great deal*. They also seemed very interested in (surprise!) boys, dating, romance, marriage, fashion, and clothes. Identity themes were traceable in these behaviors and among them with greater integrity and greater fidelity to my participants' voices.

This is how domains of behavior emerged as vehicles to represent how Muslim American women handled the radioactive elements of campus sociability and how they identified themselves and categorized themselves vis-à-vis Muslim and non-Muslim Others. For example, almost every participant raised the issue of alcohol consumption, her position on it (whether she drank or not, whether she occupied drinking spaces), and her opinion of others' alcohol-related practices. Every participant deeply pondered the problem of clothes, her own sartorial practices (whether she wore hijab and what she considered modest garb), and a survey of Muslim and non-Muslim sartorial practices. And everyone wanted to thrash over gendered behavior, the opposite sex, and various gendered practices such as courting and dating. Drinking or not drinking, clubbing or not clubbing, dating or not dating, observing current fashions or not—these factors were significant determinants of how one became an integral member of core peer culture and of Muslim community culture/s. These three groups of practices emerged as the most salient expressive principles or heuristic tools in the data, and three data-driven chapters grew around them.

But What about Academic Concerns?

You may ask why academic concerns are not salient in my book. I asked the same question as I approached my field data: why did my research subjects talk endlessly about bars and clubs (or not going to bars and clubs), about headscarves and not wearing headscarves, and about boys, but not so much about that fascinating seminar or that final exam? The issue at stake is what scholars believe should preoccupy undergraduates at college as opposed to what really consumes them. While my research subjects studied hard, academic work was not so much at the heart of their *Who am I* journeys. Undergraduates' academic and social lives were profoundly social. Therefore I concern myself with Muslim students' experience of the social dimension of college, but, for all that, my participants' academic lives are integral to the book (e.g., in chapter 4, see Latifa's engagements with classroom spaces and Amber's engagement with the politics of political debate in class.)

The importance of peer social cultures informs scholarly work in education in general and in higher education in particular, and it is reflected in the sexy course titles to be found in college course catalogs today. Social connections are important to youth. Moreover, it is in the social spaces of educational cultures that youth identities are most vulnerable to symbolic violence. In the United States, being "normal" is closely coupled with being white and Christian, or at least with conformity to majority cultural practices of a social nature—among those, drinking, sartorial style, and dating.

The Research Sample

I have provided a table with participants' basic demographic information in the appendix. The members of my research sample differed in age, race, ethnicity, and types and levels of religiosity. My participants included hijabis and non-hijabis who would be described as pious and, on the other end of the continuum, very liberal participants who were unrecognizable as Muslim, as well as a number of middle-of-the-road Muslims. I chose to steer clear of an essentialist view of "Muslim" while not draining the term of all meaning. I therefore made sure to select participants who self-identified as Muslim, whatever their religious practice. Some questioned the fundamentals of Islam, others were devoutly pious, and most took a position between these two points.

From an initial reliance on convenience sampling (recruiting "whoever I could get"), I started trying to obtain maximum-variation sampling as soon as my fieldwork took off, locating research participants of divergent racial, ethnic, and religious backgrounds and employing snowball sampling as I was introduced to potential participants by existing ones. In terms of representing a diversity of racial and ethnic backgrounds, I was generally fortunate, but I could not hope to be comprehensive: my participants encompassed some of the range of the Muslim American population, as I had black, white, and Hispanic Muslim women, and Muslim women of Pakistani, Bangladeshi, Indian, Iranian, Arab (Libyan and Iraqi), and African (Somali) origins. Examining my sample of primary participants critically in early 2003, I found it to be composed mainly but not exclusively, of rather religious undergraduates who were associated with the MSA. The range of Muslim religious identities on campus was far wider than I had initially generalized from my previous experience of Muslim student communities. In the course of data collection, I also discovered that some potential participants had gathered from my initial e-mail (recruiting "Muslim students" for research) that I was looking for "good Muslims." These potential participants had then decided not to volunteer since they were not good Muslim representatives. At this stage, however, my desperate eagerness to find "less religious" participants was borderline laughable. I tried every strategy except outright requests for introductions to Muslim women who drank and slept around. I searched university e-mail directories, using common Muslim last names of South Asian and Middle Eastern origin, and selected women's names. In a recruitment e-mail to students with last names like "Khan" and "Mohammed," I asked them if they would be interested in participating in a research project, and purposely toned down the "Muslim" element in my letter. This staggered and reflexive search for participants resulted in far more participants than I had originally intended to interview, twenty-six to be exact. Scheduling all the interviews into my participants' busy schedules and into a comparative study of two campuses was somewhat onerous, but such are the unpredictable vagaries of fieldwork.

Most participants were born and all were raised in the United States. Most of my research participants were of immigrant background, while others (and this was a deliberate choice) were not. The *Americanness* of Muslim Americans complicates the racism and nativism that easily relegates Islam to foreignness but also illustrates the power of Orientalism in trumping the racial and indigenous advantage of white and black Muslims. Four participants were converts: two whites, one black, and one mixed race (Hispanic and black). I had eleven Pakistani Americans, five Bangladeshi Americans, two Iranian Americans, two Arab Americans, one Somali American, and one Indian American. I had participants from all academic years of college. Most of my participants were Sunni, but I had two Shi'as from each campus. Two of the Georgetown and six of the GWU participants were hijabi during the fieldwork: the numerical difference results partly from sampling procedures and partly from the respective MSA's cultures. Although non-hijabis held office in both MSAs, non-hijabis felt more comfortable in Georgetown's MSA than in the one at GWU. I had four commuter participants, while the other parties were residents in dorms or in off-campus apartments.

All the Muslim undergraduates I encountered during my fieldwork were academically and professionally driven, and most had relatively clear plans for future careers. Most of my participants were quite ambitious in terms of career plans: Washington, D.C., was a city hospitable to professional development in the foreign service, law, development, and academic careers in religious and area studies. Since students in the sciences tended to be too engrossed in their own academic and social networks for participation in a research study, I had only a few such participants—Muna, Faiyza, and Roshan. Almost all of my twenty-six primary participants had a strong sense of combined religious, cultural, and civic mission to be exemplary, productive, successful, and "normal" as Muslims, students, and Muslim American women.

In addition to the primary participants, I interviewed other female Muslims, some Muslim male students, and some non-Muslim students and conducted observations of the broader campus community. The rich data I gathered in the field strengthened my certainty of focus on Muslim American *women* due to the unique gendered nature of Muslim religiosity and its interactions with campus culture. But my research also whetted my appetite for future research that would include male Muslim American youth and other faith groups.

Most of the success of my research project must be attributed to the trenchant analysis, the tremendous candor, and the excellent good humor of my participants. These young Muslim American women wanted to fit in, to resist and transcend assumptions, to be happy in romance and marriage, to be high achievers, to have successful careers, to serve, to change, to be safe, and to rock the boat. They experimented with different ways of being ethnic, cultural, American, Muslim, successful, and "normal"—all at the same time. In order to build a picture of their campus lives, I use their own words culled from interview data—hard-hitting, often hilarious, never one-dimensional, acidly realistic about their challenges, and irrepressibly ambitious in their desire to break the molds within which they often found themselves trapped.

In this book, you will find an ethnographic portrait of Muslim women's identities as they *become* on two East Coast metropolitan, private, elite campuses—in their own accounts and in my observation. As a portrait is inevitably somewhat static in nature, it cannot capture motion, process, or change over time. Today, my participants may not identify with all their identity work and their comments in the past. But in this book, I attempt to capture that fleeting yet powerful moment of their college lives, demonstrating how the processes of becoming Muslim, women, college students, and American youth are multifaceted, complex, and widely divergent for Muslim women. Like many researchers entrusted with intimate musings, I remain intensely invested in my participants' success and their happiness. In many cases, we have long transcended the research moment and become close friends. I root for them as, today, they complete graduate and professional studies, enter career fields, gain promotions, and are rising stars within their various professions— medicine, diplomacy, religious studies, area studies, law, international development, and so on, many of them also falling in love, getting married, and having children. In more recent conversations with them and with other Muslim American students, I find that the concerns appearing in this book regarding identity, campus social cultures, gender, and Muslim religiosity remain a constant.

A Map of This Book

In chapter 2, I discuss the powerful campus culture of hedonism and sociability and how this focus gives the lie to the college narrative of freedom and pluralism in Muslim American women's experience. I also name the Orientalist and essentialist discursive construction of Muslims on American university campuses and discuss what

Muslim students do to comply with, resist, adopt, and exploit the prevalent Orientalist discourse that threatens to "spoil" their identities on campus.

In chapters 3 to 5, I discuss the ethnographic data closely, zeroing in on particular areas of campus social experience. In chapter 3, I explore how participation in alcohol culture informed Muslim American women's identity construction and participation in campus culture. In chapter 4, I examine how Muslim undergraduate women sought to be authentic and normal while constructing third spaces of hybridity with *and* in spite of particular kinds of attire. In chapter 5, I show how my participants constructed normal, different, and fusion identities with reference to sexual and gendered behavior. In the conclusion, I discuss my research findings pertaining to Muslim women's identity work, pluralism on university campuses, and broader American culture.

2

Muslim American
Women in Campus Culture

A Perfect Identity Storm: Muslims at College

For undergraduates, college is a life-change that can be exhilarating, terrifying, and confusing. For youth already in the throes of physical and social change, shuttling between their roles as dependents and adolescents, on the one hand, and financially independent adults and voting citizens, on the other. Add Muslim identity to the mix, fold in a post-9/11 nativist racism, and we find that Muslim American college students have some painful growing up to do. Muslim, American, and youth—these identities effervesce and simmer in many Americans' minds like a chemistry experiment gone wrong. How can these different ingredients harmonize? How will the balance of identities shift, teeter, and settle? This book unpacks how dysfunction and confusion may result from not being free to *be*—to be American "like everyone else"; to be Muslim, Arab, or Pakistani; to be authentically American *as well as* a Somali (or white, Arab, or black) Muslim woman; to be Pakistani American and American simultaneously; to be a religious Muslim American, and/or to be an *irreligious* Muslim. *"I can't get anything right,"* my research participants seemed to say; "I'm damned no matter what I do."

In the United States, Muslim identity is typically a source of "stigma" (Goffman 1963). Conversely, behaving like a "normal" American youth can be a source of stigma in Muslim communities. In terms of American identity politics, young Muslim American women are beset by a perfect identity storm. The experiences of Muslim American women serve as a distinctive lens whence to examine the social spaces of

American campus culture. Let us start with Latifa, an effusively cheerful Arab American freshman trying to find her way at Georgetown.

Limited Liberty: Marginal Identities on Campus

LATIFA: Yeah, I came with some baggage, but my whole approach to college is, I'm starting on a new slate, so whatever I was taught in that home is definitely not being reinforced here.

College is popularly visualized as a world of freedom, mobility, and personal maturity. This is where girls become women and boys become men. Moreover, in the liberal narrative of college, there is an inherent claim—a promise, a "university imaginary," an individualistic, universal dream of full humanity that is accessible to all regardless of their particular characteristics (Abelmann 2009: 1–2). Yet this supposedly egalitarian community where diverse individuals may come together, share, and celebrate is not equally hospitable to all student identities; rather, it is a ranked array of decidedly unequal cliques and coteries. Latifa swiftly recognized that her home identities and cultural capital were identity possibilities blocked off in campus spaces and repackaged as "baggage." Latifa's religious, civic, youthful, and gendered identities stretched the conceptions of majority Americans and traditional Muslims; the "freedom" within self-consciously pluralistic campus cultures was not a very meaningful commodity to her.

Through Muslim women's narratives, I call attention to the noiselessly marginalizing processes in campus social spaces that constrain Muslim American women's identities and turn home cultures into baggage. I investigate how Muslim American undergraduates engage with the college environment and how these girls become women, negotiating multiple norms under the twin towers of surveillance by Muslim communities and the American majority. In this chapter I discuss the Orientalist discursive construction of Muslims and contextualize my research findings relative to the scholarly literature on campus culture and Muslim Americans.

Sociability and Hedonism in College Peer Culture

Peer culture is one of the most powerful factors in shaping the behavior of college students (Renn and Arnold 2003: 263; Renn 2000: 400;

Astin 1997: 53), whether majority American or minority youth. Beyond university policies, regulations, official documents, and course syllabi, it is the people on campus who co-construct and consume campus culture. Since the late 1960s, when universities relinquished the *in loco parentis* role, sociability and hedonism have grown ubiquitous in higher education, so that "many campuses have come to be seen as increasingly chaotic and dangerous to a number of students and parents . . . places where men and women share dorm rooms and where drugs and alcohol are easily available" (Miller 2006: 6). Sociability and hedonism, which play central roles in the marketing of college brands, are manufactured and indulged in by college undergraduates.

In American popular culture, college—at the corner of adolescence and adulthood—represents a selective mimicry of "adult" hedonistic behaviors combined with youthful imprudence. Undergraduates are customarily described as being frivolous, "'drowning' in a campus sea of secularism, hedonism, and materialism" (Magolda and Gross 2009: 315), and immersed in an "anti-intellectual student ethos" (Renn and Arnold 2003: 263). Getting trashed, flirting with abandon, (aspiring to) wild promiscuity, cutting classes—these are all familiar tropes that popularly represent the college years in the popular imagination (CoEd Staff 2008).

Peer culture constitutes marginality for many who are ugly, uncool, frumpy, unpopular, nonwhite, foreign, or poor. With important regional and rural-urban variations, "cool" students are (or seem) mellow or blasé in relation to, well, everything: academic work, sex, religion, morality, politics, and regulations—everything except having a good time. Nothing is supposed to faze normal youth, and certainly not a judicious measure of debauchery. If you were significantly disengaged from such "normal" youth behaviors, you would be marked as "different." And if you simply performed being drunk at parties the way my research participant Heather did during her high school days, well, "everyone else is being ridiculously drunk, so the fact that you're screaming, really no one knows whether you're drunk or not." You would *want* to do "being drunk" when "everyone" is doing the same.

When sober, youth could only *pretend* to be part of the real fun. As for non-participants in hedonistic campus culture—and Latifa did not even attend parties, let alone feign inebriation—they were particularly marginal. To use a heuristic spatial metaphor, the social world of undergraduate culture comprised a core, a periphery, and a semi-periphery. Members of campus culture who possessed the requisite cultural capital could locate themselves in the core, and others would be relegated to a lower status. Latifa was *peripheral* to campus culture. Even Heather—white, attractive, non-immigrant, and upper class—was in the cultural periphery. Within the secularity of campus culture, religiosity—particularly Islamic religiosity with its distinctive racial, political, and historical connotations—is commonly represented as "weird," incongruous, outdated, and marginal (Magolda and Gross 2009). This cultural placement of individuals was a shifting affair, as the same person could be core, peripheral, or semi-peripheral depending on her actions and contextual factors.

College Peer Culture and Unauthorized or Informal Policy

The undergraduate social world is the site of crucial identity work and the source of what Levinson, Sutton, and Winstead describe as "unauthorized or informal policy" (2009: 768). Whatever "authorized policy" in the form of university policy statements may claim about diversity, student life, and alcohol, "normal" students drink: the designation of university spaces as "dry" and of underage students as non-drinking is often meaningless because "everyone" drinks in dorms and in bars with fake IDs.

Many persons of admirable intent (myself included) are drawn to policy studies by the emancipatory promise of virtuous power, believing that, when delivered top-down (by authorities within government, the policy community, higher education, etc.), policy promises to rid the world of injustice and create triumphant spaces of liberty and equality for marginal individuals and groups. Policy is a creature far more unpredictable and slippery and far less tractable and pliant than it is usually imagined. Rather than this top-down (unrealistic and incomplete) conception of policy, Levinson, Sutton, and Winstead (2009) conceive of policy broadly, unpacking it "as a kind of social practice, specifically, a practice of power" or a "complex set of interdependent sociocultural practices" (767–68). In shaping undergraduate identities, the street-level practice of student leisure culture is far more compelling than university regulations. As peers are "the single most potent source of influence" (Astin 1997: 398), the student community's unspoken consent forms much of the "unauthorized policy" world of undergraduates (Levinson, Sutton, and Winstead 2009: 770). Systemic and powerful, unauthorized policy defeats Band-Aid solutions that are incompatible with cultural ideology and neutralizes the theater of much "diversity work."

The Discursive Construction of Muslim Americans

It does not take much scholarly research, ethnographic or otherwise, to know what most Americans tend to think when they meet a Muslim man, or a Muslim woman. In social encounters, the Muslim and the non-Muslim are both aware of a set of notions about Muslim traditionalism, fanaticism, antimodernity, xenophobia, violence, and gender oppression. In that shared psychological space, battles are won and lost; but the accusation hangs in the air, and the power differential remains. When an Arab or an African American is *essentialized* and assumed to have an essential, unchanging, fundamental, core identity—for example, being prone to fanaticism or violence—the awareness of this stereotype can inflict symbolic violence and inwardly reduce the stereotyped individual (Bourdieu 1977). The stereotyping gaze, manifested through a fearful glance, a racial slur, a snide joke, or a thoughtless remark exercises power over stereotyped persons. People *construct* what we know about Others through *discourses*, or sets of ideas, expressed in words, attitudes, beliefs, and practices (Foucault 1980, 1979; Fanon [1952] 2008). People who circulate racial stereotypes in everyday speech, books, newspapers, television shows, movies, and music can be said to possess the discursive power to construct the truth about people of color and their supposedly *essential* identities.

Among these essentializing stereotypes, *Orientalist* stereotypes project Muslims and Muslim societies as racially and religiously homogeneous and predictable and the opposite of the "West" (Said 1979; Haddad, Smith, and Moore: 2006: 21–40). Muslim men are exoticized and assumed to be homogeneously primitive, religious, threatening, misogynistic, oversexed, xenophobic, and violent, while Muslim females are perceived to be oppressed, fragile, immobile, shy, and hyperfeminine. As "the Western episteme, supported by administrative, corporate and academic institutions, has enabled the West to simultaneously represent and dominate the Orient" (Kapoor 2003: 562), Orientalism operates freely in diverse cultural and educational spaces in the multicultural metropolis (Mir 2009c: 250), remaining unnamed by virtue of its pervasiveness, exerting "intellectual authority over the Orient within Western culture" (Said 1979: 19). So, whether a woman is jailed for adultery in Nigeria or a suicide bomber blows up a bus in Israel, the surveillance of Muslim Americans is ratcheted up, because they are symbolically representative of a worldwide Muslim community.

A racist Orientalist image of the Muslim Other is the necessary corollary to an idealized self-conception of "the West" (Said 1979). Orientalist notions posit "us" as egalitarian, free, secular, and progressive, because "they" are authoritarian, backward, religious, and traditional. "We" are, in part, constructed by the Other's representations of us, and by our construction of the Other.

My Muslim American female participants continually encountered in the gaze of the Other this conviction about Muslim women's inferior status and underdeveloped personhood. Muslim women's religious identities were hypervisible in their social encounters on campus, and they were assumed to be "Muslim"—purely religious beings—*rather than* "American," in that exclusive binary. For Muslim women, continual *double consciousness* (Du Bois [1903] 1995) meant awareness that Americans believed Muslim women to be oppressed, immobile, weak, and hyperfeminine (as Muslim women) on the one hand and threatening, primitive, xenophobic, and fanatical (as Muslims) on the other. It meant that Muslim women were constantly aware of being considered irrevocably *different* and alien.

Besides being a source of psychological strain for the minority individual, double consciousness and the internalization of stereotypes can be a useful tool for comprehensive control by the modern nation-state of population groups that are subversive, suspect, or just plain eyesores. Since overt oversight and inordinate enforcement can be costly and violent, a system of internalized psychological self-surveillance can cause marginal groups to feel as though they are always being watched, with a minimum of state effort. In Foucault's words: "There is no need for arms, physical violence, material constraints. Just a gaze. An inspecting gaze, a gaze which each individual under its weight will end by interiorisation to the point that he is his own overseer, each individual thus exercising this surveillance over, and against, himself. A superb formula: power exercised continuously and for what turns out to be minimal cost" (1980: 155).

Covering to Be Normal

While Muslims, blacks, Latinos, Jews, and gays are stereotyped and imagined as having fixed core identities, identities are socially *constructed* rather than inherent, essential, and unchanging. Anthropological analysis indicates that our behaviors are not a pure manifestation of some inner unchanging core and that social interactions result in complex combinations of identities that, moreover, change in composition in different environments. Socially, we engage with people's opinions of us and with others' views on acceptable behavior. No one is entirely "free" to be who she is or wants to be. We are wrapped within a matrix—of social connections, roles, personae, rituals, and expectations—that blocks entire worlds of possibility, in the manner of the Keanu Reeves blockbuster. The roles and personae we adopt do not stay frozen forever; situationally, we don and remove roles like shoes, but—unlike a pair of shoes—multiple identities may be worn at the same time in particular circumstances.

Certain types of identities are more stigmatized, more radioactive than others. In the United States, Muslim youth, like women and gays, learn to "play down" their "outsider identities to blend into the mainstream." The American dream holds out a promise: "Just conform, the dream whispers, and you will be respected, protected, accepted" (Yoshino 2007: 20–21). This (usually) unspoken *demand* to conform—the reason why "outsiders" play down racial, religious, sexual, and gendered identities—is wrapped into a promise for better things. Blacks, Latinos, Muslims, Asians, and professional women learn to disguise, or *cover* (Goffman 1963), stigmatized identities in order to survive and succeed. Today, discrimination targets not entire racial or religious groups, but subgroups that fail to tone down awkward identities, to "*act* white, male, straight, Protestant, and able-bodied" (Yoshino 2007: 17–18), and to blend into the majority, conforming, harmonizing, and becoming all but indistinguishable. In this book, I explore Muslim American female students' responses to identity *constriction*, or to the demand to cover and mute their identities in campus culture.

Muslim American women regularly experience such identity silencing demands on campus. This is not to say that all Muslim American women who are indistinguishable from their peers are always responding to the demand to cover. It is to say that the *choice* to be openly, publicly Muslim is not an easy one because the stigma against Muslim identities breeds ambivalence, contradiction, and disavowal vis-à-vis their identity backgrounds (Bhabha 1994; Khan 2002). Under the oppressive awareness of the stigma they bear, Muslim women often try to be "ordinary" (Sacks 1984) by projecting "normal American" (mainstream Anglo, Judeo-Christian) identities. In table 1, I show the dominant constructions imposed on Muslim American women (left column), and their corresponding attempts at being normal in response to stereotypes (right column). This performance entails downplaying or "covering" their Muslim backgrounds, and sometimes even concealing Muslim identity to "pass" as "normal" (Goffman 1963).

White Christian Americans are typically unaware of the existence of racism or of "covering demands" on racial and religious minorities. Minority persons, on the other hand, are acutely aware of the content of "normal American" identities, of what norms they must obey and what behaviors they must choose and reject to adopt or approximate such American normalcy. These choices form the generally hidden assumptions of a culture. Most people work to be "normal" in various ways, but through a fine-grained ethnographic analysis of marginal individuals' identity strategies I examine the process of becoming so. Ethnographically investigating how religious Muslim students *work* to "pass" as normal drinking and dating college students reveals "the strategies of the stigmatized" and how marginal individuals are unobtrusively silenced within college cultures. Such ethnographic analysis also shows how we all conform within "the routines that we all use unconsciously each day"—a clue to "every life's inevitable existential compromise" (Rymes and Pash 2001: 280). Minority students frequently *perform* conformity, resistance, and accommodation to the hidden curriculum of campus culture. By so doing, minority students explicate

Table 1. Stereotypes of Muslim Women
and Their Performative Responses to Them

STEREOTYPES	"NORMAL" ATTRIBUTES
Marginal	Core
Restricted, oppressed	Free, independent, exercising choice
Uptight, boring, a "stickler"	Uninhibited, easygoing, fun, broad-minded
Shy, timid	Confident, adventurous, extroverted
Naive, provincial	Sophisticated, worldly, cosmopolitan
Terrorist, pugnacious	Peaceful, friendly, "mainstream" activist
"Extreme"	"Moderate"
Weird	Normal, ordinary

the hidden curriculum and the implicit assumptions and norms buried in everyday campus interactions. Ethnographic analysis of these performances reveals the cultural checkpoints that obstruct certain persons, behaviors, and ideas from crossing over into normalcy.

Agency Portrayed and Problematized

In the social spaces of campus, my research participants commonly passed as "normal" and covered Muslim identities. But often, too, they countered normalized discourses about Muslims and projected identities tailored to challenge common stereotypes. "Spoiled" but not broken, they constructed identities in new combinations, keenly aware of the gaze that fixed and curbed them. My participants became objects to themselves when they met the "Muslim Woman" in their peers' heads and internalized this image (Mead 1934: 142), but this objectification created possibilities of agency against symbolic violence. The possibility of agency is in fact catalyzed from the mix of conflicting Orientalist stereotypes that cast Muslim women as objects of fear and objects of pity, as sexual objects and virginally chaste: this repetition and doubling, these contradictions, betray the weakness in Orientalism, and they engender the possibilities for stereotyped persons to transcend inscribed identities (Kapoor 2003: 562–63). Thus Muslim women become not mere victims of cultural processes but participants in them, "active appropriators" of majority discourses and practices "who reproduce existing structures only through struggle, contestation and a partial penetration of those structures" (Willis 1981: 175).

Research on Muslim women's agency has "provided a crucial corrective" to Orientalist scholarship that represents Muslim women "as passive and submissive beings, shackled by structures of male authority" (Mahmood 2001: 205). But resistance, like oppression, is located within power. Limited choices of identity are realizable for Muslim American women in mainstream American cultural spaces. Orientalist stereotypes are inscribed on them, compelling them to engage with these constructions in their identity work, to comply with and/or resist them (Holland et al. 1998). The catch is that if they resist dominant stereotypes by projecting "normal" identities, they are at risk of becoming assimilated and invisible, whereas if they comply by performing identities in accordance with stereotypes, they acquire hyperreligionized identities. In my analysis, I conceptualize "agency not as a synonym for resistance to relations of domination, but as a capacity for action that historically specific relations of subordination enable and create" (Mahmood 2001: 203). Muslim American women who would resist Orientalist stereotypes are "enabled, if not produced, by" these constructions (Butler 1993: 15). "Although this constitutive constraint does not foreclose the possibility of agency, it does locate agency as a reiterative or rearticulatory practice, immanent to power, and not a relation of external opposition to power" (15). In other words, it is not that Muslim women rediscover or uncover a primal, "undominated self that existed prior to the operations of power" in some romantic tale of absolute freedom, but they "are themselves the product of those operations" (Mahmood 2001: 210), as we are all enmeshed within webs of power.

My research participants "did agency" vis-à-vis multiple forces and centers of power. Their identity goals varied and shifted contextually. They resisted secularity, resisted conservative Muslim gender norms, countered Orientalist stereotypes, and deployed Orientalist stereotypes. In my ethnographic analysis, "a Foucauldian view of power is indeed quite useful, because it does not prestructure the forms of dominance/opposition in the operations of power, but sees them as shifting categories whose meanings and significance are constantly in flux" (Hoffman 1999: 680–81).

Self-Essentializing

We put stereotypes on ourselves. Everybody does that. But I think it's just a little harder for black kids to just be who they are. —Donald Glover, on NPR in 2011

Stereotypes are utilizable not only to out-groups but to in-groups as well; they can be used not only for symbolic violence but equally for asserting the community's power and presence. My participants often "[played] up ideal values" that the majority expected them to embody (Goffman 1959: 38), employing "officializing strategies" (Bourdieu 1977) as they resisted and internalized but also adopted, employed, and stretched the static essentialism that was "externally imposed and often connected to negative sanctions and discrimination" (Abu-Laban 2002: 461). Many population groups play to stereotypes, but, as Glover puts it in the quotation above, it is harder for some groups than others to "just be who they are."

In adopting and employing Orientalist stereotypes and religionized identities, Muslim American women perpetuated the hypervisibility of Islamic affiliation and projected essentialized "Islamic" gendered identities that reflected their peers' stereotypes of Muslims. This self-essentialism took several forms that can be traced to several layered identity purposes and projects. Muslims appropriated stereotypical assumptions in part to meet the expectations of the gaze, and in part for political purposes of representation. We are not counted unless we stand up and make the appearance we are expected to make. *Muslim American* is so much more instantly recognizable than, say, *Pakistani American*. For another thing, Muslim ahistorical essentialism is about deculturalization. Muslim Americans hail from a dizzying variety of immigrant and indigenous origins, and Islamic identity helps neutralize potential cultural conflict, and unites (or, rather, congeals and constructs) the community, and turns it into a culturally *American* population group. Muslims may also self-essentialize and project total difference to nurture piety and religiosity. But adopting essentialized identities traps Muslims in reified identities and subjects them to "domination by social relations of power" (Holland et al. 1998: 5).

Drawing on the words of my research participants, I explore the dialectical relationship between essentialism inscribed *on* Muslim American women and self-essentialism adopted *by* them. Through an analysis of the dialectical relationship, we can explore "the fundamentally contested and strategically constructed nature of Muslim identity" that is "actively produced, reproduced, and transformed through a series of social processes." While the "ahistorical essentialist assumptions of 'Orientalism'" frequently obscure the "strategic nature of identity" (Kahani-Hopkins and Hopkins 2002: 289), Muslim American identities are constructed through improvisation, as Muslim Americans "piece together existing cultural resources opportunistically" (Holland et al. 1998: 276–77). Muslims use whatever limited range of "cultural resources available, in response to the subject positions afforded [them]" (ibid.: 18), attempting to stretch the range of these subject positions, but also not infrequently *adapting* to the limited range of possibilities within reach.

In the "third space" (Bhabha 1994), Muslims construct hybrid identities that are neither stereotypically American nor stereotypically Muslim but shed light on the reified nature of those descriptors. This third space demonstrates the incompleteness of hegemony, as marginal individuals use the cultural resources at their disposal— including Orientalist discourse, dominant majority practices, stereotypes, and slurs—to perform and to reinvent identities, and to represent communities, ideologies, and themselves.

Real Angry, Sexist Muslims

Ironically, while Westerners view Muslims through ethnocentric, Orientalist lenses as inherently xenophobic and alien, so Muslims who perform overtly anti-Western identities earn privileged positions as the default Muslim representatives, possessing the discursive power to *make* "pristine Islam." Neo-fundamentalist Muslims have frequently used the terms "pure" and "pristine" (or "mere") for their versions of Islam, implying that they possess an Islam practically untouched by human hand and human interpretation, while other versions of Islam are corrupted, diluted, and inauthentic. Westerners tend to regard such neo-fundamentalists as "real" Muslims, and progressive or moderate Muslims as mildly hypocritical or menacingly disguised. The scarier the Muslim, the more authentic he or she is considered. These Muslim performances are granted certificates of authenticity by the Samuel Huntingtons and Robert Spencers of Western academe and political punditry, while moderates and liberal Muslims are regarded as "fringe" apologists, their discourse slammed as dissimulation. A Muslim is not a real Muslim, many Westerners assume, unless he (usually he) is frothing at the mouth, shouting *Allahu Akbar* with his fist in the air, vowing either to destroy America or to impose shar'iah on it. Ecumenical Muslim advocates of understanding, peace, and justice are assumed to be either nominal Muslims or closeted jihadists. Orientalist-inspired Westerners and neo-fundamentalist Muslim "representatives" co-construct the public performances of radicalized Muslim fury and mute Muslim womanhood. While Muslims continue to struggle to *show* Westerners that they are *not* angry, hateful, and misogynistic, their struggle is labeled *false*—while the performances of angry and misogynistic Muslims are labeled *real*.

The primary message of this book—that Muslim identity is constructed, not "essential"—opposes popular and highly destructive notions of Muslim identity as Other, as pathological and as "given" and unchangeable. Pundits and popular journalists frequently probe Muslim Americans to scrutinize an imaginary subterranean core of identity, a molten mass of Qur'anic strictures and Middle Eastern customs. Following such scholars as Erving Goffman, I suggest that Muslim identity is not some static inner Islamic core with a discrete geological crust of visible social action. Through critical ethnographic research with a diverse research sample, I fracture the essentialism that (mis)informs how Americans "know" Muslims. I show how contested constructions and identities jostle with each other in the same spaces. Muslim Americans are often asked whether they are *more* American or *more* Muslim. The question is all wrong. It is inapplicable to these inheritors of multiple cultural legacies who are Muslim, American, and youthful, all at the same time. In examining different types of Muslims at college and their parents, I show the varied construction of identities that cannot be put in boxes, and I scrutinize how Muslims, non-Muslim Americans, the media, politicians, faculty and students in higher education, theological scholarship and lay discourse, community leaders and youth all together construct Muslims and Muslim women.

Religion Unnamed

In the 1990s, when I first expressed interest in researching Muslim Americans, I was asked why I would not choose to study my immigrant community of Pakistani Americans—a safe, American *ethnic* choice. Religion and religious identity were not respectable subjects of interest in anthropological and educational scholarship. Religion? What a quaint idea! Trust an international graduate student to come up with it. Why choose *Muslims*? Why separate out religious identity, when it does not really matter (or rather, we *hope* it does not), when we American academics have been hoping, trying, and pretending not to care about religious identity for decades?

Although race, ethnicity, class, and gender are vital to my analysis, I bring to my study that component missing from many anthropological studies of education—religious identity. Despite the secularity of campus peer networks, religious identity remains prominent in students' cultural production. Historically, while anthropologists have identified class capital as a main determinant of status, I illustrate how race, culture, religious identity, and religiosity can trump social class in youth social cultures and relegate aspiring members of the cultural core to the periphery or semi-periphery. I challenge the relative invisibility of religion in much Western anthropological analysis and call for attention to the ways that religious identities are powerful forces in society.

The United States has a unique love-hate relationship with religion and religious identity. Despite the Constitution's Establishment Clause, religion—usually Christianity—deeply pervades political, legal, cultural, and social life, and a vigorous religious Right jockeys for increased power and visibility. As problems of representation are core to this tug-of-war between religion and secularity, my study of Muslim American identity and self-representation on campus is distinctively American. Muslim American women's experiences shed new light on the limitations of American pluralism.

The great secular leveler at the heart of American individualism, higher education in terms of its structure and culture is pointedly blind to religion (Patel 2010: 48). Where the individual is king, why should your home community be a focus—or even recognized? Would that not *mute* your individual identity? "Let us liberate you as individuals from your communities," America exhorts its cultural and ethnic groups. And yet, when unacknowledged, religion leaks like radiation into cultural spaces. Middle-class white Christian values, norms, and assumptions operate in the background; since they are not clearly articulated, they are rarely challenged or even recognized as being the "fishbowl" we dwell in. Diverse faith groups, however, must audibly request entry, and "use up credit" when accorded grudging (minoritized) visibility.

As I examine in the subsequent three chapters, Islamic identity is perceived as almost overshadowing other identities, rendering them invisible or insignificant in comparison to it (case in point: my book is about *Muslim* Americans). Religious identity and practice were intensely significant to my Muslim American female research participants' social status and belonging in campus culture.

Religion, Islam, Education, and Women in North America

In studies of religion, youth, and education, we know something of parochial Christian schools (Peshkin 1998; Lesko 1986) and Islamic schools in North America (Zine 2004, 2008). The identities of American religious minority students remain understudied: there are some positive examples (Gibson 1988; Smith-Hefner 1999), some of which focus on Muslim youth (Grewal 2013; Sirin and Fine 2008; Maira 2009; Haddad, Senzai, and Smith 2009; Sarroub 2005; Abu el-Haj 2007; Ghaffar-Kucher 2009). Some ethnographers, too, have turned their attention to higher education in order to examine the construction of religious and ethnic and gender identities (e.g., Magolda 2000; Magolda and Gross 2009; Abelmann 2009). The study of Muslim women in North America has been a small but growing field (Haddad, Smith, and Moore 2006; Hammer 2012; Bullock 2002; Khan 2002).

In terms of Muslim immigration, we have come a long way from African Muslim slaves and early Lebanese and Palestinian prairie settlers. Today, the children and grandchildren of the professional immigrants of the 1960s and beyond often publicly keep their faith, even while they develop hybrid identities as Muslim

Americans and ethnics. Like Gibson's (1998) Sikh American participants, Muslim Americans ordinarily accommodate without assimilating, adapting Muslim and ethnic practices within American lifestyles.

My Muslim participants contextually constructed their presentation of self within the interaction *between* Muslims and others (as we see in the work of George Mead, Charles Cooley, and Erving Goffman). Cultural assimilation is, therefore, "not a simple performance on the part of an agent, but rather a dialectic between an agent and her audiences" (Yoshino 2007: 74). Performances of self by Muslim American undergraduate women are tangled with discursive performances of cultural, racial, and religious selves by Muslim and non-Muslim others. American fear and desire of religion play significant roles in these discursive identity performances. When dominant majority religion pretends not to be in the room, minority religious groups become conspicuously present by contrast. As "color-blind" attitudes in effect favor the white majority, "religion-blind" attitudes may also privilege a peculiarly American brand of secular Protestantism, one that grows spicier inland, further south, and in the "square states." I shall explore the texture of such religion-blind moments when majority religion silently (or not so silently) enters the picture not as religion per se, but as an invisible force of marginalization. When majority religion flexes its muscles most powerfully *because* of its invisibility, religious minority students experience both invisibility and hypervisibility qua religious minorities in campus communities. Yet the marginality of religious minorities is unacknowledged since it does not fall neatly into the existing compartments of class and race.

I examine the workings of power in American popular cultural discourse, on college campuses and their various social pockets at cores and peripheries, and in Muslim student groups. Through critical scrutiny of broad American cultural trends that actively engage in negative cultural production for Muslim Americans in general and Muslim women in particular, I confront the flawed pluralism in higher education—pluralism that permits only a limited range of difference yet veils its scars and shortcomings under the rhetoric of diversity. The critical scrutiny of Muslim American women's campus experiences poses a broad challenge to the cultural conditions of post-9/11 America.

In the next chapter, I show how Muslim American women undergraduates construct selves at "party schools" in which alcohol culture surfaces as a main character and a backdrop for campus life. These Muslim American women conform, resist, and construct authenticity, with alcohol culture as a powerful shaping factor in their social interactions and identity construction.

3

I Didn't Want to Have
That Outcast Belief about Alcohol

Walking the Tightrope of Alcohol in Campus Culture

Ladies and gentlemen, it is our pleasure to announce that
alcoholic beverages are now available as we have cleared the
Iranian airspace. —Swissair flight attendant in the film *Argo*

Muslim Participation/Marginality in
College Drinking Cultures

Fatima was an adventurous designer of third space identities, a non-hijabi who was at the same time religiously devout, socially liberal, sexually conservative, and politically aware. When Fatima entered the gates of Georgetown, having newly graduated from a strictly Islamic school, she was horrified to find that some of her Muslim friends drank alcohol. Though the overwhelming majority of Muslim theological opinion agrees that intoxicants (beer, wine, and inebriating drugs) are forbidden to adherents of Islam, this ban like most religious taboos is violated as well as observed. Such is also the case with Muslim American college students, men and women. Indeed, in the world of Georgetown, encountering another Muslim drinker was not a momentous discovery. In a world-weary monotone, Fatima said: "But now it's just, 'Oh, he drinks: OK, he's another one among so many.'" As numbers are crucial in any cultural change, this is significant for the future of American Islam. Religious Muslim American students at Georgetown became more nonchalant with alcohol culture over time, even if they did not drink (and, in this book, I do not even tackle the sizable contingent of liberal postcolonial elites, students from Muslim countries who filled college bars). Fatima was a proud though jaded teetotaler, profoundly aware of the social consequences on campus of not drinking. I met many Muslims like her, and many unlike her. The contours of Muslim religious identity clouded over in the spaces of youth culture, pregnant with multifarious possibilities—drinking; not drinking; drinking with regular breaks for teetotalism; periods of drinking; hanging out with drinkers; avoiding any spaces with alcohol; and not drinking but passing as drinkers. Being Muslim in alcohol cultures is, like the Facebook status, complicated.

The extent to which my research participants self-identified as religious depended tremendously on how they related to drinking, dating, clubbing, and clothing. Alcohol was the most frequently mentioned obstacle to Muslim nondrinkers becoming "normal" on campus. It bears mention that the prohibition of alcohol is not the most central preoccupation in Islamic *theology*, but it is very prominent in the cultural production of Muslim religiosity. In the United States, it functions among other things as a form and a tool of resistance to majority behaviors that may lead to religious and cultural assimilation.

Alcohol (drinking, declining, or avoiding it) serves as an expressive principle that illustrates how Muslims walk a tightrope of identity construction in the United States. In this chapter, I examine how Muslim students' participation in alcohol culture yielded status and emotional rewards while nondrinkers were poignantly uncertain regarding their placement by non-Muslim peers (Goffman 1963: 14). Yasmin identified as an insider within campus culture because she was intimately familiar with alcohol culture. But Fatima's marginality continued through the weekdays after the alcohol culture of weekends and evenings had passed. She remained within her peripheral spaces and reflected with trepidation on the prospect of similar marginality in her future workplace. Sarah managed to belong in alcohol culture on some level by extroverted sociability and dancing in nightclubs, but as a nondrinker, she was blocked from an additional layer of social intimacy at parties. And then at parties where "there's so many people crammed into such a small space, and everyone has drinks," for the tiny Sarah, alcohol was literally inescapable since "if you're short, people like, run into you, their stuff is going to spill all over you." As a certain quantity of alcohol spilled on it renders a garment impure for *salaat*, merely attending a party can become a symbolically abhorrent act by obstructing prayer and ritual purity.

College and Alcohol

Drinking together is valued social capital important for social success on campus. More socially acceptable than other drugs, alcohol is in its effects (getting buzzed, getting trashed, or acting drunk, etc.) public and social, and heavy drinking is "ritually scripted" (Hoyt Alverson cited in Brady 2005). A "buzz" is so important to sociability that underage students practice "pregaming," drinking heavily before going out (Brady 2005), so they are not the only one at the party "without a good buzz" (Pederson and LaBrie 2008: 409). The image of Georgetown and GWU students discursively portrayed in campus newspapers and student talk normalized the notion that students "work hard and play hard," that "normal" students want to date and drink (Magolda 2000: 38–39).

About 1,825 college students between eighteen and twenty-four years of age die from alcohol-related injuries annually. Nondrinkers, too, suffer the "second-hand effects" of drinking: half of campus crime is linked to alcohol, and 97,000 students between eighteen and twenty-four years of age are victims of alcohol-related sexual assault or date rape (NIAA 2012). Among sexual assault victims, 55 percent had been drinking, as had 74 percent of campus perpetrators of sexual assault. Every year 159,000 freshmen drop out because of alcohol or drugs (Weitzman and Nelson 2004; Wechsler et al. 2003; Wechsler and Wuethrich 2002). Despite all this, many universities accept money from the alcohol industry for campus alcohol-awareness programs, while claiming that they are addressing the problems (Wechsler 2002). University policies encourage individuals to drink responsibly and in moderation, yet dry social opportunities can be rare and university authorities frequently overlook violations.

The Narrow Path of Crazy Freedom

Campus leisure culture is centered on sociability at college bars, clubs, Greek housing, and campus parties—a core of "crazy," or intense, hedonistic activities regarded as the pinnacle of college entertainment.

Campus fun is not just *any* fun: it is a brand marketed and promoted to students by economic and cultural forces. These student consumers then narrate these experiences to perform specific constructions of "a fun person." As a consumer of alcohol culture, Yasmin spoke caustically of the construction of college leisure as "marketed and packaged to us so we can consume large amounts of alcohol [and cigarettes]."

In my participants' college experience, college seemed to *mandate* craziness; indeed, there was an unbending set of expectations at the heart of college fun. Overall, dangerous drinking and other risky behaviors tend to fade after college—usually. "*Why* are they here?" Yasmin wondered at the adults "stuck in their college years" and still hanging out at college bars. Mahnaz, a talented dance artist and a self-confessed "party girl," claimed that she did not *enjoy* drinking but merely drank in fidelity to the total college experience. As we sat chatting in Red Square, Mahnaz mused that, since by then drinking had already facilitated her social networks, she no longer got trashed because she wanted to, but drank "more like a social, party, let's-go-have-fun type thing." Two years later and gainfully employed, Mahnaz drank the odd glass of wine while watching football but could not understand why she had enjoyed getting drunk in college. College students were free to go "crazy"; at the very least, they were *freer* to be crazy. Crazy fun was closely intertwined with individual freedom from parental monitoring. And religious Muslim American women were asked why, when college bestowed freedom from their parents and communities, they would not choose to fit in, become insiders, become normal, and have some crazy fun.

Not everyone responded positively to this newfound freedom from home communities and curfews. Once her college choice had released her from her small-town life and curfew, Sarah leaped with freshman enthusiasm into the social and leisure activities she had heretofore been denied. But under the hegemonic glare of "crazy" alcohol culture and without the buffer of a parental curfew, Sarah felt unable to *choose* to distance herself from peer leisure culture. Since she was a relatively liberal Muslim who aspired to be at the center of the action, Sarah's resentment of leisure culture surprised me. Within the very embrace of that environment, where campus parties were "all just about drinking," she experienced a new marginality. But the glorified liberty of campus culture meant that Sarah was free to occupy alcohol-oriented spaces repugnant to her—"you're free to do whatever you want"—*and* what you *don't* want. While non-Muslim American youth were free to do whatever *they* wanted, religious Muslims desired a freedom that was not so crazy. And they wanted a saner form of freedom without marginality.

Muslims who reported drinking during their high school days felt that they were freer to abstain as college students. The highly structured social world of minors is characterized by a lower degree of individual choice and is capable of being far more culturally homogenizing than college, despite the legal restrictions on minors. Faiyza and Heather, who used to drink (or had pretended to be drunk) at high school parties now felt that they had a newfound option to decline. Faiyza, a Pakistani American young woman in the premedical program, had never been to an MSA event. We met in a GWU classroom and hit it off immediately, as she regaled me with tales about how she used to drink to try to be like everyone else at her predominantly white high school. Then she graduated and joined her family, expatriates in the Middle East, for some time. She "really re-evaluated everything," and came to both embrace and defend her difference after coming to college: "Because [now] I'll talk more about Islam and stuff." At college, where many Muslims felt that their religious backgrounds were objectified, Faiyza turned that overemphasis to her advantage. To Faiyza, a year in the Middle East gave her access to third spaces of identity and alternative identity models. She met and became friends with religious Western Muslim expatriates and discovered a way to seam the American and the Muslim together. Now comfortably a member of leisure culture, she became adept at interrogating her peers' assumptions about Islam and the Muslim world, constructing third spaces of identity at college clubs and bars. At college, she tried drinking as a freshman but within a month lost interest in it. Faiyza's prior exposure to crazy fun may have helped her get over it sooner. But to do so, it was important for her to have access to alternative freedoms and models of "healthy," integrated Muslim American youth identities.

Learning to Drink

Alcohol culture is based on interlocking narratives, myths, rituals, norms, and expectations. For example, the myth that "everyone drinks a lot" in turn perpetuates alcohol abuse (Benton et al. 2008: 859–60). Much of the pleasure of drinking is constructed in association with rituals of sociability, particularly on such "special" occasions as drinking games, St. Patrick's Day, game day, spring break, twenty-first birthday parties, general parties, pre-parties, and after-parties. In general, the further away students are from college, the safer they are from the excesses of alcohol culture, as most drinking happens among Greek students, then dorm residents, and then among off-campus residents, and least of all among commuters living with their families (Presley et al. 1996a, 1996b; Wechsler 1998 cited in NIAA 2002). Dating, drinking, and clubbing in public places where novice participants can be *seen* are essential rituals of alcohol culture, especially for freshmen "as they face the insecurity of establishing themselves in a new social milieu" (NIAA 2002: 1). Existing members of alcohol culture repeatedly initiate novices into the idea that drinking activities are enjoyable. Novices then possess tales of participation, and the narration of these tales in turn perpetuates the lifestyle and its construction as fun, free, and crazy.

Alcohol culture was built on an extensive web of cues and rituals: "People who have parties and—yes, at the party, before the party, people have posters of drinks on their walls, and they talk about how much they drink, what they drink and how good it was and how much it cost," Yasmin explained. Yasmin, a warm and thoughtful sophomore, chatted with me regularly, usually in the comfortable and companionable student lounge. I enjoyed her critical musings on both conservative Muslim religiosity and majority youth culture.

> YASMIN: It's pretty dumb what we do for enjoyment. But then everyone keeps telling you it's fun. And then you start believing it's fun. "Oh, clubs are fun!" And then you have *a story to tell someone*: "I went to the club last night." "Oh, was it really fun?" "Yeah, it was great!" Was it really? Nooo. People dancing, you don't even know any of them; it's dark, it's smelly. [emphasis added].

Having "a story to tell someone" reinforces novice membership status and perpetuates the culture. "Yes, I have the same values as you do! I think alcohol is good! Alcohol! Beer! Yay!" With mock enthusiasm, Yasmin ironically rehearsed her social performance in alcohol culture.

For novice members, alcohol was an omnipresent force for sociability, a centering subject of conversation and experience. Once Yasmin had started drinking at college under an ex-boyfriend's pressure ("What do you mean you don't drink?! Come on!"), the momentum of college culture reinforced her drinking because "after that, people drink all the time, so—." In American social culture, alcohol is central to forging sociable informality. The drinker earns a core space in the group by co-constructing that informality.

Drinking and Belonging

This is not to say that peers who did not drink were rejected from leisure spaces. Nondrinkers were generously tolerated, and I heard no reports of outright meanness or ridicule. Peer pressure and social control were experienced not through penalties of intolerance or ridicule for refusing drinks, but through *not* receiving that additional acceptance and camaraderie that result from joining the community of drinking: "Just not like as if I was joining in," as Haseena described it. Just because you were "in" did not mean you could not be kicked out. Once an individual had mastered the art of "alcohol talk" and the connective power of alcohol, giving it up became more difficult than if the individual had never gained an "in" in the first place. Yasmin worked at reinforcing her cultural core position.

> YASMIN: [If I refused to drink, other people] wouldn't care, I don't think. . . . But *you* would just be like, "What do I have to talk about now?" Whereas *now*, I always have a topic of conversation. I can be like, "Yeah, what's your drink of choice?" . . . "I like white wine!" "I hate beer!" . . . And it's really stupid. But especially once you get started and once you already know how to have conversations like that, it's hard to just stop.

Yasmin had been fully integrated in a predominantly white high school and not in a religious Muslim community. The gravitational pull of alcohol culture on her was strong, and it was "hard to just stop" belonging. Previous acculturation was significant in determining whether you drank at college. If you were acculturated in religious Muslim sociability, you probably would not drink. If you were immersed in mainstream American sociability and disengaged from religious Muslims, you might end up drinking.

Fatima, however, felt that her presence was not core to a drinking group of friends ("I'll be an inconvenience"). New to dominant youth culture, she had been raised in a conservative Muslim community, was utterly bored in alcohol culture, and was doing her best to belong in campus culture without losing her religion. So she accepted invitations to "just come and sit around" (*around* and outside the main activity of drinking). Given a choice, she preferred to watch movies with Muslim girlfriends because she felt "wanted" with *them*. Though she sought out majority American friends, more out of duty to multicultural America than for sociability, she felt no gravitational pull toward majority leisure culture. And even Yasmin, who drank, experienced the "slow, cultural" normative "pressure of fitting in where everyone else is drinking" as a force that acted "passively" simply when "I go out with my friends and everyone's drinking. *That* kind of hostile. No one's telling me *drink!* or pushing it in my face."

Fatima, as I have mentioned, was fully socialized in Muslim contexts and felt out of place in majority culture. Yasmin had long been a full member of mainstream campus culture. Elizabeth, black and recently converted, felt uncertain in the mostly immigrant Muslim student community. A brilliant and exuberant young woman, Elizabeth had a foot in several communities of interest. But the black and multicultural student groups had dance events and met at bars; the sororities had beach parties. New to Islamic religious practice, Elizabeth started avoiding parties where she feared possibly slipping up. Where Fatima was trying hard to belong in alcohol culture (and yet not drink), and even Yasmin, with her easy drinking, was consciously working at belonging, Elizabeth belonged in alcohol culture but was trying *not* to. Her alternative social space—the Muslim student group—was mostly immigrant. She felt uncertain in both Muslim and mainstream cultural spaces. Over time, she succeeded in detaching herself from alcohol culture by immersing herself in religious Muslim sociability.

White and upper middle class, Heather had belonged in alcohol culture during her high school days too. At college, she became immersed in religious Muslim youth groups. Still, she acutely felt the pinch of loss, realizing that she no longer quite belonged in mainstream sociability. Heather avoided alcohol culture like Elizabeth, but because she felt invisible, not because she felt vulnerable. She wasn't afraid of temptation: she just resented her newfound outsider status.

Semi-Peripheral Participation in Alcohol Culture

A nondrinker who attended bars, clubs, and parties was a marginal or semi-peripheral participant in alcohol culture. So why would a nondrinker attend parties where she did not belong? The *why* was tangled in necessity, utility, upward mobility, and the quest for integration in majority society.

Social Purposes

Being friendly, "the central code of etiquette in student culture," comprises "acting friendly" by smiling, making casual physical contact, and making friendly inquiries about the other person's wellbeing (Moffatt 1991: 53–54). Undergraduates were eager to make friends and socialize in person, by phone, and virtually. Like many second-generation immigrants, some of my participants felt that they had to build from scratch the sociocultural capital that their wealthy white peers had inherited. Fatima was working overtime in the disparate borderlands of her conservative Indian Muslim family, a religious Muslim inner circle of friends, and core college culture. Fatima's immigrant parents, who had eschewed such frivolities as hobbies and sociability to build a new life for their children, were not much help: they did not understand why Fatima needed to hang out with friends. As for Fatima's close friends, all strict, orthodox Muslims, they completely avoided alcohol culture and proximity to intoxicants. But to be friendly, you spent time together in sociable spaces. Extracurricular and social events punctuated the college week, but during the weekend, which constituted a concentrated chunk of sociability and enjoyment, religious Muslims often became quite disconnected from mainstream social networks and majority peers. Unlike these friends, Fatima never drank but pragmatically accepted that, work or leisure, "there is going to be alcohol" in American sociability. Fatima selectively accommodated aspects of majority culture by attending parties where alcohol flowed freely, but by abstaining from alcohol, she did not assimilate (Gibson 1988).

A young Arab American woman of sunny temperament, Latifa had attended Islamic school with Fatima. Keen to explore the social possibilities on a diverse campus yet nervous about the risks of this new world, Latifa only had *some* non-Muslim friends on campus, and "probably one or two closer ones, in the sense that we'd go out to lunch together, we do this together, that together." But "come Thursday, Friday, Saturday night, what do we do? Different things, of course, because she wants to go clubbing and drinking and I want to do something else."

Before her religious conversion, in high school, Heather had wanted to be an insider—"the one who knew everyone" and was "friends with everyone." She was white, attractive, intelligent, and academically successful. All doors were open to her. Then she became Muslim. She found that she faced an awkward choice: she could remain suspended and adrift as a semi-peripheral participant in alcohol culture or become a core participant in tight-knit religious Muslim enclaves. Heather agonized over how "you can't be friends . . . no matter how cool or funny or outgoing you are" with people whose leisure plans feature "drinking, partying, hooking up randomly."

"Weekday academic" and "weekend social" lives became separated, as "the people you're going to be cool with in class, you aren't necessarily going to hang out with on the weekend." Why? The afternoon sun streamed in on us as we gazed out of her dorm room windows to the gates of Georgetown, and Heather explained in her soft voice:

> It's always sort of traumatizing when you're walking on campus and this very drunk student that you recognize or sit next to in class Tuesdays and Thursdays comes by, completely drunk and screaming at the top of their lungs! . . . There just aren't very many opportunities to do anything that doesn't involve drinking. . . . If I go out with [non-Muslim] people, normally I'll go to dinner [with them], and they'll go out later [without me], then I'll just either meet up with Muslim friends or—.

Ephemeral workweek relationships expired on Thursday or Friday because Heather could not share the world of her classmate once she had become a screaming drunk. Teetotalers like Heather, however, were quite invisible to the screaming drunk.

Pedagogical Participation

Muslim American students were constantly aware that, though marginal, they bore the responsibility to educate stereotypes out of their majority American peers. In this way semi-peripheral participation could yield pedagogical returns. Fatima tried "to go out of her way" to socialize in spaces that her conservative Muslim friends labeled *haraam*.

> FATIMA: I don't feel that it works when you go to people and you're like, [sternly] "No, I don't do it, and I'm not going to show up at your party, and I'm against it, and I think you're like, bad because of [it]." . . . I think the better approach is, "OK, I accept you for what you're doing, and *you just accept me* for what I'm doing." . . . And I feel that you can influence people that way more, and people respect you more, than [you] being obtuse and being, "Oh, that's totally against what I do and I'm not going to do it at all" [emphasis added].

Though Fatima optimistically assumed that her peers would respond to her compromise and "just accept" her teetotalism, the *tolerance* proffered by her peers was far shallower than the *acceptance* they received from Fatima because of the cultural power differential. Fatima accepted alcohol cultural norms as dominant but also unconditionally accepted peers' right to cross-examine her about her refusal to drink. "Being accepted" by majority peers could be a strenuous endeavor.

Still, Fatima refined her peers' interrogation into a positive opportunity to change their image of her "from *this stereotypical Muslim* to someone who's *like everyone else*, who goes through the same trials and tribulations, and likes to have fun as well" (emphasis added). This *stereotypical Muslim* was the ever-present Other to which Muslim Americans constantly projected a *contrast*. The stereotypical Muslim (a religiously and culturally foreign outsider) was *not* like everyone else, did *not* have fun, avoided non-Muslims and (what Fatima's friends called) "non-Muslim environments," and did not have shared experiences ("the same trials and tribulations"). To avoid being a stereotypical Muslim was risky though. Fatima's cultural accommodation in fact frequently approximated assimilation as, like Heather, she attempted to project a persona of "someone who's *like everyone else.*"

Since the range permitted a Muslim persona was rather narrow and quirkiness was not a real option, Amira and Fatima carefully tailored their demeanor within alcohol culture to their pedagogical purposes, and celebrated their success in doing so. At bars, Amira graciously declined drinks without "acting insulted" or offering explanations. Her friends did not realize until later that she was a teetotaler. This subtle and self-consciously mellow approach was meticulously customized to her non-Muslim peers.

> AMIRA: And it shows to these people who probably have this perception that all Muslim girls cover their heads, all Muslim girls don't talk to people that are not Muslim, all Muslim girls are very intolerant or uncomfortable, it sends a message to these people that you can approach someone like me about it.

Muslims *worked* hard to come across as confident (not oppressed) yet socially "comfortable" and friendly (unlike the Muslim terrorist), and *just* Muslim enough for white folks to find both stimulating and non-threatening. Amira represented herself as a necessary bridge between Muslims and America, as an exception to *these stereotypical Muslims* (Fatima's words). In their identity performances, Amira and Fatima contested their peers' stereotypes but they used these images as being generally applicable to Muslims—just not to *them* as individuals. They accepted the dominant construction of Muslim women as *generally* xenophobic, hostile, aloof, unfriendly, uncomfortable, intolerant, and veiled, and offered their own personal examples as exceptions. They were "normal" Americans who were Muslim. Amira and Fatima were in a mental argument both against stereotypical Muslims, who did not nicely attend parties, and against their non-Muslim peers, who perceived Muslim women as intolerant, uptight, and universally veiled outsiders. For a Muslim to become "like everyone else" in America was a meticulous and endlessly persuasive performance.

In a post-9/11 political climate, being a low-key Muslim in mainstream social spaces was more than merely good manners: it could mean personal and physical safety. Georgetown and GWU Muslim students were fully aware of the dangers that could visit *those stereotypical Muslims* who did not drink or attend parties *and* were being hated, raided, detained, and deported. Fatima and Amira criticized Muslim American insularity as a political failure and a stigma in multicultural white America. They projected exemplary, moderate Muslim American identities and performed immigrant discourses of successful cultural accommodation. They declined alcohol yet represented Muslims in spaces where they were the only religiously observant ones. As for their conservative Muslim friends, they tacitly disapproved of going to parties even for pedagogical purposes. But it was her non-Muslim friends who *openly* interrogated Amira about why she did not isolate herself from alcohol spaces the way *normal Muslims* did. Why did she attend alcohol-oriented parties and *then* decline drinks? "So people always are like, 'You don't *drink?* Oh! But you come to the parties anyway?!'" Why did she not remain within her box of nondrinking and avoid the parties? Why mix Muslim religiosity with "normal" sociability? Religious Muslim teetotalers were *expected*, both by conservative Muslims and by majority peers, to distance themselves from majority culture.

For a group as vulnerable as freshmen, youth that desperately want to fit in, be normal, and connect, the "choice" to be either normal or different is not a genuine one. In her high school days, Faiyza used to drink to erase the sense of difference between her and her peers, and to generate intimate camaraderie. Despite close friendships, "there was this certain aspect that I couldn't click with them— just because they weren't from the Middle East, and I couldn't talk to them about certain things, you know?" And then there were stresses associated with being "so interesting" when she said "all these things they'd never thought about." Perpetually in the diversity showcase, Faiyza felt that she was "missing something"—full belonging, conformity, wholeness of identity, normalcy. "I was just so—so tired with everything being how it was; like, me not drinking at every party. I was tired of being the only person." Yearning to be "just another girl in high school," she started drinking.

Though Sarah did not start drinking to be normal, she, too, complained irritably of being reduced to teetotalism: "The Muslim girl who's not drinking. The Muslim girl who hasn't lost all her inhibitions and gone crazy." In a culture where drinking and being uninhibited constituted the heart of leisure activities, this label was a stigma and "just kind of stupid." Sarah became invisible *when* beer began to flow and collective enjoyment became more intense.

> SARAH: It's annoying because those situations aren't really fun for me and most people that partake of them—like, most of my friends—*that's* considered fun! . . . And they *want* you to come because they want you to be there. But I'm like, after some point they won't even remember you're there.

Alcohol culture made Sarah invisible to her friends because she was not a part of the fun at these parties. Moreover, the centrality of drinking at these parties made her religious identity hypervisible. Where "there's a lot of drinking, a lot of like, that stuff," the flow of sociability came to a sudden halt when drinks were declined: "So there's a lot of 'Oh! [pause] You don't drink, so you must be Muslim.'" Even being identified as Muslim was like being put "in a box." "I mean, it's not like I don't want to be associated with being Muslim," Sarah fumed. "But it's kind of like looking at any white girl and going, 'She's a Christian.'" Since few others were identified by religion, otherwise proud Muslims sometimes resisted being identified by Islam on campus. The Christian, Jewish, or secular identities of white girls operated invisibly under the surface and not as "a person's first identity" (as Amber put it). Primary identification by religion did not happen for white students; the categories of "Muslim" and "Christian" did not operate in comparable ways. Muslim religious identity was not only marginal and weird but reductive and essentialist. Sarah's attempt to treat the two religious affiliations similarly, and to make *Muslim* silent like *Christian*, came to naught. Sarah was a Muslim teetotaler, and her friends were just people. So Sarah downplayed the religious identity that was a source of stigma.

Cool Difference

Being different from everyone else could make you stick out in a sea of faces—either awkwardly or memorably. Faiyza's Muslim and Pakistani identities had been stressful during high school, but sometimes being different could generate possibilities of some limited power in metropolitan campus cultures. Students could be "cool" and "interesting" if they *appropriately* displayed their cultural wares in the diversity showcase of college. At predominantly white campuses, some minority students performed difference that was cool. "Cool difference" constituted a tastefully exotic resistance to majority culture, just a dash of flavor to create a pleasant contrast. Being different *can* be cool, but it is not always so. Not all kinds of difference were necessarily acceptable or popular. Cool, exotic, and colorful cultural activities, such as the South Asian dance show based on Bollywood's global products, were wildly popular on campus and far more marketable than, say, the "more religious" wearing of headscarves (and teetotalism). Certain kinds of difference are more *different* than others. The "undercover teetotaler" and non-hijabi Amira was more likely to possess "cool difference" than the hijabi Amber, with her "loud" Muslim identity (see chap. 4). "I actually kind of savor the idea that they offer me a drink and I say, 'No, thanks,'" Amira remarked. Amira was memorable. Amber was just conspicuous.

Though Amira felt empowered by her refusal of drinks and performed belonging in alcohol culture, she made a conscious choice not to openly *say* why she did not drink. She did not possess enough membership in majority campus culture to do so. She requested juice when beer was served, without volunteering her reasons for not drinking, and it was only later that her friends realized that she did not drink alcohol. Some of her friends did not guess that she was a teetotaler "because I'm not someone who's just, like—who makes them feel bad." Her normal Americanness was evinced in her studiously nonchalant, understated manner of declining drinks. A person who reacted with overt hostility to alcohol, she argued, would never get invited to parties anymore because they "ruined the mood." In the fragile spaces of American pluralism, an immoderate assertion of difference could be perceived as a competitive assertion of cultural superiority or an ill-bred disruption of normal sociability. Muslim identity, above all, had to make a cautious and unassuming appearance for it to become a part of campus culture. Difference could be cool, but it was not always an authentic, "healthy," or free identity choice.

However "cool" or understated, teetotalism was somewhat awkward in campus culture. To invest it with coolness, Amira stripped teetotalism of its religious connotations and framed it as a joke within alcohol culture: "My friends always joke around. They're like, 'Let's go, Amira, you and me, we'll get drunk!' And it's a joke, a big joke." Muslims at drinking parties were funny. Not drinking at parties was a big joke.

Difference in a Box: Sex and Booze

If you had subtle Muslim identities, you might blend in but being inconspicuous put you at some risk from the encroachment of hegemonic youth culture. Total and encompassing difference in multiple cultural areas was neither subtle nor cool, but it could be easier to legitimate and preserve than subtle, fragmentary, selective difference. Such total difference reinforced an individual's cultural boundaries against incursions by hegemonic dominant culture.

Yoshino describes how the pressure on him to convert to heterosexuality ended only after he came out "broadly." This is because "conversion demands were made most aggressively on sexual waverers—individuals whose sexuality seemed ambiguous or unformed" (2007: 44). Yasmin, with her doubts and her shifts in behavior, was a religious and cultural "waverer," liable to accept drinks when she did not want to. Sarah, on the other hand, refused to drink and to have premarital sex, so she felt somewhat buffered from peer pressure by the combined force of these two forms of abstinence. Sarah's close friend Jennifer, a white woman who fancied herself something of an authority on Muslim culture, considered it "very weird" that Sarah had a platonic relationship with a boy she liked. Jennifer's condescension aside ("Oh, you're inexperienced, and that's just the way you're going to be because that's your choice until you get married"), Sarah's teetotalism cushioned her from Jennifer's pressure to become sexually active. Much as alcohol consumption and sexual activity in college are closely linked (DeSimone 2010; Grossman and Markowitz 2005), so, too, sexual abstinence and teetotalism go together for Muslim American women, creating *total* difference. Sarah, who neither drank nor had premarital sex, was in a third space where she was not accountable to dominant norms: "That's not as big a deal because I don't drink, I don't do any of that [sex], so it's just kind of like, this all kind of comes in its own box." Both forms of abstinence could be marked off as "in their own box" and as legitimating each other. This box, protective of Sarah's religious observance, also created a wider gap between her and her non-Muslim friends.

Shallow Sociability

There were two main problems with semi-peripheral participation in alcohol culture: First, it was a poor substitute for social intimacy. Second, how could someone position herself at the center of alcohol culture and remain untouched by it? Participation in alcohol culture gave access to peer friendliness *and* membership, and drinking together was a bonding experience. Teetotalism situated many students on the cultural periphery and blocked access to moments of bonding with mainstream peers when these were, importantly, in the mood to bond. But by socially embracing or integrating an individual, the community also exercised influence on her, as in the case of Yasmin. Friendliness with non-Muslim peers reinforced conformity to the group, while becoming an outsider to the group reinforced difference from it. Elizabeth's social integration into a religious *Muslim* community coincided with the growth of stronger religiosity and abstention from alcohol.

Semi-peripheral participation in alcohol culture was not just a slippery slope; it also did not prove particularly rich in emotional intimacy for religious Muslim teetotalers. Though "*trying* to work on reaching out more to make non-Muslim friends," Fatima could only claim tentative success in marshaling "an eclectic group of *Muslim* friends." Without white non-Muslim friends, a group of Muslim friends, however multicultural, did not necessarily count as "diverse." The "still pretty difficult" labor of making non-Muslim friends was exacerbated by Fatima's lack of mainstream American social repertoire. To start with, "I don't drink; what am I going to *do* to socialize with them?" She resolutely planted herself in parties, but when her friends ended up dancing or making out, Fatima squirmed uncomfortably and felt utterly out of place. She did not get companionably trashed, and was uncomfortable with the sexual activity associated with alcohol ("they'll end up—you know—"). Since she lacked Yasmin's alcohol-based cultural repertoire ("stories to tell") and shared no drinking memories with these friends, Fatima could not move beyond a superficial connection with her peers.

FATIMA: So how can I be friends with this—*close* friends with this person? I can be friends on a day-to-day basis, like "How are you? What's up?" . . . And the way that . . . everyone relates to each other is through like, "Hey, do you remember how we got drunk and threw up on each other?" I'm not going to relate to that, you know.

She remained a casual acquaintance ("What's up?"), unable to graduate to a deeper "Hey, do you remember—?" The conversation centered on these events: "'Do you remember the keg we had, do you remember—?'" "I mean, I can't bond with them," Fatima laughed dryly; "I can't talk about my water."

Enduring shallow sociability, Fatima proffered it in turn. She occupied alcohol culture, but would not drink, did not dance, and, worse, did not enjoy herself. Moreover, she did not contribute financially to providing alcohol. Defining the boundaries of her choices in financial rather than spatial terms, Fatima rejected Islamic injunctions against being in proximity to alcohol altogether and, instead, cleaved rigorously to the prophetic tradition that forbids the buying or selling of alcohol. So when expected to pay her share toward alcohol for a student club event, Fatima stipulated that she would buy food rather than alcohol for the party and managed to "get out of that": "I would never supply alcohol; I would never put my money towards it." She positioned herself *with* the friends who drank but distanced herself from the alcohol that constituted the site of bonding. By doing so, Fatima made her allegiance clear without coming across as distant and "obtuse." In Fatima's comparative perspective, drinking or buying beer ranked as far worse in a hierarchy of Islamic prohibitions, and merely socializing with beer drinkers ultimately did not seem so bad after all.

With the convoluted avoidance strategies involved, these "mixed-contact" parties ("when stigmatized and normal are in the same 'social situation'") were emotionally unsatisfying and therefore unsustainable for religious Muslim teetotalers. Most of the consequences and most of the labor of such social rearrangements fell to Fatima rather than to her majority peers. Still, "The very anticipation of such contacts can of course lead normals and the stigmatized to arrange life so as to avoid them" (Goffman 1963: 12). Although pragmatically willing to accommodate majority behaviors, Fatima remained an outsider to "fun" in alcohol culture. She was not regarded as a fun person by her non-Muslim friends, and she had no fun with *them*. In Muslim social circles, however, she could be a full participant: "That's why most of my friends are Muslim."

So omnipresent was alcohol on campus that most non-Muslim students did not grasp the meaning of Muslim teetotalism. Peers interpreted "I don't drink" as "I don't drink *much*," "I don't binge-drink," or "I don't drink for pleasure." This meant that Fatima had to explain about not drinking *at all*, about how and why: "It's just the explaining yourself, and just that awkwardness of, 'Oh, we shouldn't go to a bar tonight because Fatima doesn't drink.'" Declining a social drink brought the fun to a screeching halt, resulting in unspontaneous awkward moments and gaps of understanding when Fatima felt like "an inconvenience to their social atmosphere, basically." Feeling "guilty" for not participating effusively in the pleasantries at a farewell party, she sat nursing her Coke instead of drinking and dancing, explaining herself repeatedly as her friends kept offering her drinks. Though Fatima powerfully forced spaces of alcohol culture to diversify, incongruent definitions of sociability rendered it hard to have fun in such diverse company. And the opportunities for Fatima's friends to *learn* to have fun with her were few because alcohol culture occupied center stage.

Extracurricular activities were more than just fun: they were essential for rounding out college students' résumés and for their social development. Apart from the academic advantages, why, after all, did upwardly mobile youth attend elite colleges if not to make friends in high places? Alcohol was the star of student club events. Fatima volunteered for freshman orientation in her quest for social integration, but alcohol followed her to the orientation team's social events. Fatima's team members socially embraced her by inviting her to parties—where she "just sat there with my Coke, and left after twenty minutes." Frustrated by her inability to connect with her fellow volunteers, she feared that this marginality within the team was a harbinger of lifelong marginality that would persist in her adult professional life: "In the future I'm going to have to deal with situations like that, in the workplace and things like that: What am I going to do then?" As early as undergraduate life, young people are inducted into the kind of marginality that costs women and minorities access to professional growth, networks, and promotions.

Third Spaces of Identity: Clubs versus Bars

Alcohol culture powerfully shaped the social lives of all students including Muslim Americans. Many Muslim American women created third spaces of praxis in alcohol culture. By means of pragmatic religious acts, they positioned themselves vis-à-vis gendered, sociable, youthful, and religious identities and ruptured such binaries as "religious Muslims don't party" and "nominal Muslims party." Sarah and Haseena chose dance clubs (where alcohol is secondary) over bars (where alcohol is dominant) "just because—I mean, yes, people are drinking, but people are there [at clubs] to dance" (Sarah).

"You should talk to Haseena," Tehzeeb urged me. Haseena had such interesting things to share that Tehzeeb even arranged the first interview on my behalf. A young and ebullient Pakistani American, Haseena was a rare case of a rather religious young woman who had a conservative, protective family *and* a steady boyfriend, Zafar. Haseena attended drinking parties but did not drink, had a sexual relationship with Zafar but intended to marry him as soon as the rather elusive parental consent had been carefully extracted without too much drama. Haseena insisted that her teetotalism indicated her observance of the "more important [religious] boundaries." In other words, Haseena's teetotalism helped offset the stigma of being sexually active and participating in alcohol culture.

"I go to parties and stuff, but I don't drink. . . . That's because I'm religious. . . . I do consider myself religious; I just don't consider myself conservative," Haseena argued with an imaginary interlocutor. A teetotaler who loved nightclubs, Haseena was a *core* participant of nightclub culture because she loved dancing. In drinking spaces, however, she was barred from the main activity. Recall how Fatima argued that by not purchasing alcohol, she was far more religious than she might seem to her conservative friends who did not even set foot in bars. In like manner, Haseena's religiosity was elevated via her teetotalism when contrasted with the heavy drinking prevalent in college bars and clubs.

But Haseena's teetotalism earned her only grudging credit for religiosity from the "no-parties" Muslims. Haseena acknowledged ruefully that "a lot of conservative people wouldn't be at the party to begin with." But then, Haseena and Sarah did not set about to *be* religiously conservative: unlike their conservative Muslim American friends, Haseena and Sarah were relatively integrated into mainstream leisure culture. They were liberal Muslim teetotalers who relinquished the option of full cultural belonging in leisure culture, an option otherwise available to them. They had almost arrived yet they *chose* not to have it all. While their semi-peripheral participation in leisure culture muddied the waters of their religiosity, this participation caused Sarah's and Haseena's religiosity to stand out in starker contrast to their leisure activities. Not drinking at parties made Muslims look more religious, like the scoundrel with the heart of gold in the stories. You did not look much of anything to the majority observer if you were not there at all.

Covering an "Outcast Belief about Alcohol"

Muslim semi-peripheral participants in alcohol culture frequently concealed or disguised their teetotalism. The way Muslim identities went underground in alcohol culture was a significant factor in religious Muslims' dislike of bars, parties, and clubs.

Disguising an Anti-Alcohol Position

Roshan, the youngest in a religiously low-key Bangladeshi American family, had launched her freshman social career embedded in South Asian alcohol culture. By sophomore year, Roshan had mostly detached herself from her former social world and was working her way toward becoming more religiously observant via student activism.

Because minority students are surrounded by majority peers, much of their social development occurs via identity performances that are addressed to these majority peers. Students with shared religious, cultural, and political commitments gather sociably in student clubs and organizations. Club officers and members engage in programming whereby the organization "meets" the outside world. Religious student programming on campus falls into the two main categories of either intra-community sociability or identity performance for outsiders to the religious community. The MSAs organized religiously framed (and alcohol-free) events as an alternative to the excesses of alcohol culture, as well as to develop community and support for Muslim students. The buffer site of the MSA was important for mediating religious identities.

During our first interview, Roshan told me about a struggle of conscience she had recently experienced. A white, non-Muslim friend had asked her to sign a petition on behalf of a student club requesting that alcohol be permitted for a campus event. Roshan had frozen for a moment and then signed the petition, torn between disapproval of alcohol culture and the fear of alienating her friend. Roshan had *belonged* within leisure culture in her freshman year of clubbing. Could she now abandon the camaraderie with majority peers in whom she had invested emotional energy? In retrospect, she agonized over the implications of her capitulation.

> ROSHAN: And I was *thinking*, no! Even if you're trying to say it's just for twenty-one-year-olds and up, I don't agree with alcohol. But I was put in this position where I didn't want to be like, "No, I don't agree with it, I'm not going to sign it!" And they'd be like, "*Why?* What's your *problem?*" I just didn't want to be put in that position, so I was like, OK, whatever. I signed it. . . . I guess, to be honest, I didn't want to have that outcast . . . that really foreign belief about alcohol.

Non-Muslim friends could not comprehend why Roshan took exception to alcohol culture: it was "just alcohol!" Faced with the binary "choice" to resist or comply (Holland et al. 1998), Roshan complied, for what kind of loser refused to cooperate with a friend on leisure and entertainment? To her non-Muslim friend, it would seem that Roshan had missed the point by agonizing over alcohol on campus. Permissive campus cultural norms and the code of friendliness both required that students ally themselves with the cause of sociability, so "even if they didn't care about alcohol, they'd be like, 'Yeah, I'll help you because you're my friend; I'll sign the petition.' But I just wanted to be like 'No!'" Roshan "wasn't strong enough to be like, 'No!'"— an overtly religious, principled, and unfriendly Muslim, armed with "hostile bravado" (Goffman 1963: 17) in the hedonistic social spaces of an elite university. She fell in with a practice that is the measure of informality in American culture (Bradley Levinson, personal conversation), covering her religiosity and her anti-drinking position.

The hypothetical "No!" certainly would not have changed alcohol culture, but Roshan covered her Muslim identity and compromised her conscience.

In the aforementioned exchange, Roshan's anxiety was centered not merely on her *personal* religious practice but on her perceived standpoint vis-à-vis the petition for a collective public event: "It's like I'm promoting alcohol." Political representation before dominant majority Americans appeared to overshadow the significance of Roshan's personal spiritual goals.

Muslim women either participated in alcohol culture at some level or did not: in any case, they did not challenge it from within. "Loud" or "obtuse" resistance, parodied by Fatima and Amira as being stereotypically Muslim, was eschewed as ineffective, socially inept, and harmful to the fragile Muslim image. The power of alcohol culture remained unchallenged. Any strategizing against it was restrained and low-key.

Privatizing the Anti-Alcohol Culture Position

Fatima focused her energies on maintaining her private religiosity where, she claimed, "Religiously I'm kind of the same *for myself*; the boundaries I hold *for myself*, I'm kind of the same" (emphasis added). Fatima held fast to her wonted beliefs and practice by retreating to her private religiosity and covering it from the public gaze. She tolerated drinking and clubbing as activities that were beneath her: "I've never seen the rationality behind dating, . . . clubbing, . . . drinking." Unlike Heather and Roshan, Fatima had been raised in a culturally isolated, conservative, immigrant Muslim community where she had learned that Muslims *were* different from the majority and that they *did not* drink and *did not* have extramarital sex. Fatima's homogeneous imagined community, with parallels in Orientalist essentialism, collapsed in the messy spaces of campus culture, where Muslim youth with diverse practices came together, where un-Islamic activities were the dominant symbolic capital of a youthful lifestyle.

Heather and Roshan aspired to bring Muslim identities to campus cultural spaces that had previously been home for them. Fatima was an immigrant, so to speak, to campus culture, and remained within it as a guest, not undertaking the project of reshaping campus social culture to make it more temperance-friendly. By dividing her public and private selves and accepting minority spaces of silence in alcohol culture, she preserved the integrity of her religiosity.

Taking Islam Out of Not Drinking

Although marginalized within hedonistic youth culture, Latifa asserted the superiority of her temperance over dominant campus culture. As she did so, however, she secularized her temperance and covered the religious underpinning of this temperance.

> LATIFA: Oh, boy, the conversations and persuasions I've got about drinking—some people just don't comprehend that not only is it religiously unacceptable but I am just not interested. To them, that's totally weird—seeing that Georgetown is a big drinking school.

Her friends saw Latifa's teetotalism as inappropriate in the context of a "big drinking school." Yet what could be stronger motivation for youth to avoid doing something than that it *bored* them? Instead of framing temperance in religious terms, Latifa framed it in youthful hedonistic terms. She avoided the *boring* and undesirable activity of drinking, so her abstention was not mere ascetic self-denial, submission to a religious taboo, or, worse, Muslim female submission to authority. She was doing what she *wanted* to do: she just was not *inclined* to drink. Latifa enacted cool cultural resistance by concealing her Islamic justification for teetotalism. In Latifa's explanation, Islam disappeared from sight entirely.

Heather knew that religiosity was not the best rationale for one's actions on campus because "when you're in an intellectual community and you make a religious argument for something, there . . . people who are going to be like, 'Oh right, because we really make decisions by what Jesus said'—you know? Or like, 'you don't take the Bible literally, do you?'" Roshan—brown and immigrant—ducked and dissembled as she signed the petition for alcohol; Heather, on the other hand, used her apparently Islam-free American whiteness to make religious temperance normal. This happened at an honors club meeting when Lisa, another club member, proposed a wine-and-cheese party for freshmen members. When Heather objected that the party was unsuitable for (underage) freshmen, Lisa countered, "Honestly though, *I* drink. We *all* drink." College students, it was clear, learned to expect alcohol at all parties, in opposition to the academic mission of the university. Sharmila and Mohammed, Muslim club members, joined their voices with Heather's, demonstrating that not *everyone* drank. In this encounter, Heather strategically wielded her power as an affluent white woman whose Muslim identity was as yet unknown to Lisa.

> HEATHER: No, I'm just going to be straight up with her. She doesn't know I'm Muslim, and quite honestly, I can sometimes get away with stuff when I don't say it—you know, when I don't say I'm Muslim, because . . . it can be a broader spectrum. I can be like, "I don't drink and quite honestly, student groups and student organizations are the one method on campus you have of getting to know people in a non-drinking environment where you can actually make contacts, make friends, and meet people with similar interests and connect on a level that's a little bit more—you know, substantive than like, being drunk on Friday night and being at a party." . . . There's so many forums in which students already are marginalized if they're not part of that culture.

Being publicly Muslim limited one's social and cultural range of possibility—for whites as well as nonwhites. White and seemingly non-Muslim, Heather could operate on "a broader spectrum" and could "get away with stuff" as aberrant and underhand as advocating alcohol-free social spaces on campus. Though claiming that she would be "straight up" with her friend, Heather strategically covered her Muslim identity. A woman belonging to the complex and unstereotypical white majority could respectably dissociate herself from select majority practices without becoming othered as an outsider. As a white female, she lent her racial and cultural power to a liberal, socially aware (still white) rejection of underage drinking and a general concern for the health and social welfare of lonely freshmen and marginal teetotalers. Freshmen needed friends, and alcohol kept getting in the way. A publicly Muslim identity would expose her opposition to alcohol for what it "really" was—particularistic, devoid of secular significance, and Islamic. Then, Lisa would know that Heather's reasoning was "just" the perspective of a controversial minority group and not applicable to "everybody." For religious purposes, Heather tacitly disavowed her religious identity and tried to rewrite campus culture by "active appropriation" and a "partial penetration of structures" (Willis 1981: 175).

Heather was outraged about the implications of such a public event as a wine-and-cheese reception for freshmen. Underage drinking has, after all, been described as "an issue of national importance" (Federal Trade Commission 2008:2). She fumed: "Why are we promoting drinking? *Granted if people do it in their own time, I don't care*" (emphasis added). As was Roshan in the case of the petition, Heather in terms of the wine-and-cheese reception was concerned about a *politically* symbolic, visible, public, and collective honors club event—not just about students drinking. And her symbolic battle was best waged by a secular warrior armed with liberal-secular political weapons (e.g., respect for diversity and force of numbers). Alcohol culture derived power from numbers, normalized as it was by virtue of demographics. Heather turned this demographic power against alcohol culture. As an ally, she spoke for "a silent population" faced with hegemonic alcohol culture, "a sizable portion of the student body who really doesn't drink, and who's not going to want to come to a party and have alcohol."

Muslim Americans were not the only teetotalers, but white teetotalers (such as Mormons) did not bear Muslim racial and sartorial signifiers of difference, nor were they politically as tainted as Muslims were. Heather cited the campus presence of Mormons, Jews, and Catholics "who all are incredibly fun, fabulous, and great people, but don't choose to drink on the weekends—or during the week." (Protestants were conspicuously absent from Heather's argument, perhaps because their majority status associated them with hegemonic cultural practices.) Peripheral participants in alcohol culture (religious minority students, nondrinkers, and academically oriented students) "who aren't necessarily going to want to—I don't know, mesh it with an honors society" added demographic strength to Heather's attack on alcohol. But clearly, in order to really count in college, the nondrinkers must be established as "fun" and "fabulous" normal youth, not cerebral, uninteresting losers. And even drinkers ought to "respect" nondrinkers, as Heather reported doing even when she was a non-Muslim participant in alcohol culture. By respecting nondrinkers, Heather dissociated herself from the oppressive political power of alcohol culture, whereas Lisa allied herself with hegemonic alcohol culture and denied the very existence of nondrinkers ("everybody drinks").

Muslim Americans' religious identities were liable to become hypervisible via teetotalism, while their peers' religious identities operated in the shadows. Dominant majority culture and "universal" norms ("everyone drinks") leaked unacknowledged and invisibly into campus culture. In the same muted manner, therefore, Heather and Latifa objected to alcohol culture, in secular terms and under the radar. Like majority culture and majority religion, Islamic religiosity also wielded political efficacy when it remained invisible. It was both a stigma *and* a cultural resource (Holland et al. 1998: 276–77).

Still, when Heather and Latifa covered and disguised their Muslim identities, they effectively perpetuated the invisibility of religion and their Muslim identities. Their short-term, guerilla tactics helped get the individual out of awkward situations, but their pursuit of legitimacy within dominant culture was ineffective in the long term since they made their religious identities invisible to peers. Indigenizing Islam in America often meant erasing it from sight. These are the terms on which minority groups integrate—the adoption of invisibility.

Muslims and Sex in Alcohol Culture

The total cultural context of parties and bars, including sexual activity, invested alcohol culture with reprehensible connotations.

> HEATHER: In college, parties were so much more out of control than high school. They're pretty dirty sometimes, in terms of people being all over each other at a party. . . . And I'm like, that's just gross and I don't want to see it. I don't really feel like being in that environment.

Elizabeth and Heather, both converts, wanted to avoid the spiritually damaging influence of alcohol culture. Elizabeth used hijab as a mnemonic aid: "I've done a lot of drinking, a lot of smoking and this [hijab] is a reminder: 'Don't get pulled into that!'" Elizabeth was constructing her own "box" of total difference (as Sarah did) by distancing herself from drinking, smoking, drugs, and sexual contact with men. Hijab helped figuratively wrap the box: "Some of the drinking and smoking is connected to one man. . . . Not only is [hijab] a signal to me, but it's a signal to him." In distancing herself from alcohol culture, Elizabeth was reconstructing her own eligibility as a pious Muslim female and turning away from men who participated in alcohol culture.

As it did Elizabeth, Sarah's semi-peripheral participation in alcohol culture brought her into the line of fire between divergent norms of mate eligibility. Her matchmaking friends, Jennifer and Chelsea, criticized her for rejecting an otherwise eligible man because of (what they saw as) her personal preference not to drink. Drinking, a mere leisure activity for Jennifer and Chelsea, was part of Sarah's total religious world: "Because for them it's like, 'Well, you can go out with this guy because he drinks but it doesn't mean *you* have to drink,'" Sarah explained. "But it's like, for me, it *matters* if he drinks." Jennifer and Chelsea perceived drinking as an individual and private act that should not affect *Sarah's* individual religiosity and private teetotalism. Religiosity had social and collective dimensions for Sarah. She saw a potential husband's drinking in a web of praxis that would affect her future life and family.

Drinking impacted, shaped, and restricted Muslim women's marriage prospects. While Muslim women's honor was tainted by alcohol, men—almost biologically configured to "make mistakes"—were swiftly pardoned.

FATIMA: Say you're getting married and someone finds out a girl has drunk before: oh my God, she's *not* going to get married. If a guy has: "Oh, you know, he's a guy. It happens. He was confused."

Marriage-market anxieties aside, the gender politics of campus culture paradoxically functioned in such a way that women were more likely to drink because "the girls who do drink, a lot of them have low self-esteem, and fitting in—self-esteem around people in general. Being able to say, 'I don't drink' is just hard for them" (Fatima). Despite the long-term social and reputational consequences, some women found it harder to decline drinks and battle social consensus. Though discursively constructed as a sphere of independence and enjoyment, campus culture produced gendered vulnerability through a combination of loneliness and an almost dangerously diverse peer group. "You're alone here, you feel like you need to fit in with all different types of groups" (Fatima). After graduation, the turmoil could be over, so that, instead of being thrown in with a motley crew, you would get married ("your spouse won't be drinking, most likely") and you would "create your own group of friends." Fatima looked to a future (teetotaler) spouse and a selected homogeneous social network to emancipate her from campus culture.

Complex Identities between Campus and Family

To abstain from alcohol was weird, yet drinking was risky for Muslim American women's reputations. And to be torn between the two practices entailed a different set of struggles. Yasmin vacillated between drinking and not drinking, but to her drinking buddies, she could not communicate her occasional ambivalence about drinking.

> YASMIN: I mean, when people ask me if I drink, I'm always like, "Um, I don't know." They're like, "What do you mean, you don't know?" That's the hardest thing to say. . . . Why do I say, "I don't know?" Because I have issues with it.

As an insider in alcohol culture, how could Yasmin publicly "out" herself as a potential outsider, conflicted on alcohol? "Diversity" at college generally supported black-and-white distinctions of identity, at least for minority groups such as Muslims, hence the relative ease of Sarah's "in its own box" sexual and alcohol abstinence. Complex and conflicting identities did not fit in the narrow range of static identity permitted to Muslims—liberal drinker or religious teetotaler. Yet as religion, social life, and gendered identities pulled them in various directions, many Muslims occupied middle spaces between drinking and not drinking. A teetotaler herself, Fatima tried to explain such behavior: "Here [on campus], it's kind of like, you're alone here. You feel like you need to fit in with all different types of groups, and one way to do it is to drink sometimes and not drink other times."

The pressures were not limited to bars and clubs. Yasmin encountered similar struggles in academic venues, even as she contemplated quitting alcohol after graduation: "Sometimes I really feel like I'm going to stop. . . . I never drink that much [anyway]. . . . [After college] it depends on what circle I fall into, honestly." But then, as an undergraduate, Yasmin found herself under pressure to drink, with students *and* with professors in a secular Middle East studies scholarly meeting. Yasmin had volunteered to manage the conference videotaping. The invitation to drink was a form of friendly bonding (of course), but the effect of this social embrace was hegemonic and homogenizing.

> YASMIN: Even if I fall into an academic circle, even if it's Muslim studies, plenty of those professors drink. After the [Middle East studies] conference, they had all this wine. Everyone was drinking. They're like, "Why don't you drink? You did so well videotaping!" . . . So I had a glass of wine, because they're like, "Oh, you deserve it!"

As Yasmin did not, after all, wear hijab or dress conservatively, she became pigeonholed as a drinker. The generous embrace of her professors disrupted her then current agenda of not drinking. Forced to comply under the pressure of camaraderie, in tumult over the American role in the Middle East, Yasmin was disoriented and overwhelmed. She wanted to avoid the stigma of refusing to drink, or even being ambivalent about it.

> YASMIN: [They're] like, "Do you drink?" And I was like [pause] "Y—eah." . . . because you're on the spot, and you're like, "Do I? Do I not? Have I stopped? Have I not stopped?" . . .
> SHABANA: But [you probably thought]: "You're a professor: can I say no?"
> YASMIN: That's so true! . . . "Because I *know* you drink. I know you drink and everyone here is drinking." But—
> SHABANA: Unless you're . . . used to saying, "I'm on the outside here!"
> YASMIN: [with mock energy] "I'm *different!*" [laugh]

Her ironic posturing on flaunting difference betrayed the difficulty of being a publicly religious Muslim in secular academe, even in a Middle East studies program on a Catholic campus. Traversing the minefields of uncertainty was more perilous an undertaking for Yasmin than it would be for a (visibly) religious Muslim teetotaler.

So she drank. Majority culture's demand for clear and "pure" minority identities created quandaries for religious *and* irreligious Muslim women.

Occasionally, family and community networks yielded unexpected spaces for uncertainty and complexity. Most of my participants' parents were opposed to their daughters drinking, and some were religiously conservative. Most Muslim women avoided defying their parents, and when they transgressed, they did so as inconspicuously as possible. For one thing, young Muslim Americans were not always resolutely set on any lifestyle point to make a statement about it.

Some parents were ambivalent on issues of lifestyle, too. Neelam was comfortably "normal" in alcohol culture, and though her liberal parents disapproved of drinking in general, she regarded postadolescent "experimenting" as falling into a protected category.

> NEELAM: Obviously they wouldn't want us to be drinking. But I don't think they would mind [us] experimenting. No, my parents aren't blatant. I know they're assuming we're going out. Because [during high school] my father would always bring up, . . ." You're going to college in a year, and when you're in college you can do whatever you want and I'm not going to know what you're doing, so just stay home now."

Even Mahnaz, who partied regularly, became quite distraught when she discovered a bottle of red wine in the refrigerator at home. Laughing, she narrated, "And we've never had any sort of alcohol anything in our house. . . . I'm like, 'Dad, what is this? What are you *doing?*' I'm like flipping out, and my dad's like, [calmly] 'What?'" Apparently alcohol belonged on the college campus and not at home. Her parents were in their own third space (her father said the red wine was for his health) and occupied—by their own choice and hers—a third space of ambiguity about Mahnaz's drinking habits. Though Mahnaz's parents became aware of her drinking when she showed up drunk at home, her father "didn't say anything really, so [laugh] he might sort of subliminally know it." The Bangladeshi parents of Neelam and Mahnaz, both drinkers, shared a "don't ask, don't tell" silence vis-à-vis their daughters' leisure practices, which left their daughters in a state of cautious but not fearful uncertainty.

Although I met most of my initial participants at MSA events, Neelam was unaware that an MSA even existed. An articulate, elegant, and poised young Bangladeshi American woman new to Washington, D.C., Neelam, was "not even sure what [her] parents would think about" her drinking. Her father drank socially while her mother abstained (this gendered difference is common among liberal South Asian families). She gathered clues from her parents' behavior to conclude that they "obviously" did not want her to drink, and "I know they have their assumptions, but *they don't want to know specifically.*" When her mother made tentative inquiries as to whether Neelam drank beer, Neelam countered cautiously with, "Well, do you *think* I did?" Her mother raised her eyebrows, shrugged, and abandoned pursuit ("just kind of dropped it").

> NEELAM: I mean she did bring it up out of the blue, so she is a little curious. *But then she doesn't want to know. . . .* I know they think about it, but they try not to. If they don't ask me, I'm not going to make it a point to tell them. If they ask me, I'll try and be as honest as—as I think is appropriate.

Neelam and her parents maintained a tacit consensus to remain in the dark about each other's alcohol-related praxes, though these seemed to be fairly similar (even her teetotaler mother did not "care" when her husband drank). Her father had allowed her to taste alcohol occasionally when she was very young. "But I mean drinking now is different than back then," as her campus drinking was unmonitored. Neelam remained moderately guarded at home, knowing that her parents might disapprove of how much she drank, because "I don't know what the line is . . . even with my father." Neelam and her sister replicated this tacit ignorance with each other: "I don't talk to her about how bad she is," Neelam chuckled.

Peripheral Participation versus the Exclusive Muslim Refuge

Elizabeth held a degree of Muslim insularity to be a natural impulse, "as long as it's not actively excluding others." Relatively insular Muslims who stuck to enclaves tended to have strongly articulated religious and/or ethnic-cultural identities. Hijabis—the epitome of visible Muslims—socialized mainly with other hijabis. Arguably, most hijabis had few other choices (see chapter 4). Female Muslim peripheral participants in alcohol culture were, by and large, religiously liberal *non-hijabis*. Some religious Muslim women felt obligated to diversify their social circles, and to participate in alcohol culture, because ethnic Americans *ought* to socialize with people to whom they were not necessarily drawn. Most moderately religious Muslim American women saw their Muslim and/or ethnic social circles as *naturally* preferable. But my participants felt that, at least sometimes, they had to resist the natural impulse to "be around people like you" (Elizabeth).

On the other hand, it was praiseworthy and virtuous to associate with religious Muslims. "Depends on what kind of person you are," Elizabeth said. "I wasn't always Muslim. I've drunk before; I've been high before; it's a real struggle not to drink and not be high." A recent convert, with cultural roots in non-immigrant black America, and a warm, sociable person of many interests, involved in a variety of extracurricular activities and social spheres, Elizabeth felt drawn to the influence of *non*-Muslim friends—"folks you like, who otherwise are like you in anything but religion." For Elizabeth, who belonged in core student culture and who had been an "undercover Muslim" for a couple of years, the pressure to drink was a centripetal attraction. Fatima felt "pressure" to drink and to go to bars. Elizabeth felt *tempted*. While (non-Muslim, irreligious) "folks like you" could be a source of temptation because of their shared (normal American) cultural background, "a lot of Muslims teach that your friends *should* be Muslims" (Elizabeth).

A Muslim's ability to socialize safely with non-Muslims and irreligious Muslims (without becoming influenced by them) depended on how impressionable she was. Elizabeth liked the idea of exclusive Muslim sociability: it could protect her from the lure of mainstream leisure culture. The romantic ideal—the embodied experience of Muslim religious community, along with its physical stimuli—meant a unidirectional progress of life (as Elizabeth thought) in a Muslim country "where the *adhan* [the call to prayer] is called all five times and you just got to do it and not be in the middle of class—that kind of thing." The perpetual battle against external influences and the physical memory, the *"Do you remember—?"* (as Fatima said) of having been drunk together, could then be replaced by external stimuli such as adhan, which would reinforce Muslim piety. Elizabeth sought visual signals (e.g., hijab) to erase drinking and smoking from her immediate memory, as well as to cool her notions of a particular man. Elizabeth overcame her former ambivalence about hijab by surrounding herself with Muslims and hijabis—for instance, at an exclusively Muslim weekend event, where all the women wore hijab.

As I have mentioned earlier, Faiyza's temporary residence in the Muslim Middle East prepared her for "healthier" and more integrated social/American and religious/Muslim identities. Faiyza had struggled with reconciling identities in her white, non-Muslim peer group at high school "because it's so hard to—you know, especially when you're Muslim, and you live with Americans, it's so hard to integrate both things." Faiyza had used alcohol to overcome the reductive stigma of being "the Muslim woman who doesn't [drink/date/party]." Things changed when, after high school graduation, Faiyza spent time with her family in the Middle East (à la Elizabeth's dream). There, she met religious Muslim Western peers who succeeded in "integrating both things"—being Muslim and American—and, no longer under the gaze of power, she wearied of being the family rebel, grew comfortable in her own skin, and stopped drinking soon after.

Muslim American networks on campus exercised a degree of social control, albeit in a low-key manner, designed to shelter Muslims from loneliness and alcohol culture. Nadira (a sophomore) reached out to Sarah (a freshman) to "protect" her from the South Asian dance show after-party. Sarah had danced in the show (moderate non-hijabis like Fatima and Nadira refrained from openly expressing disapproval of "dancing in public") and afterward Sarah's Hindu Indian roommate socially embraced her by telling her "it's time to get drunk" and "oh yeah, you need to come with us." Nadira asked the Hindu roommate if Sarah was going to the party (yes, she thought so). Anxious for Sarah but keen not to be pushy, Nadira left a message on Sarah's voicemail.

SARAH: And I got this message [from Nadira] on my phone, it's like: . . . "I don't want to tell you what to do, so if you're going [to the after-party] then, OK, and just be careful. But I really don't think it's a good idea, and it's Ramadan." [affectionate laugh] . . . No, I'm *glad* that she was looking out for me. . . . That's really cool.

And that's something I like about the Muslim girls here: they're really close. . . . They have a sense of like, taking care of you.

The South Asian dance show and the after-party had been scheduled on the most significant night of worship in the Islamic year, the twenty-seventh night of Ramadan. Sarah, who had resented as unwelcome interference Jennifer's suggestions to be more forward with a boyfriend, welcomed Nadira's advice as sisterly protectiveness.

As a freshman, Roshan had been a regular in the leisure culture scene. She described this as the only social option at that time, the alternative being what my participants frequently mentioned as the worst disaster of college life: loneliness. The MSA drew her into its fold, away from her non-Muslim friends, and terminated her initial awkward attempt at integrating teetotalism with leisure culture participation.

ROSHAN: If [MSA members] didn't welcome—. Because I felt really lonely as a freshman. I would say I was stuck in two boats. Both of my legs [were] on two boats, and I couldn't get on one boat because I was just one thing and I had to agree with that, and I couldn't get on the other boat, but I was struggling not to fall in the river. Because I was stuck here not going out with my friends, and my non-Muslim friends would go out clubbing, they'd be drinking: they would be doing all these things. So I would hang out with them but I wouldn't do everything they did. So I couldn't go on exactly their road. But at the same time, I was here with Islam, and I knew I shouldn't do those things. And I was trying to follow Islam, but there wasn't really anyone to support me there. . . . But I couldn't go there completely because I felt so lonely.

For Roshan, as she grew in religiosity, the Muslim refuge and mainstream alcohol culture appeared to be mutually exclusive options. You could not sail in the two boats—of total religious practice and complete immersion in campus culture. This was limbo— neither an entirely Islamic lifestyle nor deep fellowship with non-Muslim friends. To be an observant religious Muslim with close Muslim friends, it seemed that you had to withdraw into the private spaces of Muslim peer groups. MSA members identified and recruited receptive freshmen like Roshan (Schmidt 2004: 100), providing a protective climate and a site of "formalised resistance" (Zine 2000) to campus culture, enabling them to "sail in one boat." So Roshan became an active MSA member and extricated herself from her non-Muslim friends, adapted to the expectations of the Muslim enclave, and became relatively liberated from the wrenching, awkward performances that semi-peripheral participation in leisure culture required. Though Roshan's withdrawal from mainstream campus culture enabled her to become more religious, this common pattern of behavior led to the absence of religious Muslims from mainstream campus culture.

Alcohol culture makes full membership in campus culture difficult for religious Muslims and especially for visibly religious Muslims like hijabis. The degree to which enclaves are inscribed on diverse students in campus culture (Tatum 2003) remains under acknowledged by critics of "balkanization."

Religious and Ethnic Strands within and without Alcohol Culture

Haseena loved to party, but preferably with South Asian Americans: "Alcohol has a lot to do with being white and going out on a weekend here . . . I feel like if you're not drugged, you're not having fun." Haseena was not comparably disturbed by the fact that "it's kind of true, South Asian people, they drink a lot!" It was the *specificities* of white and brown drinking cultures that separated Haseena from white peers, and not the fact that they drank.

> HASEENA: For some reason, with them [South Asians], I feel like [pause]—*more* like it's OK that I don't drink. Because there's other South Asian friends that don't drink. Whereas it's really hard—. [Pause]. But *they* understand more that you're not drunk, like, why you're not drinking. . . . Because [pause] this is actually a really basic thing, but white people, when they drink, they just kind of sit around and get drunk even if they're in a party. And the South Asian thing, dancing is a very big part of their social life. . . . So I can just go and dance and have fun, whereas here, everyone just kind of sits around drunk and that's just not fun!

In South Asian alcohol culture, Haseena could legitimately occupy herself with dancing and not drinking, as compared to Fatima
who nursed her Coke awkwardly as she fielded questions and, eventually, left the (white) party. Haseena's belonging was not perfect by
any means; Yasmin, who certainly had a more acute awareness of
the South Asian drinking corps/core than Haseena (a teetotaler),
described South Asian social scenes as marginalizing of Muslim
teetotalers. Even Haseena acknowledged that there was *some* discomfort in South Asian alcohol culture, but it was better than white
alcohol culture: ("with them, I feel like—*more* like it's OK that I don't
drink"). Haseena loved dancing in clubs, while Fatima did not; Haseena felt more comfortable in South Asian alcohol culture because
Fatima, who did not dance in nightclubs and was not acculturated
in a secular South Asian community, had no place in *any* alcohol
culture.

Moreover, at the heart of Haseena's relative comfort in South Asian
alcohol culture lies a clue to the alienation that engulfs Muslims
in white alcohol culture. Strong temperance traditions *and* ethnic-
cultural and historical connections made South Asian alcohol culture relatively hospitable to teetotalers like Haseena. For Elizabeth,
the non-immigrant recent convert, alcohol culture was more *tempt-
ing* than alienating. Racism and cultural alienation (rather than pure
religiosity) could be a partial source of religious Muslim students'
antagonism toward alcohol culture. But both Muslim Americans *and*
majority Americans play down the racial, ethnic, and cultural foun-
dation of their alienation in white alcohol culture, while amplifying
the Islamic underpinnings of teetotalism.

Ethnic-cultural bonds coiled their way around religious solidarity
so that, while "new" bridges between individuals of different racial
groups were built with effort, friendships with "your own kind" felt
"natural" and not "fake." Still, most of my participants—except Haseena when she discussed her club attendance—framed the "natural"
sense of belonging in terms of religious identity, not shared ethnic or
cultural background. Though Fatima felt a strong sense of belonging
with her Muslim friends and alienation in white spaces ("I'd feel like
a person who's definitely wanted there, and it's not fake, you know"),
she never mentioned how sharing a racial background and ethnic
culture contributed to this sense of belonging. Like whites, Muslims
construct their identities as primarily religious, and they construct

the difference between Muslims and non-Muslims as purely religious as well.

Quite confusing were settings where nonwhite peers, who shared geographic origins with Muslim students, frequently drank as much as (sometimes more!) than white peers. Muslim American college students had a lot in common with the affluent, secular (foreign) Arabs, who marched in pro-Palestinian demonstrations and smoked hookah with them. But it was more awkward for a Muslim to decline a drink by saying "I'm Muslim" when it was proffered by an Arab nightclub proprietor who countered with "So am I!"

And when a Hindu Indian drank, the non-drinking that came in a "box" with *racial* difference became unpacked from that box, and the Indian or Pakistani Muslim stood fragile and conspicuous, teetering precariously on the tip of religious identity. The South Asian club (predominantly Hindu Indian) was a *culturally* similar but religiously diverse space where Sarah's "boxed" and "total difference" was no longer an option. Yasmin described the club as "like a mini–high school" where "mostly, Muslims aren't in the core" and the parties were "*very* drinking-oriented." Like mainstream youth spaces, these minority peer groups that should be spaces of comfort and of community turned into sites of marginalization for Muslim American students.

Zeinab, a deeply thoughtful and politically aware Iranian American, also unpacked the reification of religious unity. She emphasized the importance of personal affinity rather than religious or ethnic kinship.

> ZEINAB: I don't think friendship—I mean of course it's good to have good friends and to be influenced by good people. But I don't think good friends mean you have to be a certain religion. I've learned so much more good things from my Catholic friends. I've learned amazing things from atheist friends. I don't think that good friends—of course someone who doesn't get drunk and have sex—these people, they're not *American*, that's just their character. . . . I like people who love to read or love to talk and be philosophical or sarcastic or funny or smart, and I can round up a group of blacks and Muslims and Jews and Christians and everything. I'm not going to limit myself to Muslims. I don't think that Muslims have—just like [Daniel]

Pipes says Muslims have this inherent barbaric—I don't think Muslims have an inherent good quality.

Zeinab refused to essentialize either Muslim or non-Muslim Americans, so she refused to see any particular faith group or ethnic group as inherently more worthy of close friendship than another.

Conclusion

At the core of leisure culture, alcohol culture on campus was ubiquitous, influential, and exclusionary. In quest of camaraderie and normalcy, a number of Muslims formed an integral core of alcohol culture. Muslim American women juggled the yearning for religiosity, normalcy, and friendship in Muslim, ethnic-cultural, *and* majority social circles, and they strategized diverse ways both to connect with others and to preserve the integrity of their identities.

A Muslim teetotaler's total "boxed difference" could preserve identity integrity and shield her from peer pressure while religious Muslim teetotalers who tried to peripherally participate in leisure culture—to belong, be normal, and therefore tap into a reservoir of camaraderie and integration—found that they were no more than "outcasts" there, suspended between "two boats," and in a cultural no-man's-land. In this in-between space, Muslim women politely declined alcohol and promoted the normalization and indigenization of Muslims in American culture. Compared with the impiety of Muslims who drank and with the clannish insularity of those who avoided (alcohol-oriented) parties altogether, these peripheral participants in alcohol culture cast themselves as acculturated cosmopolitan Americans—"good Muslims" (Mamdani 2004), between the religious flaws of overly impressionable Muslim drinkers and the cultural flaws of stereotypically intolerant, socially inept, and awkward Muslims who cannot or do not socialize comfortably outside Muslim enclaves.

Conservative Muslims, however, decried such in-between strategies as sandwiched in an untenable middle space. And indeed, despite their strategizing, their compromises, and their selective silences, semi-peripheral participants neither achieved full status as normal nor succeeded in fully accessing majority networks of camaraderie.

In a variety of ways, Muslims covered their teetotalism (and their religious identity) and assumed normal youthful personae to counterpoise their temperance: Roshan concealed, Heather secularized, Fatima privatized, and Latifa disguised her opposition to alcohol, each young woman representing herself as compatible with, offended by, immune to, or bored by alcohol culture, respectively. Yet, as Heather demonstrates, this muting of religious identity was mediated by race, as was individuals' power to effect cultural change. While muted religiosity could be a "cover" for cultural change, such covering also perpetuated the invisibility of Islam and of Muslims in campus culture.

While Muslim and majority students all tended to focus purely on religious Islamic teetotalism as being the root of the problem, teetotalers' relative comfort in South Asian alcohol culture suggests possibilities for campus social culture: in a predominantly non-white and relatively "healthy" student culture, peer practices such as drinking may lose some of their power to alienate and exclude. Haseena and Sarah preferred ethnic cultural spaces, which, though capable of being hegemonic, may offer a more diverse and less exclusionary experience.

The quest for camaraderie was a reason either to seek full participation in alcohol culture or to avoid it altogether: a full participant in alcohol culture could possibly acquire normalcy in it, but a peripheral participant risked her status both in Muslim *and* in alcohol culture. The choice between insularity and Muslim "clannishness" was not a genuine one: as the exclusivity of alcohol culture, its demands for conformity, the shallow sociability it offered teetotalers, its sexually permissive norms, and its corrosive influence on desirable spiritual states drove Muslim American women away from leisure culture.

In fact, as I will show in the following two chapters, Muslim women's identity options appeared to be more restricted or starker in alcohol culture than they were in terms of dating culture and sartorial representation. Either Muslim women tried to assimilate by participation and/or semi-peripheral participation in alcohol culture, or they isolated themselves from that culture. Muslim American women's experiences in alcohol culture suggest that leisure culture overshadows and deflects official university policies that purport to enhance campus pluralism. The hyperreligionized identities that Muslims deployed in dating culture and in campus fashion culture were absent from their identity work in alcohol culture. Alcohol culture was king: you complied completely, put your Islamic identity under the table, or made yourself scarce.

4

You Can't Really Look Normal and Dress Modestly

Muslim Women and Their Clothes on Campus

"'Dammit, Jim, I'm a Muslim woman, not a Klingon!'" That cry comes at the climax of Mohja Kahf's satirical poem "Hijab Scene #3." The speaker discovers, though, that she cannot escape the perception of her being from another planet: "—but the positronic force of hijab / jammed all of her cosmic coordinates" (Kahf 2003). Like the hijabi in the poem, Muslim American women encounter in their peers' eyes the vision of the foreign, alien Muslim woman, veiled and subservient to men (Bilge and Aswad 1996), like a pervasive, elongated, distorted self-image in a house of mirrors. As a trope in Western discourse, the Muslim woman is a "subordinate figure suffering from religious oppression," and her veil is "a sign of mystery (in accordance with centuries-old Western stereotypes of exotic Orientalism) or of submission and oppression (the traditionalist view of an anonymous, backward woman, subjugated by religious obligation)" (Martín-Muñoz 2002). In reading the veil as gender oppression, Janice Turner exemplifies the Orientalist perspective: "The head is the site of our brains, our faces, our individuality. To cover it in public implies sublimation, a need to be hidden, disregarded, subordinate to male authority under the guise of religious observance. The degree to which women are covered in any Muslim country is a reliable index of their oppression" (2008: 4).

In this chapter, I discuss the role that clothes, including hijab, play in how Muslim American women construct identities and are perceived by their peers. I illustrate how my participants engaged via clothing with the religiosity, hyperfemininity, exoticism, and otherness inscribed on them; how they used clothing to construct normal and hybrid Muslim American identities, and how they often even constructed identities to match the hyper-Islamic images they saw in the house of mirrors that surrounded them. Under "scrutiny from the colonial, Orientalist, religious, multiculturalist, academic, and feminist gaze" (Khan 2002: xxi), my participants wrestled with the attempts to categorize and define them. Even as they are "constantly pressured to identify [their] single truth," and as they "express [their] desire for flexibility and the right to be contradictory and confused, which more fully reflects the hybrid nature of [their lives, they] receive subtle and sometimes not so subtle messages that [they] do not quite fit" (xxi). My participants "did not quite fit" in dominant majority circles, nor did they fit the one-dimensional mold of the religious Muslim woman generated by Western liberal, Orientalist, and feminist perspectives. They did not quite measure up to the expectations of Muslim communities either.

In chapter 3, I interrogated how alcohol culture constructs marginality for Muslim American women. Knowing that teetotalers are marginal, many Muslims enhance their social lives by drinking or associating with drinkers. Along with drinking, my participants mentioned clothes repeatedly as key to being Muslim as well as to fitting in (or not) as a normal college student. Most undergraduates want to be popular, attractive, and romantically and/or sexually successful: dressing attractively and fashionably is a primary strategy for attaining these goals. Most Muslim American women participated in the intense and expensive fashion scene at elite colleges, but women who retained religious identifiers in their clothing usually relinquished conformity and cutting-edge fashion and socialized almost exclusively with Muslims. On U.S. campuses, hijab, alongside yarmulkes and WWJD (What Would Jesus Do) pins, stands out as one of few visible religious signifiers. Many Muslim American women pursued fashion, status, and attractiveness within a complex mold of modest dress that incorporated long sleeves, tailored Dolce and Gabbana jackets, Banana Republic dress pants, decorous yet entirely fashionable necklines, and/or hijab. Many Muslim American women were indistinguishable from their majority American peers in terms of clothing. But whatever their sartorial choices, most of my participants had been interrogated on many occasions, both by Muslims and by non-Muslims, for being too Muslim or not Muslim enough, for being too modest or not modest enough, and for crossing borders of fashion, culture, and religion.

Sartorial choices, particularly the decision to wear hijab or not, were momentous ones. These choices were seemingly *religious* ones but were closely connected with competing notions of race, class, sexuality, and femininity—the scene of intense body politics. A dizzying range of Muslim scriptural and juristic interpretations exists on the topic of sartorial modesty; it is a subject that generates much heat and light among Muslims. The simplest way to think of Muslim women's modest dress is in the form of a continuum: Muslims at its conservative or orthodox end believe that a woman's body (including arms, legs, and cleavage) and hair must be fully covered, and some feel that the face should be veiled as well. Muslims near the liberal end of the continuum insist that women only need cover their private parts and secondary sexual characteristics, or that Muslims must observe the spirit of modesty, culturally and contextually interpreted. Though the representatives of each perspective can marshal large quantities of scriptural evidence, for many religiously conservative Muslims, especially for neofundamentalists, the modesty continuum is a figment of overly liberal Muslims' imagination. These Muslims believe that men and women are religiously required to dress a specific, recognizably Islamic way, and non-compliance means breaking *the* Islamic code of modesty.

Critical Islamic interpretations could be vague, confusing, and unsettling. From a youth perspective, rigid mandates were less palatable but seemed to stand on surer ground and to have a greater following among religious people. For the convert Elizabeth, rigid and strict dress codes helped reduce the uncertainty of a modesty continuum and defused such difficult questions as, "When you take off the headscarf, how much else do you take off?" and "I mean, it don't keep me up at night, but if I choose to go to the beach again this summer [and wear swimsuits], what if [I'm wrong]?"

Whatever choices they made, Muslim American women were "wrong" from one perspective or another. Whatever positions they occupied on the modesty continuum were evaluated by both Muslim and non-Muslim peers, and whatever choices they made resulted in *some* kind of fallout.

The Unbearable Weight of Hijab

Sister Outsider

It encompasses a myriad of meanings and purposes (Mir 2008), but majority Americans typically read the veil as having had a single, universal meaning for Muslim women throughout history. Muslim American women are imagined as oppressed, traditional, essentially *religious*, foreign, and fanatical fundamentalist followers of a creed that is inherently antithetical to modernity and gender equity.

In chapter 3 I described how Roshan, a Bangladeshi American sophomore and MSA officer, had blended into leisure culture during her freshman year. With her Sanskrit last name and her physiognomy, Roshan frequently passed for a Hindu Indian. But when she became involved in MSA activism rather than leisure culture, her link with campus culture became tenuous. How, then, to purposefully don the symbol of a hated group and become entirely visible as Muslim? Roshan "wanted" to wear hijab but lacked the "strength" to assume the hijabi identity.

> ROSHAN: But I'm worried about the way I'll be accepted, the way my professors are going to react to me. . . . I know some of the non-Muslims: they look at hijabis and they're just like, "Oh, she's one of *those*; she's an outcast."

Hijab could make you an *outcast* just as being uncool about alcohol could. You could "cover" your temperance, but hijab was inherently conspicuous. Roshan's conservative (and less socially integrated) Muslim girlfriends urged her to wear hijab and be undaunted by peer pressure. Roshan's fear of ostracism was based mostly in the potential loss of social connection with majority American peers. The fundamental desire for camaraderie and belonging within peer culture is the centrifugal force that pulls Muslim women away from hijab, visibly Islamic clothing, and unsubtle Muslim identities (and, as we saw in chapter 3, toward alcohol culture). As long as Roshan retained some degree of connection with majority American peers and mainstream campus culture, she did not wear hijab. As she became more religious and closer to the Muslim group, she disengaged from her non-Muslim friends, first as a function of time spent together, and then from a desire for different leisure activities. Being a visibly religious Muslim appeared to exclude the possibility of acceptance among mainstream peers. Muslims had to remain somewhat invisible *as* Muslims to become integrated in the majority peer group, so like others, Roshan turned to closer involvement with Muslims to feel whole.

Sure, hijab made it difficult to connect with majority peers, Zeinab acknowledged, because in their gaze, hijab reduced Muslim women to their clothing. But this was a *good* thing, Zeinab asserted, and a powerful catalyst for change: to achieve the everyday human connection others took for granted, hijabis helped "[break] ground and [promote] a much-needed awareness of Islam" among apathetic majority peers. As an icebreaker, Latifa claimed, hijab motivated non-Muslim peers to ask questions about it: the topic of Islam and Muslims was swiftly broached, and Latifa could then address stereotypes that non-Muslim peers might otherwise never knowingly interrogate or articulate. Hijab broke the ice that it helped create in the first place, forcing Muslim women to transcend comfort zones and reach out for the cold, unwilling hands of potential friendship.

In a dialectical relationship with the observer's stereotypes, hijab not only marked a woman externally as Muslim but it intensified her inward consciousness of difference and cultural distance, according to Diya, a Pakistani American freshman: "They [Muslim American women] feel more different and more distant from everyone else, and I think they feel like a lot more people are watching them, especially because it's almost like a stigma."

DIYA: [Hijab] has these connotations for American people. They [Muslim women] feel like everyone is judging them. . . . American people look at Muslim women and think, "Oh, they're oppressed. . . . Maybe they don't speak English" [laugh]. Or maybe terrorist-related things.

Hijab made Muslim women seem more oppressed to Americans since hijabis were *visibly* Muslim women, unable to downplay their religious identities. Hijabis were associated with victimhood but, paradoxically, also with "terrorist-related things." Compared to

Muslim men, Muslim women were *related* to terrorists—rather than terrorists themselves—since Muslim femaleness is associated with victimhood, while Muslim maleness is associated with violence. As a public symbol, hijab is a chilling reminder of Muslim women's vulnerability in the United States post-9/11, where—as Sarah said reverently, with unconscious irony—"from a mile away, someone can tell that you are a Muslim."

Unreliable Testimony

Thirsty for knowledge of their heritage, Muslim American students were keen to enroll in courses on Islam, Muslims, Muslim women, and Middle Eastern politics. But in a troubled political climate, these courses could be psychologically stressful environments where Muslims were subjected to critical and academic scrutiny. As the only hijabi in a class on the Arab-Israeli conflict, Amber was in the hot seat, the designated Muslim spokesperson who had to consistently voice the prototypical Muslim standpoint. If only she were not hijabi, Amber wished, so she could escape the responsibility of defending Islam—and defending it, probably, in vain! Hijab put Muslim women in the default position of representatives, and it also turned them into questionable representatives.

> AMBER: I feel like what [non-hijabis] say is taken more seriously. . . . So when I speak, I feel like my words don't mean much, because I'm [considered] biased automatically. . . . And if I can't do that [Muslim advocacy], then I need to, like, go into medicine or something. Because when you're defending opinions, you're ultimately constantly defending your identity. It's a constant battle between them and yourself.

When debates about Islam cropped up in class, Amber saw heads turn toward her. If she failed to provide *the* Muslim perspective, or if her opinion did not show "hostile bravado" (Goffman 1963: 17), she would be perceived as a "wishy-washy" sellout. Amber was cornered into the hard work of Muslim advocacy, trapped by her hijab in an assertive, politicized identity.

But equally labeled as blind followers of community belief (Khan 2002), hijabis often foundered in their efforts to change their peers' minds about Muslims. Semi-invisible Muslims who seemed to keep a distance from their religion, like Heather the partly undercover Muslim (see chapter 3), had more credibility. Muslims were already seen as primarily *religious* beings: *visible* Islamic identity indicated excessive investment in Islam, while, to non-Muslim peers, the absence of hijab often (incorrectly) indicated secularity and nominal religiosity. Hijab seemed to project a primarily or exclusively religious identity. Religiosity sullied a person's objectivity. Non-hijabis' Muslim identity was private: they were more credible as representatives, yet they did not *have* to represent Islam.

> AMBER: Yeah, and you know people say, "Because we're wearing [hijab], people listen to us because of who we are, not because of what we look like?" [laugh]. That's not true. . . . By looking at us they're going to think they know who we are. . . . So they're not really listening to what you're saying but who you are as you're saying it. That's what annoys me.
> SHABANA: So they're almost predicting what you're going to say.
> AMBER: Before you say it!

Amber was mocking the pro-hijab Islamist claim that hijabis powerfully render their bodies secondary to their intellect. And indeed, in some ways, a hijabi unsettles social expectations and reconfigures gendered expectations. But a hijabi's covered head garbed her words in predetermined meanings even before these words left her lips. Amber could not win the argument against her own hijab. Hijab weighed Muslim American women down with the representative burden, turned them into targets, and at the same time, hamstrung their ability to represent—indeed, to *be*.

The Conspicuous Absence of Hijab

Hijab and fanaticism, inseparably attached to each other, were negative attributes, but at least they authenticated Muslim identity. Non-hijabis had a better chance at social integration within campus culture, but they were often asked, "Are you religious?"

> DIYA: And that's always an awkward question because . . . if they're thinking in the orthodox sense . . . then they're like, "Well, why don't you cover your head?" I guess they have those

ideas about—I guess fanaticism, or that you'd be really critical of what they were doing . . . like, you're very judgmental and you have moral superiority, attached to being religious.

"There are definite barriers between being religious and being normal in society" (Heather) for almost all faith groups at East Coast urban colleges. But Muslim religiosity probably wins the weirdness award, as most mainline Christian American women do not dress in distinctively religious dress, and neither a Mennonite bonnet nor a nun's habit has quite the political baggage that hijab does. "*Are you religious?*" was a non-question: the interrogator was already armed with a set of assumptions. How to respond? If Diya were to adapt her response to the interlocutor's ignorance, and say, "No, I'm not religious," they might not consider her a real Muslim. If Diya said *yes*, "then they're like, 'Well, why don't you cover your head?'" Worse, the interlocutor might *believe* she was religious (i.e., a fanatical Muslim). Non-Muslim peers simply did not see the complexity of Islamic religiosity and the diversity of Muslim practice to be able to process a Muslim response. Besides, they thought they already had the answers. Weird, outlandish, and antifeminist as hijab was, non-Muslim peers *expected* Muslim American women to wear it. The absence of hijab signified nominal Muslim affiliation at most. That was why non-hijabis surprised friends by their temperance and hijabis shocked teammates by being athletic. Muslim women were stuck between the "seemingly unbridgeable duality of Orientalism and Islam that encourages an allegiance to either one or the Other and thus discourages the in-between gray zones from which progressive politics often emerges" (Khan 2002: xxiii). Creative, personal religiosity like that of the Muslim feminist Diya and the devoutly religious athlete Intisar is constructed in in-between gray zones of praxis, and it does not flourish in spaces where Muslim = religious = fanatical = submissive. Muslim American women's campus peers interrogated them for being different, as well as for being indistinguishable from the majority. Inconvenient Muslim American women who did not fit these categories were stopped at identity checkpoints.

Heather did not wear hijab because she did not wish to alienate her white, Christian parents entirely. But even Heather's professors interrogated her for not wearing hijab.

HEATHER: A lot of them [my professors] assume I'm half-Arab or something like that. They'll be like, "Oh, is your dad Arab?" Or, "Where are you from?" and I'll be like, "No, I converted." So they'll be, like, "Oh, interesting." And it's sort of hard to tell someone. [Dr. Taylor] says, "So, are you religious?" And I'm like [pause], "I hope so, but it's not for me to decide!" She's like, "So, you pray five times a day?" I'm like, "Generally, yes, I make the effort." And she's like, "You fast?" And I'm like, "Yep!" She's like, "Wow. You obviously don't wear the scarf, so how do you feel about that?"

When Heather first revealed that she was Muslim, Dr. Taylor (like student names, all faculty names are pseudonyms) racialized her as nonwhite. After a few false starts, the professor was on her way to filing Heather away correctly, marking off key Islamic practices (ritual prayer and fasting). But Dr. Taylor accorded hijab an importance it does not have in Islamic theology, and tentatively categorized the non-hijabi as a nominal Muslim. In this error, many majority Americans support the case of conservative Islamists in treating hijab like a "sixth pillar" of Islam (Wadud 2006: 219). Americans interrogate hijabis about their choices; but then, they also interrogate non-hijabis about *their* choices.

Leila, a non-hijabi Pakistani American from New York, believed that since the Qur'an did not mandate burqas and face veils, loose-fitting "regular" attire were sufficient for correct Islamic practice. But for the non-Muslim morality police, nothing but a burqa would do. They constantly challenged Leila about the absence of a top-to-toe covering.

LEILA: But so many people [Americans] associate being properly covered with just burqa. Like, you can't just wear loose clothes and cover your head and you're fine. They're still like, "Oh, that's not good enough." . . . [B]ecause people constantly say, "Oh, why don't you wear it?"

Conservative Islamic notions of modesty and Western Orientalist notions about Muslim women often feed into and support each other, as Westerners accept the hegemonic representative status of conservative Muslims in their rigid stance on female modesty (Khan

2002). Muslim and non-Muslim Americans tended not to accept as authentic Muslim women who did not wear conservative attire (Mir 2008).

Why Are You Weird? Why Are You Normal?

Muslim American women, whether hijabi or not, and whether modestly clothed or not, inevitably failed to measure up to *some* set of expectations. Why were Muslim women so passive and withdrawn? And why was a Muslim woman like Intisar a proficient athlete? Why did Leila not wear a burqa? Why was a Muslim woman like Latifa so extroverted? And then, why was such a normal young woman as Latifa disinclined to go out with men? Why was Heather, a normal white woman, dressed in those frumpy clothes, like a foreigner? And then why was Heather, a non-hijabi, so religious? Why did she like Bob Dylan? Why did Amira, a Muslim woman, attend parties? Why did she dance in clubs? And then, why did she decline drinks?

Hijabis were under particular pressure to fit the Muslim woman mold. Hijab publicly marked Muslim American women as Muslim and established expectations for their behavior. Haseena did not like having her behavior options limited in this way.

> HASEENA: Well, I guess [if I wore hijab] I wouldn't have a boyfriend anymore. Because that would be weird. . . . I guess this is a bad thing, but it's more fun not to be hijabi. Because you wouldn't see a hijabi at a club, you know [laugh].

Hijab did not *match* sexual encounters, sports, dancing in public, smoking, and nightclubs. American peers' inability to process or digest Muslim women's incessant border crossings limited hijabis' flexibility of behavior.

From a religious Muslim standpoint, hijab facilitated personal piety precisely by limiting assimilation within mainstream culture. The first step of donning hijab was often painful because Muslim women knew the social and leisure costs of this action. Restrictions on gendered behavior were harder for converts like Elizabeth because "having grown up with [freedoms], it's hard to do without." Reminiscing about frolicking at the public beach with friends, for instance, Elizabeth was forced to pause, "look back and think, how much am I giving up?" She did give up, though, and her sacrifice seemed to reinforce her religiosity, diminish her doubts, and give way to alternative leisure activities. Private Muslim women's parties and spiritual retreats displaced clubs, basketball, and beaches. It was a complete paradigm shift.

Teaching and Dodging

How did Muslim American women respond to stereotypes and Orientalist assumptions? Some tried to educate their peers about Islam and Muslims, but many sought invisibility and to evade the gaze that fixed them. Muslim American women confused and unsettled the gaze, combining disparate cultural ingredients—both religious and secular—in their clothing. Their strategies were oriented both toward *teaching* others about Islam, Muslims, and Muslim women and toward *dodging* the stereotypes and assumptions that majority American peers inscribed on them.

Working against stereotypes was not always a simple matter of supplying information to peers, nor was such a straightforward approach always expedient or persuasive. Instead, Muslim women sometimes crowded stereotypes out with stereotype-contrasting behaviors (like extroverted conviviality). At times, too, Muslim women eluded the stereotyping gaze by being silent, passing as non-Muslim, and/or acting less religiously. Clothing could help reconfigure social arrangements: modest clothing without hijab could bridge Islam and youth culture (or could it?), and even sports could help relegate Muslim identity to the background (or could they?).

Da'wah as Teaching and Dodging:
The Shifting Meanings of Cultural Terms

Many "apparently 'core' cultural commonplaces" (Kahani-Hopkins and Hopkins 2002: 291) in Islam (such as jihad, hijab, and modesty) are shifting rather than fixed in their meanings. The specific meanings of the veil and da'wah, for example, are "contextually shaped, fundamentally contested, and strategically constructed" (Kahani-Hopkins and Hopkins 2002: 291) though frequently Muslims and non-Muslims construct these notions as fixed, static, and singular in meaning.

Roshan yearned to wear hijab but was apprehensive that non-Muslims would shun her. She worried that, thus ostracized, she would no longer be able to enter into ecumenical dialogue with non-Muslim peers, that she would have "to give up da'wah to them." "Da'wah" is literally translated as preaching, calling to someone, or as *balaagh* (conveying the message of Islam). But many young Muslim Americans were repelled by the notion of preaching and, in practice, generally adapted the term "da'wah" to refer to the project of normalizing and indigenizing Muslim Americans and combating stereotypes about Islam, rather than to religious missionary work. Da'wah in the context of MSA-organized educational events was usually defensive, focused on apologetics related to gender and violence.

Roshan's conservative friends disagreed: visible, impeccable religiosity and observance of hijab were integral to *their* interpretation of da'wah. Roshan's friends described hijab as a form of "silent da'wah," a banner of Islam and an unspoken call to learn about (and possibly embrace) the faith. Roshan, they charged, was *forsaking* the work of da'wah to non-Muslim peers by not wearing a hijab. But from Roshan's standpoint, hijab would obstruct her kind of da'wah: hers meant dialogue, shaped by *her* strategic concern, the normalization of Muslims in America. She preferred a vocal, interactive da'wah to the silent da'wah of the hijab, which cut off opportunities for more active exchange. Conservative Muslims disapproved of Roshan's desire to "please others" (as they put it). Their oppositional religiosity was at odds with Roshan's project of normalizing Islam and Muslims, rendering them safer, more acceptable and citizen-worthy in the United States, rather than preaching Islam *as a religion* to non-Muslims. To many conservative Muslims da'wah meant rendering Islam visible, whether it was palatable to others or not. Roshan's da'wah, on the other hand, meant rendering Islam either palatable to majority Americans, or simply invisible. Depending on the speaker, da'wah can variously mean verbally *teaching* non-Muslims about Muslims and the nonverbal representation of Muslims, or it can mean *dodging* or covering Islam and doing verbal representation or *teaching* under covered Islamic identities.

Extroversion as Teaching and Dodging

Of all the preconceived notions they encountered in their peers, the idea that Muslim women were shy and withdrawn—a handy package for an array of assumptions—was the most widespread stereotype that Muslim women had to disprove. Diya, a Pakistani American non-hijabi, had to battle stereotypes, but not as much as Latifa did.

> DIYA: I think people do have a different image of a Muslim woman when they see Latifa. I think because she's more outgoing. And usually, first of all, people think you're oppressed, and if you're very quiet, then I think that sort of [confirms it]. Or they think you're traditional, Eastern, backward. . . . [Latifa represents the idea that:] "I can wear hijab, but it doesn't mean I'm any of the things you think I am." . . . [Latifa] sort of compensates for that. . . . I think people forget that she wears hijab. Ideally, I think that's what should happen.

Despite her successes, the work of "anxious unanchored interaction" (Goffman 1963: 18) was stressful for Latifa, who wanted nothing more than to be "a regular student." Extroverted behavior and "artificial levity"—"the familiar signs of discomfort and stickiness" (19)—were cultural resources Latifa deployed against the "oppressed Muslim woman" stereotype. While a timid white female college student is simply *shy*, a quiet and self-effacing Muslim woman represents a global imagined community of subjugated Muslim women. So Muslim women may be generally oppressed, but a quiet, shy, hijabi Muslim woman is regarded as *extremely* oppressed. Performing extroverted friendliness to subdue the impact of her hijab, Latifa *dodged* people's awareness that she was Muslim by making them "forget that she wears hijab." No one, of course, ever really forgot— just as no one is ever racially "color-blind."

Conforming, Reassuring, and Confounding

Non-Muslim Americans tended to be tense and uncomfortable around hijabis. Intisar's preferred wardrobe—"baggy jeans, shirts, sweats"—was initially a way to "put non-Muslims at ease" and to fit in. Now, her sartorial choices were a complex, shifting bricolage of images.

> INTISAR: It's not really fitting in; it's almost myself out there in a new perspective: "I'm not your regular Muslim girl. I'm really *not*. I'm not the conservative quiet—whatever. I'm so different

that I will wear different things so you really couldn't figure me out until you come to me and embrace that difference."

Intisar framed her casual grunge as neither conformity nor resistance but as a continuous redefinition that changed the terms of the social encounter. It was "almost [herself] out there in a new perspective," a refusal to be classified as she typically was. Intisar's youthful wardrobe belonged in campus culture, but her hijab challenged the onlooker's attempt to "read" her. Intisar forced peers out of their assumptions on multiple levels, until they abandoned their notions and came to "embrace that difference." She continually *dodged*, and then she *taught*. Intisar was so different from the stereotype that the gaze had to be educated to encounter her, as it could rest neither with a stereotypical Muslim woman nor with a typical youth.

Yet while she forced her peers to "embrace that difference," on one level Intisar also *accepted* that the "regular Muslim girl" was veiled, conservative, and quiet. Recall how Amira and Fatima represented themselves as exceptions to "this stereotypical Muslim" (chapter 3). The stereotype was too powerful for Intisar to dislodge: as an individual, though, she could still fight her own way out of it. On another level, she treated the "regular Muslim girl" as a mere image that, mixed up with Intisar's other images, no longer conveyed a singular meaning.

Like Intisar, most of my participants, in asserting that they were normal, argued that they were "differently normal": that they were "normal" American youth as well as hybrid agents, creating third spaces in American youth culture. Such Muslim women created novel pedagogical experiences of the kind that Piaget argued were cognitively effortful, productive of a "disequilibrium" that resulted in cognitive growth (Denson and Bowman 2011: 2) for their non-Muslim peers. In *dodging* the Muslim woman and the youthful image, Intisar *taught* peers to forsake their assumptions and to listen to her.

Hybridity: Different and Normal

Latifa worked hard not to be "your typical, traditional Muslim female," but being supposedly normal had baggage of its own. When peers accepted that Latifa was (as she said) "a little normal" like them, they assumed that she must resemble them entirely. Like

Intisar, who was not "really fitting in" but was "out there in a new perspective," Latifa wanted to communicate that she was neither a stereotypical Muslim woman nor the complete opposite of one.

LATIFA: And sometimes it does come with baggage—the head-scarf. But I think, once people talk to me . . . they realize I'm a little different. . . . And then I mean, yes, I'm cool to chill with and talk with and be friends with, but [that] doesn't neces-sarily mean—. Like, I do have my limits and sometimes they mistake me for—because I am a little normal, that—.
SHABANA: [slyly] That you'll do anything?
LATIFA: [relieved that I had said it for her] Yeah! No, no, I do have certain values!

Latifa's hesitant pauses indicated a reticence regarding alcohol and sex. Once people engaged with Latifa in person, they cautiously granted that she was "a little normal" and "a little different" from their stereotypes (emphasis added). At this point, they assumed that, as a normal college student, she was "cool" with the usual hedonistic youth activities. Then she had to clarify that there were "limits" to her "coolness." Latifa had to teach peers, in a multistep process, that she was a (new) hybrid with American and Muslim/Arab elements and moments. Along the way, they learned (she hoped) that "nor-mal" contained a greater range of possibility than they had thought. Many Muslim women lived in a third space of creative combinations and approximations, transcending the cultural expectations of their non-Muslim American peers.

Silence as Dodging

When I observed Latifa's freshman "Women in Islam" discussion class at Georgetown, her deer-in-the-headlights demeanor per-plexed me, as she was usually a jovial, vivacious woman. During her interview, Latifa spontaneously unburdened herself about how she felt in class.

LATIFA: But I didn't want people to look at me in the classroom as a Muslim female learning about women in Islam. . . . [Or as] your typical traditional Muslim female, the type you see on TV, very conservative . . . in the sense of ideas, lifestyle.

At the heart of academic study, images from popular culture remain intensely present, pervading campus culture. The image of heavily veiled, downtrodden Muslim women is ubiquitous in popular culture and a vital element in the Orientalist discursive construction of Muslims. What would Latifa's peers think of her, the only hijabi in sight, in a class on Muslim women, learning about herself, her status, and her history? What was her position on Muslim women's plight worldwide? Did she agree or disagree with the critical, secular, scholarly discussion as her (mostly white) peers busily hammered away at Muslim women's issues? Was she learning to escape Muslim women's oppressive circumstances? The banner of hijab made her intensely self-conscious of being watched and defined: "Because I was a Muslim female, with a head cover, then people naturally would assume I have a certain perspective." She "didn't want there to be any expectations," but her hijab had already announced a "certain perspective" to her peers, so that the noise of her hijab in their minds silenced her in person. "I want to say something, but I don't want to sound stupid," Latifa recalled thinking.

> LATIFA: But all I wanted was to be a regular student learning about the subject like any other student. . . . Perhaps it was my sensitivity to that that prevented me from participating more, from taking an active role in classroom discussions.

Latifa's veiled appearance rendered her naked, generated assumptions about her, and opened the door to her private life. If she spoke, halfway to her interlocutors' ears, her half-heard words would be overcome by the cavalry of interpretations already present in the media and the Orientalist imagination. Refusing to provide data that might disappoint or confirm observers in their assumptions about her, she remained silent as her (mostly non-Muslim) class members blithely discussed Muslim women's "plight" and "issues." The application of secular academic frameworks in Islamic and Muslim studies risks rendering Islam and Muslims predictable and homogeneous, granting scholars and students the power to define the subjects of study.

Heather, too, found herself turning away from majority Americans and *dodging* the social encounter. The dearth of parking in the Georgetown area led Heather to respond to an advertisement and to contact a Georgetown homeowner about renting a parking spot. Dressed modestly at the height of summer, Heather had walked a considerable distance to the spot. The woman's catlike attempts to pry data out of Heather distressed and embarrassed the young woman. In her first question ("So, [pause] you're at Georgetown?"), the very pause injected doubt and suspicion as to whether Heather, with her atypically modest, unfashionable clothing, was actually affiliated with the elite university. Sexy fashion and wealth were closely related on O Street.

> HEATHER: And she's like, "Do you take any foreign languages there?" And I was like, "Spanish!" And she's like, "That's it?" I was like, "Yep." And she's like, "What's your major?" I'm like, "Anthropology." She goes, "Do you study any certain region of the world?" I was like, "Not really." She's like, "Eastern Europe?" I was like, "No, I have no reason whatsoever to study Eastern Europe." And then she's like, "Well, you walked here. It's such a hot day." . . . She's like, "The way you're dressed: you look Amish!" And she didn't say it like a statement. . . . It was very much like, "Are you Amish?"

Heather's clothing seemed to give the woman leave to breach white American upper-middle-class norms of polite abstention from direct probing into strangers' religious or cultural background. The woman tactlessly exposed Heather's otherness, peeling off her attempts to "pass" and subtly opening Heather's clothing to ridicule, but all this in a manner that prevented Heather from returning fire. Since Heather was white, the woman tested her for Eastern (and not Western or Northern) European or Amish origins, either of which could have positioned her as relatively marginal and Other. Anticipating a negative reaction to Islam and pinned in the corner, Heather was unable to maneuver her way out of the interrogation. Still, Heather dodged and almost triumphantly flashed her credentials in small victories: she studied an *American* foreign language, Spanish, and *not* a foreign culture. The woman was dissatisfied ("That's *it?*"). Heather resented the new Muslim marginality inscribed on her: her modest clothes brought class, race, culture, and citizenship together in the othering of her body. Heather chose not to do business with the woman instead of using the encounter as a teachable moment.

HEATHER: Some people would be like, [with mock ebullience] "Actually I'm Muslim, and this is why I dress this way." And I was more like, "You're really annoying, and I'm not going to provide you with any further information." I mean, that may not be the best way to go about things, but I was just like, no! This woman is clearly not the most tolerant or sensitive of people, and I was like, if I'm going to be parking in this parking space somewhere, I don't feel like having her spying out the window at me every single time I come, and she's like, "Woo-hoo, these *Moslem* people!" And I was like, she'd probably be really freaked out by that, and I wouldn't be surprised if she caught up tomorrow and [said] like, "The spot's not open anymore," you know? So I was like, I'm just going to leave it alone.

Heather's response may reflect her status as a well-to-do white American. In a parody of the hypothetical response of Muslim women ("Actually I'm Muslim, and this is why I dress this way"), Heather rejected *teaching* and opted out of the encounter. But Latifa and other immigrant women celebrated their small victories and the ways that their hijabs and their names were "icebreakers" (appropriately, since they regularly encountered icy reception). Muslims who chose the *teaching* option half-satirized by Heather perhaps accepted a certain degree of otherization. Perhaps such Muslim "teachers" accepted the necessity to normalize Muslims in America, but Heather—white and wealthy, after all—rejected right back the woman who had othered her.

Individuals who are marginalized, whether on racial or religious grounds, have a nose for predicting negative situations, eluding predators with the instinct of animals in the wild. Ethnographic analysis of the daily minutiae includes what happens, what does not, and why, as well as how individuals interpret those events. Statistical reports on the number of overt physical and verbal attacks omit negative encounters that are predicted and avoided and therefore cannot convey the essential experience of everyday life for those on the margins as can ethnographic analysis.

Acting Irreligious

Knowing that their non-Muslim peers seemed to avoid them like a contagion, hijabis tried to overcome the religiosity inscribed on them and worked harder to belong. "If there are two girls sitting in class, one hijabi and one not, students may be more inclined/ comfortable to interact with the non-hijabi," Zeinab, herself a hijabi, wrote in an e-mail, adding, "In some ways, which I believe is totally wrong, hijabis feel they need to prove that they are not as religious as they look." Hijabis bore the burden of proving that they were not wretched, foreign, or fearsome, but also that they were as secular as anyone else. They did so by performing what I call *religiosity lite*: this could be in the form of mild impiety, irreverence, worldliness, self-indulgence, high fashion, or talk about popular culture. Muslim women in general engaged in such social performances that involved "halal hedonism." But hijabis in particular sought camaraderie and everyday friendly interaction by behaving in a manner that seemed irreligious in contrast with stereotypical religiosity.

Normal-Modest Clothing

Religiously observant non-hijabis typically seek a midpoint between normal American and Muslim dress: this usually involves wearing no hijab; modest necklines, long sleeves, and long pants to cover skin; and clothes of a loose fit to cover one's bodily contours. Stylish layers such as jackets were in common usage to cover the chest and buttocks, but also to counteract the single baggy layer appearance. Hijab certainly is not the measure of modesty or dowdiness. As the trends of "hijab chic" and "sexy hijab" have grown in popularity, I have observed, on the one hand, hijabis wearing daringly skin-tight jeans and shirts, even low-cut necklines, coupled with minimalist headscarves, and non-hijabis, on the other hand, wearing loose clothes and bulky hoodies.

But even non-hijabis who wore modest "American" dress could not escape othering. It was no surprise that for Heather, a recent convert, "the biggest thing"—the greatest challenge—was her Muslim wardrobe.

> HEATHER: Because you can't really look normal and dress modestly. . . . You can pull it off to some degree. But you'll never— [trails off]. . . . There are definite barriers between being religious and being normal in society. And you can make up to a certain degree with personality or knowledge of popular culture—or

being interested in having a fun time that's not necessarily *ha-raam* or something, but—[trails off].

Like teetotalism, both religiosity and modest clothing were *possible* at the elite campuses, but that did not mean a person would be seen as normal, or that she could inhabit the cultural core. Majority society may provide minimal space ("to some degree") to dress modestly and/or be religious, but this space must be earned. In the diversity showcase of college culture, being Muslim or ethnic was said to offer a certain "cool quotient," but religious Muslims had to exhibit (as Heather put it) "personality or knowledge of popular culture" to offset their modesty and religiosity.

On a summer day, Heather stood among her peers in their short skirts and lacy tank tops. In a woven long-sleeved shirt and an ankle-length Gap denim skirt, Heather's skin was conspicuous by its absence.

HEATHER: It's so annoying when you go to class . . . and I just went in a buttoned-down long-sleeved shirt and a skirt—a khaki skirt. Like, *"Are you hot?"* The most irritating question in the world!

"Are you hot?"—the tentative attempt to pry into her well-being—cast Heather as a dupe of a sexist religion and only betrayed the interlocutor's lack of tact: "Plus, what sort of benefit are you deriving out of asking me if I'm hot?" she chuckled bitterly. "'Yes, I'm absolutely burning up. It's really unfortunate that my religion is so oppressive, and like, I'm suffering here.'"

A Muslim woman in the classroom came to Heather's aid. This woman did not practice conservative Muslim norms of modesty ("she had on capris and a short-sleeved shirt," Heather explained), but she stepped in to strategically offer sisterly support, saying, "No, look, this [clothing] is so light." The fact that the aid came from someone who was not invested in similar norms of modesty made it not only "sort of nice that she defended me" but also provided more persuasive evidence in defense of Heather's "legitimate" clothing; Muslim women who were invisible as Muslim were more credible, after all.

Heather tried to prevent such encounters by strategically planning outfits, though she remained dissatisfied with the partial conformity that resulted.

HEATHER: And so, definitely this summer I'm a lot more inclined to wear, like, light-looking things or things that might fit in a little more—like, skirts that don't look like they're hot, or pants that just look like khakis. Because you can sort of get away with wearing khakis in the summer and nobody's going to ask you *"Are you hot?"* for the most part. Because at least you're like—you know, it's a legitimate thing to wear. The problem is when people wear long skirts or long pants they normally wear, like, a tank top on top.

Heather could "get away with" khakis and long skirts but when not paired with tank tops, this alternative to skin-baring summer fashion marked her as hot, weird, and oppressed. With her modest attire, Heather would never be perfectly normal or free from the pressure to defend her clothing choices.

Putting Muslim Identity in the Background

Basketball served Intisar as an indigenizing cultural resource and gave her entrée into a basketball clique. Friendliness and sports are wholly American routes to the heart of youth culture. The sport redefined her as an athlete, rather than as "some Somali outcast."

INTISAR: I didn't feel like I had to say who I was, where I came from. . . . It defined me. It made everything easy. . . . I didn't have to feel different. I could just play basketball and be Intisar who plays basketball and who also happened to be Somali and Muslim, when those things would at first define me.

Basketball covered the stigma of her racial difference, her religion, and her Somali refugee origins: it made these identities secondary and almost rendered Intisar an honorary African American. But as Heather said, once you stopped working to counteract the social impact of Muslim identity, your normalcy could slip away. When Intisar turned fifteen, "suddenly" and "out of nowhere," her mother told her that she had to become a more decorous Somali Muslim, rather than "Intisar the normal person who plays basketball."

Subject to competing demands, Intisar complied with both. She continued to play basketball, resentfully dressed in the newly mandated hijab over her athletic attire. This combination of the Islamic and the American was "natural" and seamless on one level, but on another level, it was a ploy that she "got away with." Still, Intisar could no longer *dodge* identification. As Intisar tried to be normal both in youth culture and at home, the cultural gatekeepers on both sides agreed that she could not have her cake and eat it too.

> INTISAR: It's really difficult to wear hijab. . . . People assume certain traits that should *go with hijab*, and the hardest thing for me to do was go along with stereotypes. . . . Like hijab and basketball: I thought it was a natural thing. . . . My [non-Muslim] friends thought, "Can you do this? How can you play basketball? Is this allowed?" [emphasis added]

Hijab accentuated Intisar's racial and religious origins. Home and non-Muslim peer groups both exacted of her the immobility of stereotypical Muslim womanhood. Eventually, her mother forbade basketball altogether.

In the manner of many African immigrants, Intisar's mother had been pressuring her to be less friendly with African Americans. Without basketball, she lost these black athletic friends. Intisar "had to create a whole new other person." Her mother was relieved: Intisar's focus shifted away from sports to academics, and her racial identity shifted from its transient African American abode. With her new studious Asian friends, Intisar surpassed what was popularly considered the academic norm for working-class Somalis. Now, alongside her affluent Arab and South Asian Muslim peers, Intisar was attending a private university, with aspirations to belong in America, develop her multiethnic Muslim American network, *and* aid the underserved Somali community.

At college, the hijabi Intisar played basketball (in secret from her family) in an elective class. She grew tired of classmates' and Muslim friends' perpetual surprise over her athletic ability. Originally, Intisar's athletic activities had gained her friends, but for the *hijabi*, hypervisibility became wearisome. "Some Muslims thought it was cute that I was hijabi *and* played basketball, but some of them gossiped about" the impropriety of mixed-gender sports. "[So] I kept my basketball thing undercover from both Muslims and non-Muslims." The pressure to be an exemplary Muslim woman bore down on Intisar: trailblazing entailed individual choices that were also collective community property. "I got tired of this teaching role," she said; "I just wanted to be myself." Under the spotlight in her hijab, Intisar had better be sure about her choices. In her sophomore year, she decided that it was "wrong" to play basketball in public and quit. Intisar renounced basketball for the sake of a representative status she did not even want.

Ideal Islamic Personae: How Not to "Confuse" Non-Muslims

Hijabis were deemed religious and oppressed; non-hijabis were seen as nominal or secularized Muslims—or just odd. Muslim American women who professed to be unsettled by stereotypes sometimes lived up to them, often to the point of exhaustion and dissonance.

Consistency and Ideology

Once they had been tagged as hijabis (or non-hijabis), many Muslim American women got stuck representing particular ideological positions on modesty and clothing, unfailingly performing correct Islamic identities to the point of appearing one-dimensional. Free-spirited, outspoken, and cynically good-humored, Tehzeeb, a cosmopolitan Bangladeshi American, maintained her own freedom from the cage of hijabi consistency, revering hijab from afar. A hijabi could never deviate from faithfully representing Islam, hijab, and Muslim women. Were she to fail, she could easily let Islam down, confuse non-Muslims, and dishonor the Muslim community in full sight of the white majority.

> TEHZEEB: It's hard to go through [religious and ideological] changes when you wear hijab, for example. . . . OK, if Nikhat, for example . . . starts rethinking [her religious ideology], she can't, like, stop wearing hijab or something like that. She really can't. . . . It's a bad move because what does it say about Islam? . . . It's all this responsibility.

A visibly Muslim and widely respected woman like Nikhat—an articulate, brilliant, young hijabi—since she was representative of and influential within the community, ought to appear static and changeless like a statue. The halo effect of hijab brought a fallible, changeable Muslim woman under the naked bulb. It was "not that hijab makes you not free to grow," Tehzeeb added hastily, not that hijab possessed some intrinsic stunting quality. But a hijabi's ideological deviation away from orthodoxy ought to be private. Personal intellectual growth and ideological change did not bespeak the unswerving *consistency* expected of Muslim women. If a hijabi publicly became less religious, dressed immodestly, or abandoned hijab, her conduct could be a symbolic defeat for Muslims in the face of majority society—against which minority communities wield only the power of symbolic defiance. Strong, "loud," audacious diverse identities demonstrate cultural integrity in the face of hegemonic whiteness.

When I stopped wearing hijab in 1997, well-intentioned white friends asked me, half in jest, why I had "sold my soul." (My Muslim friends with the same question were not joking.) The half joke betrays how Western observers perceive hijab, as a form of conspicuous differentness and resistance to the Western status quo. Many years ago, a white woman in my graduate classes was infuriated when I argued that hijab was a spiritual act for many Muslim women, not just a political one. Surely a woman dressed like that was *trying* to thumb her nose at *us*, a British professor at Cambridge University suggested to me, in my former incarnation as a hijabi. This vision of hijab as a political statement has considerable circulation among many Muslims who treat the quitting of hijab as "capitulation to Western cultural imperialism" (Kandiyoti 1991: 3). Progressive Muslim critiques of hijab have been widely criticized by traditional Muslims as assimilation and "Westoxification." Colonial and neocolonial interest in emancipating Muslim women produced "in the minds of many Muslims, a close association between feminism and cultural imperialism" (Kandiyoti 1991: 7).

For Tehzeeb, a bohemian non-hijabi, it was quite inconsequential "to go through all these different changes and do all these different things." Good girls stay put; bad girls explore and experiment. Tehzeeb was "low-key and on the fringes," and she had "probably made so many mistakes, so [she] wouldn't want to influence anyone to take [her] path." Ideological change could be contagious, and inflicting it on impressionable fellow Muslims was dangerous, heavy with responsibility.

Even as the stultifying Orientalist gaze belittles the Muslim woman's alleged inertia, such essentializing focus on her effectively *restricts* her freedom and perpetuates her alleged immobility and lack of agency. Whether French or Italian bans on headscarves, burqas, and burqinis, or Olympic bans on Iranian women's athletic attire, the effect of such purportedly pro-feminist policy is to restrict Muslim women's movement and agency in new ways, as maligned Muslims dig in their heels against Western condemnation of Muslim ways of doing gender and Western imperialist pressure to be good feminists (Mir 2011).

The demand that Muslims simulate liberal white Western feminism can serve as a tool of cultural imperialism. This situation means that certain strains of liberal feminist posturing result in Muslim resentment and reactionary entrenchment against feminist ideals. To accusations that Islamic gender was illiberal, Tehzeeb reacted with *antifeminist* posturing that in no way matched her personality.

> TEHZEEB: And [Christina was] like, "Oh, why don't *men* have to cover?"—already assuming—. Like—they always have such an aggressive attitude. . . . They're too *out*, [mock earnest tone] like, women's rights, and political correctness, and everything. . . . And I was like, "Men have to cover too; they have to cover like from their knees to their bellybuttons." OK. And she's like [sarcastically], "Oh, that's a big difference!"

Assuming that the wearing of less clothing is a form of freedom and status, Tehzeeb's friends Laura and Christina mocked Islam's sartorial restrictions specific to women (as if Islam were the only religion that chooses women for particular focus). Tehzeeb was no traditional Muslim, but whatever her own opinion was, she confronted and challenged Western feminists' ethnocentric paternalism. In her resistance, we see how the moments within which "feminism collides and colludes with Orientalism" (Stephens 1990: 93) often harden Muslims' position on gender issues. The strong cultural and political bias of much Western feminist thought begets "polarizations that place feminism on the side of the West" and sets up an unending "cultural opposition between Islam and the West, between fundamentalism and feminism" (Abu-Lughod 2002: 788).

> TEHZEEB: And I was kind of trying to piss her off too, because I wasn't even going to try and appease her. I don't like these

Muslims who try and appease Western interpretations of like, feminism and stuff. So then I was like, "Yeah, it's because women's bodies are sexier than men's." And I *knew* she was going to hate that. . . . [laugh] But the problem is, because I'm not being aggressive either, and I'm so chill . . . so she doesn't know how to handle it either. . . . And her friend's like, "No, that's actually just a social construct, that women's bodies are more sexual." . . . And I was like, "Yeah, OK, don't say it's a fact, that's what people believe now, and it's becoming accepted, and being delivered like it's a fact, but it's not a fact. That's your opinion, and it's my opinion that women's bodies are more sexual." And she didn't have anything to say after that. . . . They're always ready to—. . . . That's why I don't feel comfortable having close friends who are American, I guess.

Tehzeeb's friend confronted her with the assumption of Western feminist superiority to "Islamic" gender norms. Tehzeeb reacted by strategically constructing an antifeminist position to "piss off" the other young woman, using the same relativism that is often deployed against religious perspectives and claiming adherence to traditional Islamic body politics. In this encounter, Tehzeeb turned around and replicated the self-assured superiority of Western critics of Muslim gendered cultures. Knowing Tehzeeb as I did, this performance of hers was quite hilarious.

Representatives

Hijabis were representatives of Muslim religiosity, whether they liked it or not. A recent convert, Teresa, explained in an e-mail, "Wearing the scarf is a statement about my level of commitment." But the (public) *statement* of Teresa's behavior overshadowed the (inward) *commitment*. Whether this image of total personal change was strictly accurate or not was immaterial ("even if I were the same person as before").

TERESA: Now I would not stand in front of the library smoking as before, if I felt like having one cigarette, and I would not possibly have a drink or go to a club as an exception. The hijab means that others notice what I do as a reflection of Islam and of my own level of religious strength, so I don't want to devalue that for one exception.

Teresa, as a hijabi under a microscope, quit public smoking because it would be perceived as the act of a *Muslim*, not just of an individual woman. A hijabi slipping up, making "one exception" that did not represent a person's overall behavior, bore weighty significance in the Muslim collective's political life. Hijab demanded Muslim womanhood so ideal that the prospect of such expectations profoundly daunted Elizabeth.

ELIZABETH: [In the past] I guess I assumed that if a woman was wearing hijab, she was faithful—like, she prayed five times a day, I assumed that she *had* read the Qur'an, that she was knowledgeable about some of the institutions of Islam. . . . Just knowing that when I wear it—not that I would *have* to—I would want to correctly represent, know about Islam as much as possible.

To Elizabeth, as to many religious Muslim youths, knowledge and religious observance comprised the essence of Islamic cultural capital, and the hijabi needed to encompass the best of such cultural capital. By fixing them within a readily conjured set of expectations, hijab ensured that Muslim women remained within the confines of those expectations.

Sarah inhabited the liberal end of the Muslim spectrum in matters of dress—she wore running shorts and knee-length skirts—but she venerated hijab as "a wonderful gift" and a challenge, since "from a mile away, someone can tell that you are a Muslim. You are a representative of your faith."

SARAH: And with [hijab] on your head is also a constant reminder of how you should be living your life, what you should and should not be doing. If you aren't ready for that, and if you aren't strong in other aspects of your faith like praying, etc., you should not take on that challenge.

As a distinction and a symbol of prestige, hijab exalted a woman above the rank and file of Muslim females assimilated, perhaps too comfortably, among non-Muslim Americans. Muslim women who were not religiously exemplary did not *merit* representative status; they should therefore remain non-hijabi along with these undifferentiated masses. Only superlatively religious people were qualified to announce, maintain, and facilitate an existing religiosity via hijab. You could not employ the tool if you did not have the requisite religiosity to maintain. Conversely, you were under less pressure to be perfectly religious if you were ineligible to be representative. As a mark of religious status, hijab was, ultimately, a highly *public* thing.

A United "Front"

Muslims, including Muslim youth, wrangle furiously on a number of social and political issues, but gender is a particular tinderbox of controversy. The Muslim students at Georgetown and GWU had their feminist vanguard and their traditionalist Muslims, with a range of uncertain and mildly opinionated youth in between. Progressive and feminist Muslim perspectives coexisted uneasily with the traditionalist scholarly interpretations that were gathering strength among Muslim American youth in the early 2000s.

One year, MSA officers at GWU had invited Dr. Abdelmalik, a Muslim feminist professor, to speak on a public panel on "Women in Islam" (a perennial favorite) during their Islam Awareness Week schedule of events. The panel had included the part-time chaplain, a traditional Islamist male.

> AMBER: And I guess people [in the MSA] didn't know her [feminist] standpoint. . . . But anyway, it turned out being like a debate between the two speakers. . . . And they were pretty much arguing the whole time. It got really heated. . . . Because it was a da'wah event and it's non-Muslims in the audience, and we shouldn't present a difference in opinion or something . . . because it looks bad.

The Muslim collective had to project a uniform theological perspective. Public disunity entailed a loss of face. It "looked bad." Multiple perspectives "confused" non-Muslims. Fed by sensationalist media images and political rhetoric, non-Muslim students could not handle the truth beyond a rudimentary, one-dimensional message. Such elementary familiarization with the message of Islam, a reassurance that Muslims were not crazy fundamentalists—this sort of da'wah alone was the purpose of the event. It was not served by fervent and erudite debate between traditional and progressive Muslims. Individual and collective representation of Islam and Muslim womanhood must be ideologically cohesive and singular. In this way, Muslim collectives could be just as frozen into hyperreligionized positions as Muslim individuals. Hijabis like Amber were expected to provide *the* Muslim voice in classroom discussions, and the MSA as an organization needed to provide a uniform, invariable, united voice on the singular Islamic outlook on everything under the sun. If MSA spaces represented multiple perspectives or nonstereotypical, politically "weak" ideologies, the community would be seen as disunited and weak. Nor could Islam, identified as a traditional and conservative faith, be associated with progressive ideologies—such as feminism. Dr. Abdelmalik was not invited to speak the following year.

Amber was frustrated by the stereotype of Muslim homogeneity: "Because I think a lot of people think Islam is such a monolith; that every Muslim's like every single other person, and it's not really like that. I mean, I guess ideally it would be like that to some people. But it's not like that." Though frustrated by this stereotype of homogeneity, in public settings, Amber maintained the collective homogeneous front in MSA spaces.

Between the Imam and the Professor

Were they properly covered in accordance with religious mandates, immersed in tradition? Were they rational and progressive freethinkers? Competing ideological demands kept Muslim American women embroiled in struggles for legitimacy. The choice to wear hijab or not was not a private one, but one of immense political significance for various Muslim ideological forces that had a stake in representing Islam.

Latifa was occasionally ambivalent about hijab and discomfited both by secular Muslim critiques of hijab *and* by the orthodox preoccupation with Muslim women's covering. She found irritating and "superficial" the local imam's bitter attack on progressive Muslim critiques of hijab. Yet because she *was* hijabi after all, Latifa dreaded the discussion on hijab that would inevitably crop up in Dr. Anwar's Islamic theology class. Amira and Fatima adored Dr. Anwar's rationalist theology, while Sharmila and Heather were unconvinced by the professor's modernist approach.

LATIFA: [Dr. Anwar will] say, "It's not written in the Qur'an, and people [hijabis] follow pre-Islamic tradition. . . . It's not a religious notion, and you're not supposed to stick out like a sore thumb." . . . Yes, [she thinks] you're just supposed to assimilate in your community. So I think I'll stick out in my class!

Latifa could not help but "feel marginalized when [Dr. Anwar was] talking about the people who are wearing hijab, that it's not an act of faith," and that hijab was a purely cultural practice of a bygone era, not rooted in Islamic theology, a practice of under-educated and culturally clumsy Muslims. Moreover, Dr. Anwar avowed, hijabis were in contravention of the Islamic juristic principle of ʿurf (respect of local customs). Dr. Anwar's claim fed into a cultural assimilationist perspective within a predominantly white campus, implying that a Muslim woman who "stuck out like a sore thumb" by her own choice deserved to be "sore" and that Muslims ought to "tone down" their identities (Yoshino 2006: 4).

While I, as a progressive Muslim, have a soft spot for some of Dr. Anwar's arguments on religion, I am concerned about the absence of hijabis' voices from Dr. Anwar's discourse on hijab and how she closed up the democratic possibilities of internal religious pluralism by voicing a singular perspective on an essentially contested matter. Latifa felt powerless to challenge the professorial authority: "I mean, ultimately, she'll have the final word, and I'll look like I'm a blind follower, you know?" Latifa gloomily said that in Dr. Anwar's class on hijab, "I'm going to end up feeling marginalized and just weird. Looking down—." Latifa looked down at the floor, as if humiliated.

Much as Latifa was stuck between the conservative imam and the modernist professor, Muslim American women are often torn between the demands of conservative Muslims and those of feminists, progressives, or secularists. In many ways, they continue to resist the expectations of fellow Muslims, both traditional and liberal, and of their non-Muslim peers.

Religious Pluralism among Muslim American Youth

Who was "judging" whom? Many non-hijabis thought that hijabis "judged" them for being impious, while hijabis were under the impression that non-hijabis disliked them for being too religious or "intimidating." Although fervently dismissive of the notion that hijab was divinely mandated, Fatima had many close friends who were hijabis. She also had a number of liberal Muslim friends who simply could not abide conservative hijabis, and who often asked her how *she*, Fatima, managed to get along with them.

> FATIMA: I don't think [hijab] is usually touched upon [between hijabis and non-hijabis]. Yes, [it's a sensitive issue] because I don't think I would feel completely comfortable telling someone wearing hijab why I don't wear hijab. . . . [Because] I don't want them to think that I think that they're doing something superfluous in their religion or something. . . . And for them to say to me, "I think it's a huge part [of religion] and I think that, like, guarantees you going to hell or something," . . . it's definitely going to be offensive to me.

Even as close friends, non-hijabis and hijabis skirted the issue of hijab as a minefield. Was this a gulf in communication? As someone who had attended an Islamic school and had hijabi friends, Fatima was quite comfortable with bypassing the delicate issue to avoid hurting or insulting her friends. Both hijabis and non-hijabis maintained strategic silences about their friends' respective practice. While the imam and the professor each had a political axe to grind and each competed for representative status, Muslim American students preserved pluralistic spaces through pragmatic silences. Authority figures insisted on singular ideological positions. Unlike Fatima and her friends, Dr. Anwar explicitly disparaged hijab as completely extraneous to religious observance, while the imam openly berated non-hijabis (albeit in general terms). But Fatima's observance of social tranquility did not quell her critique of hijab. Peace and politics could coexist among Muslim women, as long as high-stakes adult quarrels did not interfere.

Inside the Family, Outside the Family

Latifa confessed that Dr. Anwar's critical interrogation would not rattle her as much if the class were not majority non-Muslim. While Dr. Anwar's bold interrogation of the religious establishment is commendable, I found her critique one-sided and doctrinaire, insensitive to the *local* impact of her critique upon hijabis in her classroom. The hijab debate among Muslims became reductive when it became public. Fatima and her hijabi friends coexisted in peace because they did not parade their differences publicly before non-Muslim Americans.

Dr. Abdelmalik's feminist discourse irked Amber mainly when the professor and the imam crossed theological swords at a public MSA event, one open to non-Muslims. In intra-community settings, however, Amber's response to the feminist critique was muted and reflective. At a Muslim conference, the Critical Islamic Reflections conference at Yale, Amber witnessed a debate on the topic of Muslim female prayer leadership between academics and traditional religious scholars. Amber was gratified that she had "got to see the debate," noting how the same texts and tools were differentially employed by traditional Islamic scholars and young secular academics. Amber's analytic focus remained on the texts and methodologies, without being distracted by a "confused" non-Muslim audience and its stereotypes, and without falling back reactively on the conservative-traditional model to preserve an imaginary "unity."

Clothes, Race, and Religiosity

As a new arrival on campus, Heather had been reluctant to announce her conversion to her friends verbally or via hijab. She had heard first-hand their unvarnished views on Muslims and hijab. Muslims were "crazy" for "dressing like that," and their claim that hijab was liberating was mere feeble apologetics. Heather hoped that her friends might come to see that she was "a strong Muslim woman, or self-respecting, or whatever, just pretty similar to who they are." Yet Heather's very similarity as a white woman, she acknowledged, framed her as an ethnic apostate and "a freak."

Black Muslim women, on the other hand, did not have to wear a Middle Eastern–style headscarf to cover their heads. Black women often wear turbans and other head covers derived from Afrocentric clothing styles, relatively free of Islam-related stigma. In this way, black women often have an advantage in terms of being normal *and* Muslim, since "blacks remain the only Americans whose conversion to Islam connotes neither cultural nor ethnic apostasy," and it is to blacks that Islam owes its "status as a bona fide American religion" (Jackson 2005: 131). Despite apprehensions as a new hijabi during the War on Terror, a woman of Elizabeth's physical stature and racial identity in (black-majority) Washington, D.C., was less physically vulnerable than many immigrant Muslim women. This is why Heather commented that though they bore the brunt of racism, black Muslim women were less likely than other Muslim women to draw attention if they covered their hair. Elizabeth's experience sheds light on the ways that religious and racial identities shape each other, and on the shallow integration of American immigrants. Yet within the predominantly immigrant MSA, Elizabeth remained "kind of undercover" as a black convert—and a non-hijabi. Loosely affiliated with the Muslim community, Elizabeth filtered ideological content—especially related to the politics of hijab and gendered behavior—through critical lenses.

ELIZABETH: I think a great deal of it is that the MSA does focus on more, like, people who are Pakistani, Egyptian. . . . So I grew up Christian, so a lot of things, my mannerisms are very Christian. . . . So, not that I don't fit in, because there are very few places where I feel straight excluded. But just that that [MSA] is not focusing [on people like me]. I come and I learn, and then I leave to think about it more.

Elizabeth's complaint of alienation and MSA's provincialism is a common one among black Muslims. Elizabeth struggled to minimize the conflict between her various lifeworlds. How could she create a Muslim persona that could function in both her new (Muslim) and old (non-Muslim) cultures? Not quite normal in the Muslim community yet *more* normal than immigrant Muslims in mainstream American society, Elizabeth was disinclined to adopt symbols of difference. She puzzled over constructing a Muslim lifestyle on her own terms, and she resisted her Muslim friends' subtle, rather condescending encouragement to wear hijab.

ELIZABETH: It's not that they [Muslim women friends] are disapproving [of my behavior], but they're *so* approving when you do something right. . . . They're like, "Oh, yes! Yay! Exactly!" Although, you know what, some sisters will be honest and compliment my hair when I'm not [in hijab]. . . . That's me, and they see me, and that's the person that they see, is OK. Like, that's what I'm looking for.

Elizabeth resisted the infantilizing pressure of some Muslim friends who tried to replicate Islamist womanhood in the convert. To Elizabeth—caught in an "in-between spot because I am American"—the immigrant flavor of their religiosity was potentially implausible, un-American, decontextualized, and culturally inappropriate.

> ELIZABETH: At the same time, I have no problem sitting next to my guy friends, hugging my guy friends when I see them. And [laugh] that drives a lot of people in the MSA community—. . . . They don't grow up like that. . . . This is one of the big things I have about being hijabi: that once I put on the scarf, I have to act—like, I would *want* to act as a Muslim woman should in front of the community. So that means when I see my guy friends, I can't hug them. . . . How do you reconcile? How much of it is in hadith? How much of it is in Qur'an? I'm struggling with it because I do want to do what's right, but at the same time—I see my parents living this way, and I can't say it's absolute wrong. . . . Because in general, African American Muslims . . . we're just more liberal anyway because we grew up *differently*. . . . Like the guys I know were born Muslim, but the girls, like, most of us are reverts [i.e., converts]. We're more Amer—.

(Some Muslim converts describe themselves as "reverts," since they understand Islam as a state of nature to which they "revert.") Elizabeth's Islam was in a cultural world different from that of her MSA friends. On campus, she balanced her life between different communities—the black students including the black Muslims (both born Muslims and converts); the mostly immigrant MSA students; the Latino student group, and other friends of diverse backgrounds. Elizabeth struggled to unravel "true" religion from the tangled strands of religion, culture, ethnic origins, and transnational ties, and to answer the unanswerable question about what was "real" religion and what was "made up," or a construction? Were MSA Muslims' religious practices derived from the sacred text of the Qur'an or from the hadith (more open to interpretation and criticism than the Qur'an)? Even if the source of a particular mandate passed muster, modesty did not function in a cultural vacuum. Elizabeth felt that the physical reality of black bodies compared to most South Asian or Arab female bodies—and Elizabeth was an unusually tall woman and not slender—placed her in circumstances that immigrant Muslim youth did not share. Perhaps, therefore, this necessitated some independent (lonely) cultural translation on her part, some peripheral participation in the immigrant Muslim community?

> ELIZABETH: And part of it is style and the whole hijab issue. . . . Part of my problem is, I just have a problem with clothes anyway. Like skirts to the floor? I have a forty-inch inseam! They don't *make* skirts to the floor! Like, jeans that aren't tight? Yeah, right! [indicates very wide jeans]. Hijab—do you know what a struggle it is to put all my hair back?

Where hijab is often portrayed as a purely doctrinal matter, for Elizabeth, upbringing, diverse Islamic theological perspectives, cultural style, diverse ideals of femininity, body type, and the American fashion industry that primarily serves women of certain body types all gathered to complicate the issue of "modest dress." Hijab was not a mere spiritual decision: it also meant the daily wrestling with nappy hair tamed into a headscarf and struggling to find clothing of specific design in her size. The mainstream fashion industry also certainly does not adhere to Islamic norms ("They don't *make* skirts to the floor!")

It did not take long for Elizabeth to figure out that the MSA National leadership felt rather strongly about hijab. Quite ambivalent about hijab during her second interview, she arrived wearing a headscarf to her third interview. She had recently returned from attending a weekend regional MSA conference in New York. When I interviewed her before she left for the event, she was disgruntled that, only one day before the event, the conference organizers had sent out (rather specific) instructions that women attendees were to wear hijab and "modest" clothing. Elizabeth had no headscarves and no shalwar-kameez that could translate into modesty for immigrant Muslims more readily than did "American" clothes.

> ELIZABETH: It just made me mad because they didn't tell us in enough time. . . . I don't mind wearing a headscarf. I'm looking at this e-mail the night before, like, you're nuts! I don't *have* any skirts. They're talking about no tight-fitting pants. . . . *These* are

the only pair of jeans I have; everything else I have is like knit, tight pants: they're rather clingy! That's *all* I have. I was freaking out.... I was like, "Imrana! I don't have any clothes." She's like, "Ah, don't worry about it." She's like, "As long as your hair's covered."

Elizabeth had not yet learned what Imrana, an MSA officer, already knew: the headscarf was a far more powerful symbol than vaguely defined modest clothing. Yet theologically, the principle of sartorial modesty is more widely accepted by Muslims, while the headscarf remains a controversial issue. Still, Muslim Americans identify hijab as "Islamic," while long sleeves and loose jeans are not immediately classifiable as Islamic. Moreover, no one in the (mostly immigrant) MSA community knew that their demands for public, immigrant-scented modesty might become a financial or logistical burden, as they did for the convert Elizabeth.

Between Elizabeth's black Christian family and immigrant Muslim friends, hijab was also a cultural burden: her MSA event wardrobe would certainly not fit at graduation dinner with her Southern, Christian grandparents. Was she to be the pride of their eyes walking across the stage—with her hair covered in a scarf? "In the American South, [wrapping your head] is *country*," she protested. "You don't do that. You're supposed to have your hair done, xyz." Elizabeth creatively and independently constructed her religiosity, and since "the purpose is modesty and the purpose is not fighting with my family," she decided, "I think I might take it off at graduation, just to [sigh] deal with this." Whatever the immigrant Muslims thought, hijab was a means to an end—modesty—and modesty and filial duty were of greater ultimate religious value than hijab itself. These goals had to shape themselves to fit her non-Muslim family.

Sexual Politics, Class Politics, and Modesty

As she went on to become a full-time hijabi, fully involved in the Muslim youth community, Elizabeth found theological hermeneutics tangled up with religious symbolism and sexual, class, and ethnic politics.

ELIZABETH: At first it [hijab] was a cultural thing, to identify myself as Muslim. Later, I read the Qur'an and I read the hadith concerning it. And while sometimes I disagree—the Qur'anic verse that's based on the commandments to Muhammad's wives, to me, it's iffy because it's Muhammad's wives [rather than Muslim women in general]—but at the same time, there's a hadith. . . . On the other hand, I like to be cute! [laugh] . . . For me personally, I've always been a modest person. Even when I'm wearing hijab, I don't want this to be halfway. I want to wear the nice coats that are long; I want to wear the shirts that are long enough. In any case, I want to be able to be professional. I see the coats, the tailored jackets.

SHABANA: It's expensive—the "hijab outfit" is expensive.

ELIZABETH: [with great feeling] I know!

Hijab does not usually blend smoothly into high fashion or career wear. Almost all hijabis I encountered—except Intisar, Elizabeth, Sharmila, and Muna—were chic hijabis typically garbed in attractive, elegant, yet modest ensembles. Creating similar ensembles was harder work and a greater financial strain for Elizabeth than for her affluent immigrant sisters. At least once I found her hungry because she had simply run out of money. Clothes that are "Islamically modest" *and* stylish are typically culled from upscale brand names and not usually to be found on the clearance rack. Cheap shirts and jackets usually follow mainstream Western trends and tend not to fashionably cover curves in an understated manner.

In the upwardly mobile environment of immigrant American Islam, hijab necessitates a feminine etiquette shaped by gendered, class, and cultural expectations. I saw reflected in the mirror of Elizabeth's imagined future her aspirations for religiosity, class status, and style, combined in the form of her desired hijabi outfit. She wanted to be an observant Muslim, "cute," and "professional." If and when she donned hijab, Elizabeth wanted to wear behavior that "matched" hijab. Before becoming a hijabi, she wanted to embody a typical hijabi persona—a decorous, visibly modest woman who eschewed physical contact with men. Her goal was to graduate from modest to *professional* "Islamic" clothing *before* adopting hijab full-time. But even as Elizabeth desired to be a typical hijabi, she interrogated the origins of the Muslim American feminine religiosity. Was it of scriptural or (immigrant) cultural origin? Until she became immersed in a group of hijabis, Elizabeth was torn between "American" and immigrant identities, and critical of both, while the class, spiritual, and sexual politics of hijab complicated the binary.

As a non-hijabi, Elizabeth could be a competitive contestant in the romantic marketplace. But valuable sexual capital in dating culture was not the same as sexual capital in the Muslim community, and marriage with a Muslim husband was better than a short-lived romance.

> ELIZABETH: Because one part of me wants to go on [and] do the parties, and look all cute for the guys. But seriously, when I wear hijab, I feel peaceful. . . . Also that, the kind of husband I would want would probably—not *insist* that his wife would wear hijab—but he would probably feel a lot better about it if she were hijabi . . . [or] didn't object to it. Yes, if I don't wear hijab, I would have less of a chance of meeting the husband that I would want. . . . A lot of times, that's one of the first things boys learn about women—that women are supposed to be covered.

Since hijab renders (Muslim) women more visible and/or attractive to many *Muslim* men, hijab could be more useful than *normal* cuteness in the long term. Elizabeth needed the Islamic symbol because she was black and *American*. Hijab helped her make the cut with young men (or, as she said, "boys") who expected Muslim women to wear head covers. As an external sign of religiosity, an identifier for Muslim women, and a source of community honor, hijab has taken on an exaggerated importance for diasporic Muslims. Conservative forms of Islam have held representative status; even liberal Muslims frequently pay lip service to the "official" brand. Musing over the gendered hierarchy, Elizabeth grew aware that her lack of hijab created a glass ceiling for her community affiliation and that a religious Muslim man was quite likely to desire a hijabi wife.

Conclusion

Distinctive Muslim attire, which could signify religious devotion, community membership, ethnic heritage, or a mnemonic device for piety (Mir 2008a), became interpreted in campus culture as a symbol of religiosity, fanaticism, victimhood, antifeminism, and/or affiliation with dangerous and xenophobic forces. For better or worse, hijab functioned primarily as a public *and* representative practice, a sociopolitical identifier of a primarily religious persona. Hijab was also a function of Muslim fellowship; women who were not core members of Muslim communities usually did not wear hijab (which is not to say that non-hijabis were peripheral to Muslim communities).

Muslim American women responded to the assumptions of the Orientalist gaze by resisting it, correcting stereotypes, avoiding negative encounters, confounding prior assumptions, covering Muslim identities, and enacting idealized Islamic identities. Though Muslim American women sought a third space of uncertainty, flexibility, agency, and pluralism, border-crossers were interrogated: both Muslims and non-Muslims interrogated hijabis who did normal "American" things as well as non-hijabis who did "Muslim" things. Mainstream campus culture *and* Muslim American cultural spaces remained limited in the scope of their pluralism, and they thus limited Muslim women's ability to creatively construct third spaces of identity. Consider the following excerpt from my field notes as an illustration of these constrained identities:

Latifa and I had just finished an interview and were walking out of the library. We bumped into a male (non-Muslim) friend of Latifa's. [After greetings and small talk,] he teasingly pulled at her hijab, moving up rather close to her in a mock confrontational manner. She and I both responded to his banter with forced good humor, though I sensed that Latifa was working hard to appear unruffled. He took hold of one end of her hijab and said, "Why don't you wear it like this?," and stretched the fabric out like a veil in front of her face: "You should do this.... I like you like this: I'd rather not see your face." She laughed with ill-concealed discomfort and said, "Well, if you want, I'll wear it like that!"

Muslim American women, like other stereotyped individuals, "wear" their identities the way "you want"—as inscribed on them by others. This encounter shows how hijab could serve as a space where Muslim American women's identities could be interrogated, challenged, ranked, and categorized with impunity, in ways that opened them up to attack on multiple levels.

5

Let Them Be Normal and Date

Muslim American Undergraduate Women
in Sexualized Campus Culture

If you want to get laid, go to college. If you want an
education, go to the library. —Frank Zappa

In this chapter, I show a partial range of voices among Muslim American undergraduate women regarding the thorniest of issues, those most fraught with anxiety—discourses about sexuality and gendered behavior.

Undergraduates imagine college as a world of freedom, mobility, sexual opportunity, and sexual maturity. Going to college and having sex are closely linked in the popular imagination. As American men and women stay single longer now than they did before, the *way* college students have sex has shifted from traditional dating to a culture of short-term sex or hooking up, with alcohol facilitating such casual sexual encounters.

Like their peers, young Muslim women teeter on the verge of adolescence, preparing for adulthood, navigating not only the expectations and surveillance of others but also their competing desires for wholeness, religiosity, love, and sex. How do Muslim American female students, just a year after high school, function at "party schools" that vigorously advertise the local nightlife? How do Muslim women engage with this environment, colored by the new political climate, and furnished with the old stereotypes thinly veiled by diversity discourse? How do they negotiate "American" and "Muslim" norms of gender and sexuality, under surveillance by Muslim communities and the Orientalist gaze?

Muslim women's overall gendered behavior is characterized by a fusion of resistance and conformity—resistance and conformity to majority stereotypes and to Muslim expectations. Muslim women forge public and private gendered and sexual discourses and identities within the social spaces of campus culture where their sexual conduct often fits neither mainstream nor Muslim sexual discourses regarding male-female interactions, friendship, romance, dating, courtship, and sex.

Traversing the minefield of sexual and gendered behavior, Muslim American women constructed third spaces of identity and combined American, Muslim, and racial/ethnic identities, squirreling away their not-Muslim-enough and not-American-enough identities from the sight of parents and non-Muslim peers. This complex project had important political, religious, and sociocultural goals in a post-9/11 United States. I will use the admittedly messy term *dating* throughout this chapter in faithfulness to my participants who use the word to refer to the broad range of sexual and romantic activities between traditional dating and hooking up (Bogle 2008). There is a wide ideological spectrum of Islamic religious belief on gendered and sexual behavior. The Qur'an forbids fornication and adultery and exhorts believers to observe chastity and modesty in behavior and clothing. Interpretations of these exhortations to sartorial modesty vary considerably. Appropriate clothing for women may range from the burqa, the headscarf, and loose clothing to jeans and T-shirts. Similar to the "modesty continuum" I mentioned in chapter 4, imagine a complex continuum of Islamically appropriate gendered behavior. Conservative Muslim Americans at one end of this continuum abjure all but the bare minimum of contact with the opposite sex: among the strictly conservative, this *can* lead to partial gender segregation (I use the term "semi-segregation") and the avoidance of many mixed-gender social, educational, and professional spaces. In my observation, middle-to-upper-class conservative Muslim Americans tend to construct moderate positions on gendered behavior that do not adversely impact their socioeconomic activities. Hijab and modest attire symbolize a highly mobile form of chastity and *enable* Muslim women's full socioeconomic participation (though Westerners frequently regard such dress as restrictive). Arranged marriage (which in the United States is rarely as extreme as imagined) is also associated with the prohibition of premarital sex, as well as with ensuring endogamy and the integrity of the extended family. Very liberal Muslim Americans are indistinguishable in their sexual behavior from most of their white Judeo-Christian compatriots, though there is a range and a continuum of Muslim liberal sexuality. At the midpoint of my continuum, progressive Muslims observe variations of "normal" American gendered behavior similar to those of Orthodox Jews or conservative American Christians. In short, the construction of any Muslim American position on the gendered continuum is a complex and highly situated matter, best explored through close ethnographic scrutiny of social behaviors.

There is no stable, consistent, universally held set of "Muslim American rules" on the socially appropriate, religiously permissible, and culturally fitting behavior to find love, companionship, and/or a mate. There is, however, no end of passionately held views on the subject, many of them described in terms of what "Islam says." Hybridity is hot and fusion is fun, but the complexity and variance of the ethnic, Muslim American positions on gendered behavior can be perplexing for Muslim American youth. How was one to be the same person on Friday afternoon as one was on Friday night? For immigrant girls and women, whose behavior is monitored by tight-knit, culturally besieged communities, the consequences of sexuality are especially significant; the very appearance of wanton sexual conduct was fraught with serious danger to a Muslim woman's reputation, gendered status, and marriage prospects. A Muslim woman could be friendly and fashionable as well as chaste and virginal, but sexualized behavior could position her as an outcast. As Muslim and American sexual norms did not "speak" to each other, it is in matters of sexuality that Roshan's picture of a person flailing with a foot each in two boats (chap. 3) took on truly explosive meanings. Just as we sometimes glance into our refrigerators and wonder how dinner might result from the ill-suited and incompatible items in there, Muslim American women faced a range of choices among the cultural practices preferred by their parents, their peers, and their Muslim and ethnic communities. How much ought one to socialize with men, and how publicly? What if one became branded as slutty? Or what if one was so inhibited that one was branded as uptight, uncool, and too religious to marry? How "normal American" and how "Muslim" should one be, and when? Where did the *ultimate* boundaries lie?

Sex and Self-Discovery on Campus

Undergraduate culture on a secularized campus is framed within the liberal individualistic endeavor of autonomy, growth, and the pursuit of novel experiences. Many of my participants eagerly looked forward to transcending personal boundaries even if they had to make "mistakes." Even before her arrival at college, Haseena had anticipated relaxing some gendered reticence, though she had not foreseen having premarital sex: "I know this is kind of wrong, but sometimes being more strict within yourself kind of holds you back from different experiences," she confessed. "For example, if I had followed the rules at home, I would never have gotten involved with Zafar." She paused, looking slightly distressed, and added, "I mean that's debatable, whether or not that was a good idea, but I'd never have that experience." One would not grow up and become a college woman unless one had experience. On one level, significant personal change was normatively *good*.

But would the college journey of experience, self-fulfillment, and self-discovery (*self* was, of course, to be found within the confines of mainstream youth culture) clash with the quest to cultivate and preserve religious identities? Sarah celebrated the circumstance of a few chaste dates and a speedy breakup with Irfan: "But I'm really glad because I think I needed to encounter something like this eventually, just because I want to have experience" before marriage. Experience "doesn't mean you have to cross lines and make—you know, immoral decisions," as Sarah cautiously clarified. But who would Sarah discover, once she "understood [her]self"?

Pressure to Date

YASMIN: *Definitely the most stressful thing for a lot of Muslims is living in a culture in which most people are boyfriends and girlfriends, and struggling with that. And I think that's the number one . . . hardest thing for everyone. And where you stand on it, defines you in a way.* [emphasis added]

Haseena was taken aback by the outcomes of her self-discovery. Who was Haseena? The conservative, religious high school girl who had refused to attend prom, or the liberal coed who had (in Leila's coy parlance) a *real* boyfriend? Freedom to have experiences in campus culture was not a neutral freedom, since it fostered particular kinds of experiences. When I interviewed her, Haseena had mixed feelings about having a boyfriend. She wanted to get married and become "respectable," but Zafar's parents did not want him to marry before his career had been established. Haseena, therefore, was obligated to keep her relationship with Zafar a secret from her own parents indefinitely. She felt as if campus culture, the absence of family and curfew, and the total encouragement of all her friends had blinded her, made her "go against herself": "I wasn't [thinking]: what are the consequences going to be of this? It was definitely college."

Friends' encouragement, to put it mildly, to find romance was central in motivating some Muslim American women to explore their sexuality at college. Sarah's allegiance to sexual abstinence faltered as her friends Jennifer and Chelsea infantilized her for her sexual reticence and looked on the Pakistani American with mild contempt as not *quite* free and not *entirely* grown up. No sooner had Sarah acknowledged mild interest in Irfan, a male student, than Jennifer and Chelsea set to pestering Sarah to approach him. Initially warmed by their interest, Sarah came to seethe at their paternalistic voyeurism. It all started when Sarah and Irfan "were set up, like an experiment. It's like, 'How will they do?'" As the relationship progressed, Sarah realized that Jennifer's entire clique knew about it, and oversaw, defined, controlled, and protected the relationship Jennifer had hatched: "And so everyone's watching us, and I *hated* that." Nor would Jennifer permit Sarah any doubts about Irfan, chiding her, "Oh, I hope you're not going to be mean to him, because that would mess everything up." Under her peers' uncomprehending, contemptuous gaze, and under painful social pressure, Sarah wilted. Non-Muslim peers demanded at least an *effort* at quality romance, and Sarah "almost had to *prove* to them that [she] could do it by [her]self." Eventually, Sarah proudly announced, her friends "knew [Irfan and I] are going out on our own now."

Though she initially complied with their expectations, in time Sarah started resisting her peers' definitions of Irfan as her boyfriend—the term had different meanings for her and for Jennifer—and she started avoiding Irfan.

Ultimately Sarah parted ways with her close friends Jennifer and Chelsea, who *knew* of conservative Muslim sexual mores in theory but were mildly repelled by Sarah's notion of a platonic pre-courtship. "They relate, like they *understand*," Sarah said, but they were puzzled: "How can you have a relationship without being, like, *very* physical?" Jennifer and Chelsea's "understanding" of Muslim sexual mores was a superficial and cosmopolitan superiority, a *mastery* of alternative and inferior lifestyles rather than empathic understanding. Diversity experiences in higher education are often precisely no more than a conspicuous consumption of disparate exotic factoids.

In the pervasive dating culture, some Muslims gradually assimilated, and others concealed the fact that they were not sexually active. Many grew ashamed and sorrowful as they watched "everyone else" pair up, thinking, "Well, if that's the way to be, then I guess I'll be that way. . . . It will make me happier; it will make me fit in; this is what everyone else is doing, and there must be something wrong with me if I'm not doing it" (Sarah). Sarah battled the nagging suspicion that she was "wrong" in dating culture, unattractive, naive, "inexperienced" (as Jennifer informed her), and somehow unskilled at the American project of the pursuit of happiness. Though Sarah "did not *want* to succumb" to dating culture, she wearied of the struggle to hold her own and came to feel conflicted about sexual abstinence. In hedonistic campus culture, she was pigeonholed as "the Muslim girl who *doesn't*" (drink, date, party, and look utterly hot). For those aspiring to be *normal*, the pressure to date was powerful (Mir 2007).

The Dangers of Semi-Peripheral Participation in Dating Culture

I have shown that Muslim religiosity was difficult to maintain if you were a *core* member of *alcohol* culture (chap. 3). Dating culture was worse: in sexualized *dating* culture, even *peripheral* participants had trouble being religiously observant Muslims. For one thing, peripheral participants in sexualized campus culture were alienated and bored. When mingling with non-Muslim friends on the weekend, even though she took care not to "leak" Muslim religiosity into the conversation, Heather was a mere observer of the actors, a fifth wheel.

HEATHER: Everyone's talking about boyfriends coming to town, or them getting a hotel room. Or, you know, the party the weekend before, or how they're going on a date Friday night, or how that guy's hot. I'm not the type that's going to be like, [mock sanctimoniously] "*Haraam*, we don't speak about boyfriends because it's a haraam relationship." On the other hand, I really don't have anything to contribute.

Heather was not *external* to leisure culture like highly conservative Muslims who would recoil scandalized at the mere mention of premarital sex. But she had no entrée into the conversation ("nothing to contribute"). Her sarcasm ("*Haraam* . . . relationship") points to the yawning gap between mainstream sexual culture and Muslim religious mores. Sexualized discourse is powerfully "naturalized" in college culture (Holland and Eisenhart 1990), but not in religious Muslim youth discourse. Intensely aware of her marginality, of the fragility of her belonging within dating culture, Heather lingered silently on the sidelines, saying nothing that would betray her religiosity and expose her alienation in campus culture. At least being hip to hookup culture was a fair stand-in for actual participation in it.

But as peripheral participants, Muslims risked the integrity of their religious identities when they sheepishly covered their sexual abstinence within sexualized campus culture.

> HEATHER: There are people who would never date . . . but they're going to hang out with the people who *do* and probably be good friends with them. . . . So what do you do? Sit around, talk with them about their girlfriend when that's [dating] something you don't even do?

Rather than observing a pious distance from sin, the religious Muslim in sexualized culture was a marginalized coward, tacitly assimilating into sexualized culture. Heather's marginality when her friends were discussing sexual plans for the weekend could have been similar, except as she argued, she was not impressionable. Such Muslims, who did not date but were close friends with people who *did* date, were also at risk of identity erosion.

> HEATHER: Some people are just not leaders, and they just don't know how to stand up for what they believe in, and they suddenly get caught up. And it's much harder to get out of a situation than it is to never get into it in the first place.

An impressionable peripheral participant in dating culture could get "caught up" unaware in the flood of youthful sexuality. Visibly Muslim identities and a degree of social distance from core campus culture could shield a Muslim from the indignity of lapsing into un-Islamic behavior, so she might "never get into it in the first place."

Some Muslims were too impressionable to withstand sexualized culture. Sarah prided herself on having been adequately prepared for college by her semi-peripheral participation in, or exposure to, hedonistic high school culture. Getting your toes wet before the tsunami of college could blunt the impact of campus culture: it could furnish you with some elementary savvy regarding romance, sex, and men. Some of Sarah's cousins had been overprotected ("they weren't exposed") during high school, "so they were [still] very naive" when they went to college. Like deer in the headlights, Sarah's cousins were so blinded by the novel intensity of campus culture that they "had very bad experiences" (probably ill-fated sexual and/or romantic escapades). But despite her early "exposure" that, she hoped, would facilitate a relatively risk-free transition to dating culture, Sarah wavered between confidence ("no, that'll never happen to me,") and trepidation: "Now that I've met [a boy], I'm *scared*. I'm like, am I really as tough as I thought I was?"

Student Culture on Top

In its dominance, sexualized campus culture overshadowed even policy accommodations for religious minority students who practiced sexual abstinence.

As with alcohol on campus, the matter of overnight guests of the opposite sex is a gray area in campus policy implementation. Georgetown University, for example, does not permit "cohabitation" ("defined as overnight visits with a sexual partner") in undergraduate housing, as this is "incompatible both with the mission of the University and with the rights of the roommate" (Georgetown University housing, e-mail message, November 29, 2010). But in this matter, too, there appears to be a gap between policy and practice, and policies on overnight guests tend to be "on paper." In the case of Georgetown, my research participants were quite unaware of them. I have observed, among residential assistants at another university, this tepid approach to rules on sexual activity ("just shut the door and keep it down, okay?"). As Heather said, "if there's a rule [against opposite sex overnight guests], it's not enforced at all." Online youth forums and campus life guides offer a plethora of tips for how to avoid social friction and simply "deal with" being kicked out of dorm rooms for boyfriends or girlfriends.

A religious Muslim woman's reputation was at risk if her room-mate's boyfriend stayed in the room overnight. Under parental and community surveillance, Muslim women students were sensitive to their roommates' activities that could damage *their* reputations. Amira's father, furious that his daughter's freshman roommate had a boyfriend, demanded that she, Amira, ban the boyfriend from the room, or acquire a different roommate. Wisely, in sophomore year, Amira chose to live in Georgetown's Muslim housing apartments, where the rules prohibited a man and a woman being alone together at any time (chap. 1).

But Amira's non-Muslim roommate Emma and her liberal Muslim roommate Salwa both had boyfriends. Both Emma and Salwa had expressed interest in a Muslim lifestyle in their housing applications, though Amira suggested that their main goal was the coveted location of the Muslim housing apartments. After one semester, Emma complained that she never got to see her boyfriend and started pressing her roommates to let her boyfriend stay overnight in her shared room without being reported to campus housing. Amira's apartment-mates were prepared to "look the other way." Amira was not. Her apartment-mates charged Amira with being a self-righteous "stickler."

> AMIRA: I said, "Why did you choose to live in Muslim housing? You're infringing upon my standard [way] of life. And I don't want to infringe on *your* standard of life, but you can easily go to his house. I can't go *any* where else. . . . I could have lived in *any* other dorm and faced this.

Being a "stickler" was not cool on campus, even if (or especially if) "stickler behavior" was aligned with campus policy within Muslim housing. Majority cultural norms invaded and occupied the safe space of Muslim housing when Emma demanded that the rules be bent for her "normal" sexual expectations.

But Emma was not Amira's only problem, as both Muslim and non-Muslim youth constituted hedonistic cultural practices. One Sunday morning, Amira, returning from home back to her apartment, found Salwa (a liberal Muslim) and her boyfriend alone together in the room Salwa shared with Amira. Alarmed that her father (waiting downstairs in the car) might learn that sex was probably being had in his daughter's room, Amira reported Salwa. Salwa was moved to a different apartment for the following year. As she packed up and departed amid a bitter altercation, Salwa taunted Amira, telling her, "They [Yasmin and Emma] wish *you* were the one that had moved out. Now how does that make you feel when you're left behind to live with them?" Amira's demeanor betrayed immense sadness and frustration during and after this episode.

The pervasive dating culture seamlessly integrated itself into the limited space allotted by the university to religious Muslims, as Emma, Yasmin, and Salwa reshaped the rules of Muslim housing and minoritized Amira's objection to overnight male guests. The conditional mobility and trust Amira enjoyed from her parents was endangered by the presence of her roommates' boyfriends. Under her father's surveillance, Amira was cornered by both Muslim and non-Muslim roommates in the Muslim housing apartment.

The Language of Limits

By the end of her freshman year, Sarah had had enough of Jennifer and Chelsea (see "Pressure to Date"). She wanted to room with Muslim friends, namely Nadira and Feroze, who shared with her a Muslim American language of "limits" that circumscribed male-female interaction.

> SARAH: And the kind of relationship [Nadira] would have with someone would be similar to the kind of relationship I'd have with someone. . . . Limits and all that kind of thing. . . . In that sense my other friends can't really—[understand].

White non-Muslim friends could not fathom the Muslim language of "limits", though non-Muslim immigrant groups such as Sikh and Hindu South Asian American adolescents often use similar codes (see Shankar 2008: 171). The language of limits was the Muslim American "normal." This code rendered dominant youth culture irrelevant and enabled Muslim students to resist majority peer pressure. Leila and her Muslim friends, for example, had opposite sex friends, but they avoided unnecessary, flirtatious physical contact with opposite sex friends. Leila automatically differentiated between influential peers (her Muslim friends) and casual friends (everyone else): "See, when it comes to [interacting with] guys, I don't really compare to like, what *all the other kids* are doing. I'll compare to what all the other *Muslim* kids are doing."

Male Friends: Non-Muslims and Conservative Muslims

Muslim Americans had strong yet varied opinions on what was *just* the right kind of correct Muslim gendered behavior. Leila and her friends, for instance, were not *so* different from mainstream youth as to avoid physical and social contact with the opposite sex altogether.

> LEILA: [Muslim students] will talk and be friends but . . . [they don't do] little things like people [men and women] always hitting each other [playfully]. If someone [a male friend] was saying something dumb, I'd push them and be like, "Oh, you're so dumb!" It wouldn't be like, "*Ooh*, that [touching a man] is so wrong!" But at the same time I wouldn't run over and be like, "Oh, give me a big hug!"

This description of the deportment of "the Muslim kids" by implication eliminated from Leila's immediate peer group those non-Muslim youth and very liberal Muslims who were crossing ultimate sexual boundaries. But Leila's description also excluded the highly conservative Muslims who frowned on physical contact between men and women. The gendered conduct of hijabis was under particular observation. When a non-Muslim male friend gave Latifa a friendly hug, Ibraheem, who had observed the exchange, approached Latifa afterward and broached the issue of hugging men. Ibraheem's critique ("There's a certain image you need to maintain") rested on the political representation that Latifa's hijab embodied. Latifa rejected the *political* reasoning, countering with religious and cultural arguments. Religiously, the hug was not sinful because the intent was correct ("It's not a hug where [I'm thinking], 'Let me feel your body rub against mine'"). Moreover, in Islam, the value of exoteric practice is contingent on the spiritual intent. Culturally, Muslim ethnic groups do not hold to universal gendered norms, and her Levantine culture certainly did not condemn a sociable handshake or a friendly hug.

Yet Latifa wanted any potential male huggers to know that, though normal, she was not *completely* normal: "I don't want people to mistake it as the beginning of something I do with a guy: 'She'll hug you, [then] she'll kiss you.'" The meaning of a hug remained suspended between the conservative Muslim norms and the mainstream American ones, and the non-sexual hug was charged with a potential kiss. Arab, Muslim, and American, Latifa skillfully but uneasily mediated the expectations of her non-Muslim friends and of conservative Muslims like Ibraheem. Though not too different, she was not *too* normal either. Latifa was differently normal, trying to find a happy gendered medium between the conservative gatekeepers and the liberal Muslims who were "full-fledged dating": "Just try to go in the middle ground in whatever you do. Just be moderate. Have that boundary."

But where was the boundary? Where was the middle ground? Sarah's platonic dating? Heather's cautious avoidance of male-female contact? Yasmin's casual dating? Mahnaz's hookups? The boundary and the middle ground shifted as they were defined by my participants, constructing viable Islamic, American, ethnic, modest, and/or normal identities at a variety of points, rather than at any one point on their gendered behavior continuums. Generally, Muslim American women self-identified as "moderate," but described *others* as extreme, conservative, or liberal. They navigated parental and peer (Muslim and non-Muslim) norms and expectations, contextually shifting between extremes and "middle grounds." Nadira, for example, defined her own gendered behavior by contrast with that of conservative Muslims who did not hospitably invite male friends to socialize in their apartments.

> NADIRA: I realize that all my friends are *guys*. . . . I mean, I don't particularly get along with the [conservative] girls across the hall. . . . I think it's just because Feroze and I lived very differently than they did. . . . Because I had friends who were guys, and we had them over to the apartment.

Yet Heather—one of the "conservative girls"—in turn disagreed with *more* conservative Muslims about having MSA meetings in her apartment. Conservative Muslims objected to male and female MSA board members conducting organizational meetings in her apartment, since "brothers should not be in sisters' apartments." Heather dissociated herself from "the conservative line," arguing that the venue of Muslim housing was morally safe and that untoward events were unlikely in a group setting. The conservatives who did not like having MSA meetings in Heather's apartment were probably former MSA officers and graduate students who were affiliated with the larger Washington, D.C., MSA and interfaced with Muslim undergraduate life via MSA officers. Their influence was felt, but local MSA officers shaped the organization's work on campus.

Fatima's conservative friends disapproved of Fatima's male friends but only tacitly (just as they avoided the subject of hijab): "I kind of have a sense that if I'm talking to them, it's kind of, 'OK, I saw you talking to this guy.' They'll say something like that, they won't say something directly," because "you know, in the end it's my decision." Fatima could handle that. She prided herself on having Muslim friends who were at both "extremes" ("friends who won't be friends with guys, who will try to stay away from men" and "friends who are *very, very* close to guys"). If there was anyone she would not abide, it was "super-conservative Muslims, who impose their views, or whose beliefs are like, women shouldn't be talking to men, women shouldn't interact much [with men]." At Georgetown I never encountered any "super-conservative" Muslims.

Muslims Do Not Date

In chapter 4, I discussed how cultural notions such as hijab, modesty, and da'wah shift contextually depending on their usage. Specific perspectives about Islam and gender as carelessly tossed around by Islamophobic pundits and columnists are in fact "highly contingent upon the strategic concerns of those claiming to represent the community" (Kahani-Hopkins and Hopkins 2002: 288). The meanings of concepts depend on which representatives are speaking. The notion of *dating* shifts in meaning contextually when used in different forms by religious liberal and conservative Muslims (even when used by Christian Korean American college students; see Abelmann 2009: 64).

Heather pointed out, for instance, how Muslim Americans often claim that Muslims do not date. But this claim constitutes an oversimplification, a heuristic tool that highlights an idealized contrast to the ubiquity of sex in American culture. Dating in American parlance usually includes sex, Heather explained. "I think that's why Muslims are like, 'We don't date.'" But since this claim makes little sense to most Americans, Heather explained to her friends, "it doesn't mean you can't get to know someone."

HEATHER: Basically when I've explained stuff to non-Muslims, I'm like, it's not totally against dating per se. It just means that there are certain things you can't do before you're married. Hanging out together in a non-public place. Or any sort of physical relationship is out. . . . They're not going to talk about sketchy things either. . . . It's one thing to talk about "how did you do on your test?" . . . But you're not going to be like, "You look hot today!"

According to Heather's explanation, though dominant majority Americans used the term "dating" to include sex, dating was not inherently sexual within the Muslim American language of limits. When associated with courtship, dating could be acceptable as long as sexualized touch and talk were avoided.

Talking with Pretexts

Religiously conservative Muslim Americans avoid the term "dating." Muslim women who adhered to the prohibition on premarital sex generally described their relationships not as "dating" but as "talking to someone." "Talking" was assumed to be for long-term purposes and often fell under the rubric of courtship. In some cases, it was part of an undefined, flirtatious, semiromantic relationship that was distinguished from "ordinary" flirting in its more highly developed expectations of marriage. Only the putative pretexts of possible marriage, MSA work, and/or academic work could legitimate "talking." "Talking" highlights the expectation that only conversation should happen.

Though it was not "really sketchy" because it did not involve random hookups, according to Heather, such "pseudo-relationships" between religious Muslim men and women were too undefined, neither full-fledged dating nor courtship. Fatima had a couple of Muslim women friends who were "dating but not—not having sexual relations, basically."

HEATHER: But it's like, "I'll justify the situation because he's Muslim, I'm Muslim: we can get married in the future if things work out." . . . And maybe it's not been *discussed* but—.

The "less religious" Muslims were, after all, dating, and the somewhat religious Muslims were engaged in "Muslim dating." Real Muslims pseudo-dated, and pseudo-Muslims *really* dated. But even though they were not heavily sexualized, "talking" relationships were not entirely "justified." They were semijustified by the couple's intent and the likelihood—however remote—of marriage. But if the intent of marriage was not "discussed," a "talking" relationship could turn "sketchy." Unless the intent was verbalized, "talking" was mere flirting and could continue inconclusively, until a woman got "screwed over" or "something [sexual] happened." Undefined relationships were religiously problematic, socially damaging, and, within a patriarchal "culture of romance," inequitable (Holland and Eisenhart 1990).

Such an inconclusive relationship was Teresa's with Faisal, a male Pakistani student. "We talk online and in the library . . . all under the pretext that we're doing something [academic], but it's not! . . . And I go and we *never* talk about [academic work]. And we sit for three hours talking, literally, in a study room, and laughing." Nothing physical (or, as far as I gathered, even romantic) transpired between them, even though Faisal sought Teresa out constantly. He never framed the "relationship" as courtship. Faisal always asked her to meet for help with his English, and never just for a chat. "They [Muslim men] *have* to have a pretext," Teresa said dryly. These little escapades continued indefinitely, as Heather said they would, but *something* did not happen between Teresa and Faisal. At length, Teresa gave up on him and moved on. Community members often set up Muslim women with eligible men, but Teresa lacked access to ethnic networks that other Muslim women had. Since Teresa—a liberal white convert—had relatively limited options in the marriage market (Mir 2008b), she was obliged to pursue "pseudo-relationships" in the quest for marriage. Moreover, she had a reputation in the community for "talking" to Faisal.

What distinguished "talking" from the "just friends" phenomenon? *Talking* was significant because religious Muslim men and women did not—or should not—routinely spend large amounts of time together. By talking too much with opposite-sex friends, Muslim men and women became talked about. As Fatima pointed out, everyone in the community knew everyone else, and the loss of reputation could have far-reaching effects. But how else could they find love and marriage here, in the culture of romance?

FATIMA: Islamically, I don't think there's like a very clear method that's ever been said. It's just *culture* that dictates it! And the arranged marriages, that's culture. *This* culture is dating, but the thing is, there's still some boundaries. I don't know. This friend of mine who's interested in a guy, everyone just talks about her, and it makes me sick. And I'm like, look, we all don't know how to—go about this. . . . I'm like, what would you do in her position? And they're like, "Well, maybe there's a time when you tell your parents." And I'm like, when—you don't tell them right away when you *see* someone, you like them, you don't go and tell your parents. . . . And then your parents are just, like, if you keep doing that over and over again, your parents will be, like, [laugh] what's *wrong* with her?! But they [the critics] don't have an answer, you know! . . . And I'm just like so we shouldn't really be—.

Confronting the conservative critics of the woman who was pursuing a prospective mate, Fatima exposed conservative Muslim Americans for having no practical mate-seeking strategies other than hope. Fatima's conservative friends cautioned against the risky road of dating or "talking," recommending instead a reliance on fellow Muslims, parents, and guardians as matchmakers. Parents, Fatima retorted knowingly, were not always equal to the task. (And, I would add, the non-Muslim parents of converts would be little help locating good Muslim grooms). Conservative Muslim immigrant parents would become quite unnerved if a daughter reported home whenever she liked a man: the unspoken part of this narrative was that parental surveillance would become intolerable if parents were involved too early in the process. In other words, a woman *had* to pursue a relationship independently, without her parents, until it approached the point of marriage. But how was a budding romantic relationship to be pursued while observing the boundaries?

Arranged Marriage or Dating? Muslim Parents

Muslim parents, like religious Muslim American youth, drew fragile lines of difference around their children's gendered praxis, claiming—as Heather said—that Muslims did not date. At high school, Heather's non-Muslim friends had been outraged that some Muslim immigrant parents did not let their children date.

HEATHER: Some of my good friends were Muslim in high school, and my friends were like, "Their parents are insane; *they need to let them be normal and let them date.* They came to America, they need to just accept the fact that their kids are American."

Not only were immigrants expected to jettison religious and cultural identity wholesale, but it was believed that the entire impetus for not dating must originate from immigrant parents and (un-American) cultures. After all, non-Muslim youth assumed, the "kids are American" and, if left to their own inclinations, must surely want to date American-style.

For different reasons, *both* majority American youth and Muslim immigrant parents regarded Muslim American youth's gendered behavior as not normal. Even most of the very religious Muslim youth therefore tended to maintain a degree of secrecy about romantic matters. Muslim youth awaited their parents' cultural adjustment to their American hybridity, but they seemed confused as to their parents' codes of gendered conduct. Many parents seemed likewise uncertain. Generally, my participants' parents accepted, and even embraced, their children's hybridity in matters of gendered behavior. They seemed to alternate between conservative strictures and liberal uncertainty, sometimes leaving open third spaces of interpretation for their children to resolve independently.

FAIYZA: [I asked my mother], "What am I supposed to do? I'm not going to have arranged marriage." She's like, "Well, I'm not too sure." . . . I was like, "Well, I don't think dating's that bad." And she said, "I don't either."

Typically, parents seemed unenthusiastic about arranging marriages for their daughters. For Fatima, who had observed her conservative Indian parents' matchmaking efforts, the "*very superficial*" process of arranging a traditional South Asian marriage filled her with dread. "The girl has to look a certain way, she's judged by whatever—I personally don't want to go through any of that, and my mom didn't like going through that when she was getting married. So, I mean, if I told her, 'Look, I found someone,' I think she'd be like, 'OK, fine. Let's meet their family.' . . . My parents are not into the whole, blind, arranged marriage deal at all. . . . My dad himself says, 'You should get to know the person before you get married, you should talk to them.'" Fatima and her otherwise very conservative parents rejected the notion of arranged marriage but availed themselves of community networks as needed.

> FATIMA: And my mom hadn't seen my dad until the wedding day. . . . Yeah, and I tell American people that story and they're just like [shocked stare]. [Laugh] But I'm like, I've seen a lot of marriages in my parents' generation, where they have arranged marriages and it's like—they're not compatible! Yeah, it's like, a lot of compromise usually on the part of, like, the wife. And I'm not going to deal with that [laugh]. I don't have to. If I don't have kids, I don't have to deal with it. I'm just going to get divorced. Because it's like, if you're not happy, what's the point?

It was one thing to reject arranged marriage, but quite another to contemplate a concrete alternative. Leila's mother wanted her daughter to "find someone"—but without dating.

> LEILA: My mom's view of dating is actually like, a phone call. Like, she's really odd, because she's like, "I want you to find someone for yourself, but you're not supposed to date."

Leila's mother's foremost desire was her daughter's happiness. While she feared the risks of dating, and technically banned it, she steered away from definitively prescribing and proscribing mate-seeking rituals for Leila. Leila's mother was vague in her guidelines probably because she lacked the expertise and did not want to block Leila's chances for finding happiness—even if it was through "*really dating.*"

> LEILA: I really think she doesn't want to set [limits on dating] because she herself isn't sure. Because she notices, I think, that people here *do* date—like *really* date—and then get married. Like, they don't just talk on the phone and write each other letters, and decide one day. . . . She doesn't want to say, "Oh, you cannot do anything," because then what if there is some guy, and in order just for something to happen—like, she stopped it, you know? Because her biggest thing is, she

doesn't want it to be arranged. . . . She's like, "Nowadays the only people that get arranged are the leftover guys. Everyone just finds someone for themselves." So she's like, "You should find someone. But if you can't find someone"—obviously she's going to find them.

Since "leftover" Muslims—the less eligible, the unattractive, and the socially inept—resort to the arranged marriage route, it may be associated with stigma for Muslim Americans. But the breezy assumption that "everyone just finds someone for themselves" neglects the growing population of single Muslims who cannot find someone, or someone Muslim (Mir 2008b).

Even parents who calmly supervised "talking" relationships avoided the word "dating" and used "seeing each other" or "talking" instead. "And you're like, 'You mean, they're dating?'" Neelam chuckled. "That is really what they're doing, but they don't like using that. . . . Because growing up here, they see what dating's like when you watch television and you see movies and you see what they do, and it's a lot more physical, whereas they don't like to think of it that way." Dating was contaminated by the sexual rituals of non-Muslim Americans. We *talk*, and *they* have sex. The terminology helped distinguish *us* from *them*.

Early Marriage?

FATIMA: I don't know what the answer is, but I think that everyone's in that kind of flux. Like I think my older sister's in that flux. She always had the kind of mentality that someone will come to *me*. And no luck. She's [older]. . . . And she looks at her friends who went and found someone, oh, they're happy and they're fine. And you're like, I was just busy thinking about, like, the boundaries.

There was a strong current of fear—"quiet desperation," as Yasmin said with a nervous chuckle—among Muslim American women—fear that they would never find the right man, fear that they would be too old for the marriage market once they had completed their education, fear that they would have to fall back on an arranged marriage, fear that they might be missing out on the best time to find someone—except that in Washington, D.C., in the 2000s, hunting for a husband in college was so uncool. But it was even more uncool to be "leftover" women who resorted to arranged marriage.

Some people did not have to hunt for a mate. For conservative Muslims who collectively shared expectations that there would be no dating, this meant that a young man's parents would approach a woman's parents, or *his* friend would send the woman a message through *her* friend, and the happy event would ultimately follow. Two religious couples became engaged while still at college: Heather and Mohamed, and Sharmila and Hassan. Because all were postponing sex until after marriage, none of the parents objected that their offspring were to marry early, that is, before they had completed their education (Heather's parents, Christian whites, though unhappy with her conversion *and* marriage, did not stand in her way).

Zafar and his parents, on the other hand, refused to agree to an engagement or marriage while he and Haseena were still in college. (Zafar's liberal family, though they knew he was involved with Haseena, was less concerned that he was sexually active.) "And [dating] is a limbo stage, and I don't want to be in that limbo stage," Haseena griped, asking why *she* could not get married before graduating but Heather and Sharmila could.

> HASEENA: [The Prophet] said [that] as soon as people become adults, . . . they should get married as soon as possible afterwards . . . [and] you're not supposed to wait, because what happens if you wait? . . . You get yourself into situations like I'm in. . . . With Mohamed and Heather, everyone understands, and Sharmila. But for some reason, I'm held to a different standard . . . *because I went out with him instead of doing what they did.* Obviously they're not dating, so what else do they have to do *but* get married?

Since Haseena went out—"*really* dated" as Leila put it—with Zafar, she was held by her community, friends, and Zafar's family to mainstream American norms of dating: these include a degree of uncertainty on the outcome of the relationship, as well as low acceptance of "early" engagement or marriage. Haseena was infuriated by the comment that she was too young to be married. She was also acutely aware that her Muslim friends regarded her plight as one of her own making. By dating, she had embraced mainstream (specifically upwardly mobile East Coast non-Muslim) norms; and these norms *also* precluded early engagement and marriage. Until men and women had established their careers and were ready to settle down, and until the chosen mates of career women had popped the question, no-strings-attached dating was acceptable. (The preferred timing of education, career, and marriage respectively is not uniform, as I found while living in the Bible Belt.) Since Sharmila and Heather did not date their fiancés, they and their relatively early marriages were not subject to mainstream American norms. As a Pakistani American Muslim woman, Haseena wanted to salvage her reputation and religiosity through marriage, but non-Muslim norms (delayed marriage, dating) and immigrant Pakistani norms (a man must become established before marriage) both thwarted her. It did seem that consistent adherence to "one" set of norms could be safer and more predictable. Being in between was precarious.

(Haseena and Zafar eventually got married.)

Surveillance

Haseena was petrified that her parents would find out that she had a boyfriend. Much as Muslim American women omitted to mention specific details to non-Muslim students, they did likewise for their own parents. Muslim Americans were too liberal for their parents and too conservative for their non-Muslim peers. The problem with parents, too, was that they were not necessarily either *liberal* or *conservative* on sex and gender, but vague and unpredictable. "Good girls" who had "never actually dated someone" did not know where their parents' boundaries lay. "Because at times she seems totally cool with everything, but other times she's like, 'No!'" (Leila). Amira was cagey with her father because he veered between leniency and strictness in terms of monitoring her behavior. His "paranoia" at times belied his cultural liberality. While her father had her playing softball, tennis, and soccer, and encouraged her to play on an all-male soccer team ("You have to learn how to push them around!"), he was uncomfortable with such trivialities as her going for a walk with her friends ("Why? Why do you need to go for a walk? Where are you going on this walk?"

AMIRA: So you get mixed messages, and that's why, you know, it's really hard for me to open up very much because I don't know if one minute they'll be joking around about something and the next minute they'll use it as a reason to not trust me! . . . My father, I mean, he gave me a new laptop, he set up this cable network in our house, but he throws a tantrum if he sees me on the Internet, like, for an hour. "What are you doing on the Internet? . . . You're chatting with people? Who are you chatting with?"

Amira's father wanted to monitor her sexuality as well as to enable her full personal, academic, and social development in the new American environment. "It's like dealing with the Chinese regime or something. They'll loosen up a little bit, liberalize a little bit, and then all of a sudden get scared that, oh no, they're going to go crazy, let's clamp down." "Parents who haven't grown up here" vacillated uncertainly since they "just [don't] understand [pause] how much they can give or take" in dealing with their *American* daughters.

Covering Muslim Identities in Dating Culture

In America, people don't really brag about not dating. Not dating is usually a failure, a lack. Some Muslim women tried to "pass" as "normal" by covering the fact that they did not participate in dating culture. The culturally mainstream "never been kissed" fairy tale was more acceptable in the campus "culture of romance" (Holland and Eisenhart 1990) than the strangeness of choosing not to have a boyfriend.

> LEILA: I'm always like, "Yeah, I've never had a boyfriend." I wouldn't be like, [mock effusively] "Oh, I don't ever *want* a boyfriend!" Or, like, "A boyfriend for me is never a *real* boyfriend!" You know what, I'm not going to be, like, explain all these details. I'll just be like, [curtly] "Yeah. Never had one."

Leila preserved an appearance of normalcy—the hint that she *could* have a real boyfriend (which implied a sexual relationship)— rather than say that she *would* not. Many Muslim women "passed" as "normal" (Goffman 1963) by keeping Muslim identities in shadowy liminality. Muslim women skillfully disguised Muslim practices in the language of mainstream culture even when it came to males who overstepped the boundaries of appropriate behavior with a Muslim female.

SHABANA: In interacting with non-Muslim guys, do you ever wish they knew what your [physical] boundaries are?

LEILA: Yes, actually that's happened to me a few times. . . . This one time [in high school], . . . I was on the computer and [a boy] comes up from behind and puts his arms around [me] and, tapping on the computer, he puts his head on my head. I was just like, "OK, I have to go to the bathroom." . . . And I didn't feel comfortable. . . .

SHABANA: Would you feel comfortable telling a non-Muslim guy, . . . "Can I have some personal space?"

LEILA: I think I'd just push them away and be like, "What are you *doing*?!" I don't think I'd be like, "Oh, I need personal space." . . . I think I'd be more inconspicuous, and more like, "Ew, what are you doing? Get away from me!" So they'd just be like, "Oh, well, maybe she doesn't like me!"

Leila managed to avoid physical contact with the boy simply by unobtrusively disentangling herself and departing to the bathroom rather than being "conspicuously" Muslim. (She would certainly not use my rather wooden, academic language of "personal space"!) Yet covering her minority identity was a cultural assimilationist strategy: "Well, maybe I do look at it from other people—white people's point of view, because I won't make a statement about it" ("it" being her dislike of close physical contact). She added that, if she were to "make a statement" to a boy who was getting too close, he might sneer, "Why? Like, you're so weird!" Leila preferred to act as if she *disliked* a male rather than divulge that she was a Muslim woman who did not want men getting too close. Sexual and political vulnerability came together in the political act of informing a man about her *minority* Muslim religious practices and asking him to not touch her. Non-Muslim students' ignorance of Muslim practice was both a cultural resource and a hindrance: on the one hand, non-Muslim ignorance of Muslim sexual norms hampered Muslims in their practice of modesty; on the other hand, Muslim youth were able to cover their religious modesty *because* of non-Muslim ignorance, rather than be ridiculed as weird.

Teaching: Normal Difference

Muslim women's quest was multidimensional: to be normal and to be authentic as Americans, Muslims, ethnics, women, and students.

But embodying authentic identities was a sticky matter when there was little agreement on what an authentic Muslim identity was in, for instance, sexual matters. Moreover, Muslim women's desire for "normal" identities was tempered by their desire to be *different*. They sought to stretch what was considered normal gendered behavior, locating it near the edges of how majority Americans conceived of it, yet transporting it close to Islamic praxis.

Heather used her own courtship and engagement conduct as a pedagogical tool to demonstrate a viable Islamic romance that was both chaste (Islamic) and somewhat romantic (American). She was doing difference in a way that might seem normal to majority peers, inserting Muslim footnotes into American youth culture. Non-Muslim students usually perceived Muslim courtship (or "not dating") as entirely foreign and conjured up a binary opposition of dating versus parentally arranged marriage. How to establish the legitimacy of Muslim sexual praxis between conservative Muslims' total gender-segregation and liberal Muslims' casual hookups? Against these projections of excessive difference and complete normalcy respectively, Heather constructed a "middle ground" that was differently normal—authentically Muslim yet recognizably American. The Muslim women who avoided all contact with men were totally "different" and not normal they fit the ethnocentric American Orientalist image of Muslims. The Muslims who engaged in "normal" dating, American-style, were conformists, lacking the difference that should distinguish authentic Muslims from the majority of Americans.

HEATHER: A lot of them [non-Muslims] have the impression that the [male] Muslims they knew in high school were totally against dating, which meant they didn't speak to girls at all. Or the kids were dating, and the parents were like [with a slight foreign accent], "Dating is not allowed!" . . . So for people to realize that there's a middle ground that's not sketchy—people are like, "Oh, that's understandable." . . . [But] I'm sure the no-hugging thing, or no-touching [your fiancé], is probably really weird to people. . . . There's certain things you explain [to non-Muslims] and certain things you just leave out.

In high school, there were two main groups of Muslims: the conservative Muslims who did not talk to the opposite sex, and the liberal ones who were secretly dating. "Dating is not allowed!" represented the position of the stereotypical, conservative Muslim immigrant parent who constructed total difference in terms of conservative Islamic gendered behavior. In contrast to these "extreme" positions, Heather constructed a middle ground of Muslim American *normal difference*. Though *normal*, Muslim American normal difference must not be "sketchy" like majority American youth. Though Heather addressed an imagined, ever-present audience of non-Muslim peers who validated this normal difference ("Oh, that's understandable"), certain features of the new normal were inescapably weird to dominant peers, such as not hugging one's fiancé. Such stigmatizing features ought to be covered for a person to become even partially accepted. In public, Heather and Leila constructed "normal" American gendered behavior, but they constructed more elaborately Muslim gendered behavior at a discreet distance from the majority gaze. Private Muslim spaces, away from the risk of symbolic violence, were essential for such Muslim identity construction.

Not Being "Too Normal": The Presentation of Muslim Selves in Campus Life

By neither being sexually active nor drinking, Sarah was constantly being defined within campus culture as "the Muslim girl who doesn't." The reductive, religionized, *different* identity rose prominently to the surface within spaces where leisure activities were central. While Sarah resented this reified difference, many Muslims who resisted dating culture performed and even enhanced it.

> INTISAR: [Male-female interaction is] really a little uncomfortable most of the time. . . . 'cause [the men have] got their *kufis* [skullcaps] on, they've got their beards on. . . . I'm just like, look, should I call you *shaikh* [a religious scholar] or should I call you "brother"? . . . Very serious, very kind of adamant. . . . They lower the gaze. I'm just like [with mock awe] oh, my *God*. . . . I don't mean we have to go *out* together, but [let's] just . . . crack a joke . . . I wish I could, but I can't. Just because it's the established norm.

More in public than in private, many Muslim American students adhered to stereotypically "Islamic" identities. Male-female

interaction was often wooden and evasive, evoking images of traditional, sex-segregated Muslim communities. Though not *normal
American* behavior, conservative Muslim behavior offered secure
Islamic status to Muslim women and therefore exercised powerful
influence in Muslim youth spaces ("the established norm").

Intisar reciprocated Muslim men's ceremonious modesty. (Some
Muslim men complained about similar dynamics on the part of Muslim women.) Though she wished she could do away with the forced
aloofness, even Intisar wanted to appear relatively conservative. To
challenge "the established norm" would visibly position her on the
stigmatized "liberal" end of the spectrum. So Intisar maintained the
performance of coy, evasive gendered behavior. This multilayered
performance functioned in part to stave off cultural assimilation.

INTISAR: When you get to this [college] age . . . Here we are, a
lovely MSA; we're a little different than, say, [majority] people
who are partying. . . . So, I suppose, most of the time *we're afraid
that our faith is going to get lost in the midst of acting too college-like,
too, too normal,* you know? So we'd rather be conservative. [em-
phasis added]

Self-conscious of the campus gaze—because the MSA was a
prominent club—Muslim Americans often maintained an idealized image that was not "too college-like," not "too normal." By self-
essentializing, by playing up their differentness in areas of life that
were most sensitive and intimate, Muslim American women "for-
tified their threatened cultural choice" (El-Or 1997: 666). They kept
leisure culture at bay to stem the flood of assimilation, exaggerated
their difference from dominant youth—the "partiers," in an Occidentalist description. The fear of identity erosion was not ill-founded: I
observed dramatic religious change among students I had known
during fieldwork—traditional hijabis became regulars in the clubbing scene and MSA activists married non-Muslims.

Elizabeth held gender-segregation among people "who grew up
Muslim" (not converts) to be an (immigrant) cultural practice, rather
than a religious one. A mixed-gender crowd of non-convert Muslims
was usually somewhat gender segregated: "You're not going to see
people [men and women] interspersed like in any kind of American gathering." This behavior was "official" (Elizabeth) because such

Muslims' *private* gendered behavior did not always match their official collective performance. Private, individual behavior diverged from "official" performances. Both Elizabeth (black) and Intisar (Somali)—not members of long-standing, high-status immigrant groups (Arabs and South Asians)—suggested that there was a gap between the "official" and the (hypothetically) "natural."

The sexual chastity of many Muslim American women *was* highly different from the dominant population. Muslim women often tried to be normal, and to cover Islamic practices from their undergraduate peers, but sometimes they performed the total difference expected of them. In matters of sexuality, they tended *not* to (visibly) adopt mainstream behaviors, but they also sometimes "played up ideal values" that the non-Muslim peer group expected of them (Goffman 1959: 38). Whether they were conservative or not, at times Muslim women maintained a collective public image of "extreme" chastity, representing reified difference from the dominant group. For many Muslim American women (and men), the image was not *always* consistent with their private lives. Recall Intisar, who *did* practice chastity; and consider her critique of the image. The image *they* and *we* constructed was inscribed on *us* and perpetuated by *us* and by *them*.

> INTISAR: [People] are going to say [about your public behavior], "This is a Muslim girl. This is what *they* do." . . . Even the discomfort between brothers and sisters in public. . . . There's always people watching. . . . Even if they're non-Muslim and they already have ideas about us—then they see us, and their image gets messed up—in a good way sometimes. But then it can be, "Oh, my gosh, this isn't what [Muslims] do. And here they are, [Muslim men and women] doing high-fives." . . . Shy, lower the gaze: that's what they want to see. That's the image *we* want people to know about Muslims. . . . *We're* the ones that don't allow ourselves to be normal. . . . It's almost like *they* want to shape you into the stereotype they've got: Muslim girls, shy, hijabi. We do it more now than ever before. [emphasis added]

Intisar's commentary painted a complete picture of interactive cultural production (Levinson and Holland 1996) that fed into an industry of Orientalist "religionized" images, collaboratively maintained by both "us" Muslims and "them" (majority Americans). These "gazes" coerced Muslims into performing one-dimensionally religious, stereotypical "Muslim" identities. Intisar traced the stilted social behavior between Muslim American men and women to the self-consciousness of being stereotyped ("they already have ideas about us"). Muslim American students' "true" gendered practices were intensely edited ("We're the ones that don't allow ourselves to be normal") to match stereotypes of a Muslim imagined community (Anderson 1983). By "normal" here, Intisar referred to "unspoiled" Muslim American identities (playing on Goffman's notion of "spoiled identities"), or to what I have also described as "healthy" identity, one that is constructed in relative freedom from the constraining effect of stereotyping (Mir 2009c). *Normal Muslim* behavior, to Intisar, would not be prim and proper sex segregation, but might connote chaste (Muslim) yet relaxed (moderate Muslim, American) interaction (e.g., high-fives) in mixed-gender groups.

"Discomfort" characterized public interactions between many Muslim men and women. But when they became comfortable, they confused and shocked non-Muslims; the diversity and complexity of Muslim American gendered behavior put stereotypes in creative disarray ("their image gets messed up—in a good way sometimes"). But the momentum of majority discourse motivated Muslims to match the stereotypes ("they want to shape you into the stereotype they've got"). Muslims did this "more now [post-9/11] than ever before" and became frozen in an Orientalist fantasy—a fantasy that they in turn promoted through their "spoiled identities."

Muslim women were sandwiched between conservative Muslim and majority American expectations, which together constrained women's identities. Conservative Islamic ideologies constrain women's identities by demanding that women fit into an idealized homogeneous community ; Orientalism reduces Muslim women to an entity both hyperreligious and hyperfeminine.

Yet there were Muslims who *did not* live reified difference and were *too* normal, excessively acculturated in the United States, or, as Intisar described them in an unconventional use of the term, "extremes."

INTISAR: We don't accept our other sisters and brothers who . . . haven't got to that level of understanding in their *deen* [see glossary] . . . [instead] of accepting who she is . . . and saying, "I don't have to agree with what you do." . . . [We] don't accept our extremes. . . . But really, they're just normal people that just grew up in America.

In Intisar's voice, I find a seamless inclusion of the oft-dichotomized "extremes" of the conservative Muslim and the lax Muslim. Both Muslim "types" have been maligned in majority American circles and in Muslim circles. Intisar variously described less-religious Muslims as "extremes," as "normal Americans," and as en route to religiosity ("haven't got to that level of understanding"). Her lenses switched between those of the dogmatic Muslim, who critically appraises the apathetic Muslim's piety, and the tolerant Muslim, who, cognizant of Muslim Americans' various cultural experiences, embraces diverse members of the community without judgment. Therefore, "outcasts" (as Tehzeeb called them), who upset the idealized consistency and homogeneity of the community image, were at the same time merely "normal" Muslims who had culturally assimilated as a function of "growing up in America."

On occasion even worldly and acculturated Muslims could not "accept" the dishonor of lax Muslims. Amira was ruffled by her Muslim roommate Salwa's audacious and suggestive behavior when a non-Muslim male friend visited their apartment.

> AMIRA: Salwa comes in and she sits in [his] lap! . . . Like, what is he going to think? And especially [since] he's non-Muslim, and we're Muslim. . . . What will this make people think about Isla— [pause] like, Muslims in America? . . . [Because] for an American, if you don't know that many Muslims, if they see them on TV, they always wear hijab. . . . I mean, what satisfaction does it bring to other people when it's like, "Oh, she's a Muslim but she drinks and she smokes and she dances—like, she goes out with men." . . . Again, inside the house, outside the house; inside the family, outside the family.

Although it was rather difficult to maintain the image of a conservative Muslim community at Georgetown, just how ostentatiously forward could Muslim women be? Amira, who danced at nightclubs as Salwa did, was no stereotypical shrinking violet. But Salwa, with the cumulative effect of her conspicuous behavior—sitting on a man's lap, drinking, smoking, and dating men—*blatantly* unsettled the chaste Muslim woman image. While private indiscretions might be less politically harmful to the community, "other people" (non-Muslim outsiders) might derive malicious "satisfaction" from a Muslim woman's flagrantly suggestive behavior.

Women's bodies are always the battlegrounds on which community politics are waged. Outlandish as the idealized overly modest Muslim image may be, an outcast "undermines" the collective mission of minority representation. Everyday gendered behavior is an integral part of this representation. A Muslim woman's belief that "it's not always necessary to be touchy-feely with [men]" was symbolically ridiculed: "When your own friends or people close to you are undermining it . . . you feel disrespected; you feel undermined." A female Muslim body fully accessible to male contact symbolically "makes you question everything. It makes you question yourself: am I being too intense? Am I being too narrow-minded or too rigid in my belief, or are they wrong?" In a non-Muslim's presence, Salwa treacherously exposed Amira as possibly the wrong kind of Muslim, too different, too "narrow minded or too rigid," turning Amira's *Muslim* gendered behavior into a mere individual choice—and a stigmatized one at that.

Match the Muslim Image with Muslim Behavior

Different Muslim campus cliques constructed widely divergent modalities of being Muslim. The South Asian dance performances were chief among campus events that provoked debate over Muslim identity and representation. Though Muslim men and women participated in such events along with non-Muslims, religious Muslims condemned dancing in mixed-gender settings as sexualized and improper. Intisar disapproved, too. Yet when Intisar's friend Aliyah invited Intisar to attend a dance event because Aliyah was performing, Intisar accepted, out of loyalty and support. Intisar wanted to offer camaraderie to a friend. She did not, however, want to be too evidently *seen* at the event: "What kind of personality am I putting out there? You know, someone who's at the *musalla* praying—and [now] she's here . . . watching something that's just not normal, in an unhealthy environment."

In the course of her seamless day, Intisar prayed in the musalla, disapproved of Muslim women dancing publicly, and attended the dance show out of sisterly affection for a performer. Her world-view accommodated multiple situational identities—pious Muslim, youthful, and friendly. But, to the (stereotyping) gaze, which demands a frozen image of intolerant Muslim piety, the implications of her actions seemed inconsistent and "messed up" the fragile Muslim image.

However, Zeinab—also a hijabi—was quite unperturbed by apparent inconsistency. She rejected contrived and stereotypical conformity to conservative and Orientalist notions of correct Muslim gendered behavior. For instance, while Zeinab's close friendships with several men were a matter of (muted) Muslim disapproval, she was "trying to break the stereotype of being a good Muslim but being friends with guys." In "Muslim" spaces, immigrant Muslims usually set the rules of identity performance and gendered behavior. This is why second-generation immigrants like Zeinab freely reconstructed ("broke the stereotype") of Muslim gendered behavior, while Intisar (a member of a socioeconomically less powerful "newcomer" group of Somalis) and Elizabeth (a recent black convert) hesitated to edit community self-representations. They avoided engaging in unorthodox ("messed up") behavior.

Elizabeth, not quite ready to provide a complete, consistent public performance (see Goffman 1963), was unwilling to don the hijab because wearing hijab would make her Muslim womanness concrete and remove her from a gray zone of elastic identity.

> ELIZABETH: At the same time I have no problem sitting next to my guy friends, hugging my guy friends when I see them. And that drives a lot of people in the MSA community [crazy]. . . . They don't grow up like that . . . This is one of the big things I have about being hijabi: that, once I put on the scarf, I have to act—like, I would *want* to act as a Muslim woman should in front of the community. So that means when I see my guy friends, I can't hug them.

When Elizabeth's religious affiliation was no longer "undercover," and immigrant-flavored "Muslim womanness" took over her persona, dominant Muslim norms would become applicable to her behavior. Being Muslim was one thing, and performing Muslim femininity for Muslims was another, more complicated matter.

As immigrant Muslim norms are by no means singular and homogeneous, the notion of immigrant Muslim gendered behavior was also a reification. False binaries abound, of American and Pakistani, American and Muslim, and modern and traditional, respectively— among majority *and* minority Americans. Many Muslim American women live those binaries—especially when parents are watching. Unlike affluent, worldly men and women in Pakistan, Pakistani American youth of similar socioeconomic background often avoided public interaction with the opposite sex.

> SARAH: [I wish] the [American] Pakistani girls and guys hung out together [since] everyone's families know each other. That's . . . what happens in Pakistan. . . . [My] parents feel so comfortable with me going out with [men] in Pakistan [when we visit], because they know their parents. In America it's the opposite, so it's weird.

It is common for immigrant daughters to experience stronger parental expectations to maintain cultural norms than sons do (Dasgupta 1998). As with Yemeni schoolgirls from conservative immigrant families (Sarroub 2005: 36) and Somali Muslim communities in Toronto and London (Berns McGown 1999), so it was with Pakistani Americans. Sarah did not attend school with the offspring of her parents' school friends, let alone with Pakistanis, so her parents restricted her interactions with boys a good deal.

Sarah's parents (who had dated as high school students in Pakistan) admitted that they had adjusted their expectations of her in the United States.

> SARAH: My mom says things would've been different if I'd gone to [their school] and grown up in [Pakistani city]. . . . I'd be going to school with the kids of the people he went to school with. . . . It would have been okay if I'd gone out with guys I'd known in high school . . . [Often] kids in Pakistan are like, a lot more [romantically or sexually] experienced, liberalized, less Muslim, than . . . kids that have grown up here.

"Muslim" norms were seen as diametrically opposed to American norms. But upper-class Pakistanis and Americans, for instance, are not so very dissimilar. Still, in the new terrain, even liberal immigrant parents guarded reified difference to keep dangerously corrosive majority culture from seeping in.

Though Sarah and Leila were not "doing gender" exactly as their parents had done, they still chose to construct their identities as recognizably ethnic, religious, and American—more religious and self-consciously Pakistani than their parents had done as Muslims in Pakistan. To observers, Sarah would seem "Americanized" because she went out with boys. Sarah was only doing what her mother had done as a young girl, and the gendered culture described as "Western" was rooted in both America and Pakistan. The diversity of behavior in Muslim cultural repertoires disappears before the simplifying Orientalist gaze, and specific cultural practices become reified as representative practices. In turn young Muslim Americans take the baton to continue this reification. As "American woman" swallows up and hides evangelical stay-at-home mothers and leftist feminist lesbians, so "Pakistani" swallows up cosmopolitan Westernized immigrants, rural young women studying medicine in Faisalabad, Marxist feminist college professors in Lahore, fashion models in Karachi, and destitute mothers panhandling in the streets of Quetta; only the binary of modern versus traditional remains. Conveniently pulled off the shelf easily for everyday use, binaries need not be explained or contextualized.

Contextual clues were mixed and ambiguous, and identity construction on gendered behavior was especially complicated. Amid multiple constructions of diasporic Muslim American identities, there was a broad range of gendered behavior. Which was the *right* kind?

> LEILA: Because we're also first generation, we don't know [where the boundaries are]. I think if you were raised in Pakistan, you'd know what limitations you really had because of people around you. Here, it's so different because there's [Muslim/Pakistani] people who will not *look* at a boy, and there's other people who are full-fledged dating.

Official MSA Islamism and Unofficial Liberal Norms

Much journalistic ink has been spilled by Islamophobes on the power of radicalized ultraconservative Muslims within Muslim American communities. Although conservative Muslims sometimes hold representative status on doctrinal matters, no single ideological force was clearly triumphant in the MSAS at GWU and Georgetown. Close scrutiny of the power dynamic in Muslim student communities disaffirms the notion of stereotypically fanatical groups holding sway over oppressed liberal ("good") Muslims. Instead, ethnographic data underscores the importance of shifting contextual factors and dynamic ideological forces.

Under the auspices of campus student groups, youth of diverse backgrounds and interests congregate, socialize, organize, and serve. Behind the face of the organization, individuals work to promote it, and in turn, the organization helps safeguard their ideologies, interests, and status. Like other student groups, MSAS mobilized, educated, and connected its members. But MSAS also took seriously the enterprise of representing Muslims, their beliefs, and their interests to the broader campus community. College students are notoriously overextended, between academic work, leisure, and social and extracurricular activities, so any representative of a "diverse" organization has a limited window of opportunity to sell its wares. A flyer advertising an event or the actual event must be tailored so as to instantly etch a positive impression upon the busy, apathetic student on his way to the game. In the competitive marketplace of ideas, a consistent minority image was quicker, simpler, and more memorable than a complex, shifting, diverse one.

On campus, MSA operated as the public official face of Islam. Many Muslims wished to see an objective, timeless, text-based Islam govern MSA practices, irrespective of the members' practice. Such Islamic behavior, moreover, should be displayed at MSA events. "Gatekeepers" (usually MSA student officers) practiced "strategic essentialism" (Spivak 1993), and employed more stringent "Islamic" gendered practices than most Muslims practiced in their personal lives. To engineer what they considered correct Islamic behavior, some MSA officers tried to construct MSA events as more gender segregated than "normal" life. Constructing highly nonsexualized spaces that were markedly different from hedonistic campus culture served both inter- and intracommunity purposes: representing Muslims on campus recognizably as Muslims, and providing community and religious education to Muslim students.

Speaking for a group entails espousing specific versions of identity that are "bound up with recruiting support for particular political strategies" (Kahani-Hopkins and Hopkins 2002: 289). In families, educational institutions, and workplaces, individuals subsume their interests and identities within those of the group, the organization, the community. The group is more than the sum of the individuals, and the individual, through participation in the organization, is transformed into something more—or even other—than herself.

Latifa took a dim view of MSA's artificial construction of a representative Islamic environment. Numbers, she argued, took priority over ideology: MSA should adapt to its members and "seeing that most [Georgetown] MSA members aren't that conservative," MSA should accommodate various ideological interests instead of engineering some authentic Islamic setting. "Just try to go in the middle ground in whatever you do," she said. "Just be moderate. Have that boundary." She imagined that a collective Muslim American praxis could be constructed in a "middle ground," some median point on the gendered behavior continuum, with the all-important (and nebulous) "boundary" between the sexes. Latifa's "boundary" illuminated the value of Islamic chastity, while the "middle ground" would simultaneously accommodate all Muslim parties at various points clustered near the "middle." But Muslim American ideological diversity defied the strategy of occupying "middle grounds" or identifying "boundaries."

The Muslim student communities at Georgetown and GWU had two broad sets of gendered norms: (1) official Islamic public norms encompassing a degree of sex segregation and slightly distant behavior between the sexes; and (2) unofficial more "liberal" gendered behavior. ("Segregation" implies that in meetings, men and women voluntarily sit on either sides of the same room, with no intervening barrier, rather than next to each other.) Outside of MSA events, men and women—gatekeepers included—usually socialized freely. At Georgetown, conservative Muslims seemed timorous and defensive. Liberal norms were dominant overall, owing in part, I feel, to the wealthier, more undergraduate-centric, and more bohemian and residential Georgetown culture. Liberal and conservative Muslim practices sometimes clashed in public MSA spaces. Stricter norms of sex segregation were somewhat securely established in GWU MSA spaces, maintained even by relatively liberal Muslims. But MSA public events were supposed to represent idealized Islamic identity, and Heather, who organized such events, was frustrated when they were not recognizably "Islamic."

HEATHER: Like, people, at least if you're going to do [sexual] stuff on the side, at least come to MSA with the right mindset—"at least we're not going to do it here," sort of thing. . . . [Sometimes at MSA events we see] the Muslim boyfriend and girlfriend . . . being all over each other at a table. . . . I just wish there was some sort of conscience that "We're coming to an event that is Islamic."

In a Muslim "haven" Muslim identities should be performed by all. Such performances served religious and political purposes. But conservative Islamic norms were minoritized in Georgetown Muslim spaces as well as in mainstream non-Muslim spaces, so that an MSA event was, at times, similar to a non-Muslim event.

Sex segregation, hijab, and MSA were like mnemonic devices or semiotic mediators that helped some Muslim women reinforce their sense of self. Muslim women negotiated not only various types of Muslim expectations and semiotic mediators but also American norms of undergraduate identity. Playing up religionized identities also served to reinforce spiritual states and religious practices. Physical Islamic spaces and visible gendered practices made identities palpable. Conservative Muslims missed the semiotic mediators (such as sex-segregation) in MSA spaces. Sharmila, for example, wished that she belonged to a more conservative Muslim community.

SHARMILA: [It would have been] very different in terms of gender relations [at a different university]. I don't think I would have made as many [male] friends. . . . Most communities are like, you come in, and you're sort of *enfolded* within an already set rubric or something, whereas here people come and . . . make their own thing.

Sharmila had hoped to be "enfolded" in a more conservative Islamic campus group, like her local community, a well-established mosque and social network in the D.C. suburbs. Such community frameworks facilitated religious development, enabling members to become more devout than they might as dispersed individuals. But the Georgetown Muslim context fostered identities that diverged from the immigrant, Islamist "rubric." The conservative "established norm" (Intisar) or "rubric" (Sharmila) was widely seen as more authentically Islamic and closer to the canon. In the mostly liberal Muslim culture at Georgetown—where Muslims had close friends of the opposite sex with whom they socialized with extensively at nightclubs and parties— Muslims generally "made their own thing" (Sharmila). This culture appeared unorthodox and inauthentic to Sharmila. The intrusion of dominant norms disrupted commu- nity socialization so "enfolded" in this new made-up "rubric," even Sharmila made numerous male friends.

Despite Sharmila's disapproval, in MSA spaces at these two uni- versities, public norms and identities were contested, and neither the liberal nor the conservative group was clearly triumphant. Latifa approved of neither the male-female physical and social closeness at Georgetown nor the gatekeepers' imposition of fabricated gender segregation. An incident she narrated points to the precarious foot- ing of conservative norms at Georgetown: it took place during a coed MSA weekend retreat. A group of men and women were playing a role-playing game called "Assassins." They must have been getting too comfortable, for in due course, the MSA president, Mohamed, tactfully suggested that everyone retire to their separate cabins "for early bedtime." This attempt to break up mixed-gender mingling failed. Then Heather tried to bring an end to the game, wistfully say- ing that she had been hoping for more time to bond with the sis- ters (i.e., in a single-sex space), at what was her last campus retreat before graduation. Still no one complied. Latifa shrugged both off breezily with an "Uh, I think we're fine the way we are," and Amina and Taher (all three were MSA officers) continued with the game un- concerned. In their discreet prompts, neither Mohamed nor Heather *explicitly* underscored the merit of sex segregation. Both used emo- tional or practical appeal to persuade retreat attendees to break up the party. Clearly, conservative gatekeepers adapted to mainstream and liberal Muslim norms, facilitating the maintenance of physical distance between the sexes by means of precedence, cultural norms, and advance spatial organization, not by openly endorsing its reli- gious value. At Georgetown, as Muslims camouflaged religious com- portment in a secular American guise for their non-Muslim peers, so they did likewise with liberal Muslims.

At the next board meeting, where only MSA officers were present, Mohamed chided Latifa for neutralizing his attempt to break up the party. Amina and Taher—who had ignored Mohamed's request at the retreat—concurred with his reproach. At the retreat—a "free place" (Goffman 1961: 205)—unofficial liberal norms overpowered the gate-keepers. But in the circle of the MSA board—a "surveillance space" (204)—they acceded to Mohamed's conservative stance.

Despite ongoing contestation, liberal norms were generally domi-nant at Georgetown. Some core MSA activists were very liberal Mus-lims; Haseena, for example, had a boyfriend and chaired a com-mittee. Since the rules of Muslim spaces were not applicable to all spaces, "when we're MSA, we're MSA; and when we're not at MSA we're not at MSA!" (Haseena). Haseena's dichotomy that posited dif-ferent priorities in different spaces was mirrored in Heather's plea that Muslims observe "Islamic" behavior in MSA spaces "at least," if nowhere else.

Many GWU MSA members half-jokingly praised their MSA for its contrast with the ("too liberal") Georgetown MSA. Amber felt "out of place" when visiting Georgetown MSA events: "It's not like, 'Oh, I'm more religious than you, therefore I'm going to look down on you,' but it's like, the opposite." Some conservative Georgetown Muslims felt like lesser members of the community. Though official and unof-ficial norms coexisted there, too, GWU MSA spaces featured relatively conservative practices in public. Roshan, an MSA member, was half anxious and half pleased about the report that "bad" Muslims felt "intimidated" at MSA events. Roshan wanted an admirably inclusive MSA ("I don't want them to think that [they are being judged]") that, at the same time, wielded full control of its spaces.

> ROSHAN: [At] other MSAS . . . people can go in there holding hands, or [men and women] hug and flirt. . . . We don't encour-age that at all. So that's why inevitably they feel intimidated . . . coming to these events. . . . You *should* feel guilty if you're doing something wrong!

Roshan's position was mixed. She appreciated the construc-tive power of religious intimidation ("you *should* feel guilty") and claimed that her MSA—in salutary contrast to the Georgetown MSA—discouraged "flirting" at MSA events. All the same, Roshan wanted Muslims to enjoy MSA as a non-intimidating space even as she tried to sustain an idealized Muslim community: "judgmentalism" is the cardinal sin that religious Muslims speak of eschewing, reflecting liberal American cultural attitudes on religion, judgmentalism, and sin (Wolfe 2003). But Roshan's personal behavior in non-MSA spaces was not consistent with the semi-segregation she enforced in official Islamic spaces.

> ROSHAN: I'll give you an example: the Supreme Court judges, they have to maintain a reputation or image. Outside of their professional room where no media is, they treat each other in meetings . . . [formally], "madam," "sir," even though they're close, like brothers and sisters, because they work so closely. . . . [Although] I'm really close with brother Jamal . . . obviously, I'm not going to act stupid with him in public as I do [in private] . . . [Impressions] can produce misconceptions about certain things. . . . [As an MSA officer] you have to be so patient, simply because you're a *representation* [to] Muslims who are struggling [with religious practice] and to non-Muslims. And . . . because you're on the board, those conservative Muslims have such high expectations for you. [emphasis added]

In private, Roshan was "really close" (read: fraternal) with Jamal, and "acted stupid" (playful, not flirtatious) with him. But, as a representative of Islam to conservative Muslims, to less religious Muslims, and to non-Muslims, she provided exemplary, decorous "Islamic" behavior in public, and observed a fitting social distance from Jamal and other men. If she were to publicly "act stupid" with Jamal, "novice" Muslims might read this as a validation of flirtatious behavior.

Muslim American students' public behavior was under layers of surveillance. In MSA spaces, Roshan structured physical arrangements that preserved semi-segregation for the edification of "struggling" Muslims; in turn, sex segregation in MSA spaces "constituted a response to internal panopticism" (Wills 2011: 237) by "those conservative Muslims." But in *private* (non-MSA) spaces, Roshan was relaxed enough to sometimes be what Amber disapprovingly called "too comfortable." Gatekeepers used hyperreligionized behavior to regulate "novice" Muslims' behavior in MSA spaces, but, in non-MSA spaces, they edited the script. The "masses" received a more austere version of the code, as did the conservative elite, who co-constructed the Islamicized code.

What, then, was MSA? To marginal members, MSA officers represented MSA. But MSA officers were by no means a monolith (consider the disparity between Latifa's and Mohamed's views). MSA members' own individual demeanor fluctuated contextually across a continuum of male-female interaction. Amber deplored "excessive" mixed-gender socializing and "acting stupid":

AMBER: [Some GWU MSA] guys and girls are always hanging out together. And the younger kids are thinking, "If they can do it why can't we? They're not *doing* anything [sexual]." They're just sitting around, chilling, whatever, or they'll have a snowball fight [laugh] . . . *Too* comfortable. . . . And [the kids] come to an MSA event where there might be segregation, and they're like, "This is kind of contradictory."

Comfort was a key theme in Muslim women's gendered behavior. Amber described herself as "comfortable" with her male MSA friends. These *other* people were "too comfortable," engaging in physical play and extended male-female fraternizing. A judicious level of comfort reflected moderation and balance (central themes in Islamic discourse) as well as integration without total assimilation vis-à-vis mainstream American culture. Excessive "comfort" in mixed groups did not sit well with MSA's agenda of creating and maintaining some physical distance between the sexes.

Since MSA activists must spend a great deal of time together planning and implementing activities, Roshan thought Amber's condemnation of "comfort" did not hold water. As Teresa pointed out, Muslims disapproved of public male-female interaction in the absence of a "pretext" (see "Talking with Pretexts" earlier in this chapter): MSA activism was one possible pretext. MSA men and women chatted via phone and online frequently in relative freedom from the gaze. There appears to be no gaze without actual seeing.

Non-Muslim observers of the sex-segregated setting perceived Muslim American women as enslaved to Muslim faith and men, penned in within "separate and unequal" harem-like spaces. Non-Muslim peers did not necessarily appreciate how Muslim American women were constructing, shaping, resisting, and deploying these sex-segregated spaces. Muslim women resisted as well as adapted stereotypes about Muslim gendered behavior, projecting Muslim identities that were recognizable as well as unexpected, normal as well as powerful. "Comfortable" with her male MSA colleagues, Amber did not feel "distant" from them when they occupied the "male" side of the room during MSA events, nor did she hesitate to cross zones and speak to them. Amber wielded creative power and control over sex-segregated spaces—spaces that she herself had constructed to prevent male-female physical demonstrativeness. Students new to MSA spaces (e.g., freshmen, younger, less religious students) had less ownership and creative control of these spaces, and were consequently diffident about traversing invisible boundaries. Although close with their male Muslim friends, Amber and Roshan upheld sex segregation. Creators of sex-segregated spaces, they were not trapped within them. Moreover, they had flexibility of praxis in *private* convivial spaces. But Amber and Roshan maintained MSA events as official representations of Islamic behavior.

> AMBER: [Some people] feel very comfortable [with mixed gender groups]: they push each other and joke around. . . . [To prevent this from happening in public] might be like hiding things . . . because it *does* happen . . . [but] I just don't think it's appropriate in a Muslim setting. So if we have to enforce [appropriate behavior], so be it!

The key factor was not whether these other Muslim American women frolicked with male friends but *where* they did so. Amber thought it "safer" to keep the Islamic nature of an event from being sullied by male-female contact. "Things" should not "happen" in public Islamic settings. In Haseena's case (of the boyfriend) too, the formula of avoiding public and brazen indecency emerged as pivotal. Heather, a religiously conservative gatekeeper, hastened to distinguish Haseena's case (she had a steady boyfriend) from others who were sexually active because of the couple's monogamous mutual commitment and their discretion in public spaces.

> HEATHER: Personally . . . if you're engaged, I don't care what you're doing. You're getting married to this person? You've made that intention? People's parents are in on it? As long as you guys don't do anything [forbidden] in front of people, I don't care what you do.

Mutual commitment and the avoidance of blatantly sexualized behavior (say, kissing and touching) set Haseena's relationship apart from "normal" majority-style dating (although the parents were not "in on it"). Private religious morality, strictly construed, was not the community's business when it did not impact the community's religious culture. If Haseena and her boyfriend were to fool around openly, this, along with public knowledge of their sexual relationship, would sexualize the community: the taboo status of premarital sex would fade, and it could become as "normal" as it is for non-Muslim Americans. A culturally embattled minority religious community was tainted by public transgressions such as "the Muslim boyfriend and girlfriend being all over each other" (Heather) at MSA events. Haseena's behavior, tempered with overall religiosity, remorse, and the future intent to marry, neither "infected" the Muslim community nor challenged its tenets, as more brazen forms of dating did. As for coexisting with peers who were sexually active, Muslim students already did that within a dominant group culture; coexisting with fellow Muslims who were (privately) sexually active was only an extension of the same.

The much-vilified *shariʿah* law, too, evinces primary concern with public rather than private immorality (e.g., the punishment for adultery applies only when four eyewitnesses attest to the act of penetration). Oddly similar is the French republic's concern with hijab, based on a perception that hijab is ostentatious and therefore "injurious to French public life" (Scott 2007, Hirschkind and Mahmood 2002: 351). Some difference is too "in your face"—even (and especially) in the supposedly pluralistic public spaces of multicultural Western societies.

Roshan's personal gendered behavior and the instructive import of her public "MSA" behavior were incongruent. Yet, since the pedagogical commitment was an integral part of her religiosity, all these behaviors—"acting stupid" with male fellow MSA activists, enforcing segregation, and being aloof toward Muslim men—were seamlessly aspects of her religious life, as were Intisar's prayer and her attendance at a dance event. The aloof and ceremonious discomfort between men and women was plainly a consequence of the multi-level cultural surveillance, which, in turn, becomes interiorized (Foucault 1980: 155), guilt ("You *should* feel guilty if you're doing something wrong!"), and "intimidation." The continuum of male-female interactions categorized individuals into "extremes" and "moderates," or "uncomfortable," "comfortable," and "too comfortable"—though, for female gatekeepers, "comfortable" and "too comfortable" (with fellow activists) coexisted with (publicly) "uncomfortable" behavior. This stilted, aloof gendered behavior was then transmitted to "struggling Muslims," as well as to non-Muslims—affirming their stereotypes of secluded and remote Muslim women.

Muslim activism was an indispensable excuse for legitimately being comfortable with opposite sex friends. Muslim community work created a framework for legitimate male-female bonding that differed in orientation from yet resembled non-Muslim peers' male-female social behavior. MSA work also shielded religious students from the condemnation of excessive male-female bonding, since many "MSA Muslims disapprove of males and females talking in public without an obvious reason, like an MSA issue or an academic issue" (Teresa).

> TERESA: But I think a lot takes place in the private sphere, in particular online and on the phone. I think that is where males and females interact and have relationships.

As Teresa pointed out, MSA Muslims disapproved of men and women talking in public unless there was an academic or activism-related reason or "pretext," but men and women, including MSA officers, chatted online and on the phone. A female MSA officer told me how a religious male student had practically proposed marriage to her via internet chat. The Muslim group's "front" operations—the "official" spaces of mosque, musalla, and MSA event—conformed somewhat to official and stereotypical assumptions about Muslims, while there was the potential for "wilder" behavior outside these core spaces, in unobserved virtual and telephone interactions. Chat, email, and phone interactions were not physical, so they appeared to fall under a modified set of rules. Without actual seeing, there was no gaze.

Gender Inequalities and Strategic Essentialism

As a Muslim feminist, I have mixed feelings about Islamicized behavior that serves purposes of cultural resistance yet also ends up perpetuating gender inequity. Certainly, many Muslims including MSA gatekeepers craved a religiously wholesome space that operated in political and spiritual resistance to the racism and the decadence of campus cultures. But sex segregation in Muslim spaces could work toward gender inequality. Elizabeth attended an MSA regional conference where male speakers lectured to mixed-gender audiences but women experts lectured to private women-only audiences. (Not all events are organized in this way.) This discrepancy did not bother her "because generally, I'm sorry, most men have the head for that [religious expertise]." A recent convert's internalization of essentialized gender roles and male entitlement to religious authority betrays some implicit gender norms in many Muslim spaces, despite the equality discourse there.

A certain discomfort with women's public roles is ingrained in the idea of women as sexual objects whose modest and withdrawn behavior "protects" collective chastity. The belief that male sexual aggressiveness is a product primarily of feminine enticement is certainly not limited to conservative Muslim circles (consider the prevalence of "slut-shaming" and fascination with the rape victim's attire). A male friend of Zeinab's, who regularly chatted with Zeinab online for instance, disapproved of women speakers at local MSA events (MSA communities were too liberal for him). A close personal friendship with a woman was acceptable, but her appearance in a highly public role was not: the latter involved display of female body and voice to a mixed-gender group. As we know, there is a fine line (if that) between conservative notions of public indecency and the disappearance of women's bodies from public spaces. Thence to women being impure, inferior, marginal, and marginalized (for the sake of collective purity) is not a stretch.

Since the manipulation of collective identities by gatekeepers can silence voices and create inequalities, Hall questions whether we are any longer in that necessary moment of strategic essentialism (1993: 110), and Spivak (1993) argues that strategic essentialism (such as MSA gatekeepers' differential application of religious principles to public and private behavior) should only be used on a temporary basis for specific goals.

"Native manipulators" such as Zeinab's chaplain friend and the MSA officers often "cover up contemporary faults, corruptions, tyrannies" and real-life fragmented identities. In critiquing such subaltern practices, we should contextualize them in their relationship with "the embattled imperial contexts out of which they came and in which they were felt to be necessary" (Said 1994: 16). Sex segregation is symbolic of "Islam," just as *sati* acquired "emblematic status" for "both British and Indians, for its supporters as well as opponents on both sides." As sati to "Indian Culture," distinctively "Islamic" sexuality "becomes a larger-than-life symbol" of Islam "in a way that radically transcends the reality of its limited practice" (Narayan 1998: 93–94). As Roshan upheld sex segregation in public but *not* in private, many Indian reformers who privately denounced sati upheld it in public as a "symbol of 'ideal Indian womanhood,' indicating a feminine nobility and devotion to family deemed uncharacteristic of Western women" (Narayan 1998: 94). Muslim American students served up the spectacle of Islamic distinctiveness to the majority gaze as the limited pluralism of campus culture offered Muslim American women limited options for constructing complex identities. "Actively produced, reproduced, and transformed, through a series of social processes" (Kahani-Hopkins and Hopkins 2002: 288–89), Muslim female identity is essentialized by global and local political and cultural powers, both Muslim and non-Muslim. Muslim women students' ahistorical essentialism was both strategic and a product of the dominant majority's definition of identity options. The subaltern appeared before the majority gaze in garb that the majority expected of her.

Conclusion

College campuses, it is supposed, are spaces of identity exploration and lifestyle choice, a diversity showcase of sorts where being different can be cool. In the spaces of college culture, Fatima and Sarah gained the new but unwanted freedom to date, as well as the permission to *not* date accompanied by mortification and marginality. The "choice" to assimilate into sexualized campus culture was a costly one for those who became "outcasts" to the Muslim community, while those who did not assimilate would never entirely belong in mainstream campus culture. The latter found private Muslim American subcultural spaces where the new Muslim normal and the language of limits might thrive and blossom.

Such private Muslim spaces were vital in cushioning Muslims from the corrosive influence of dating culture. Yet sexualized

campus culture even seeped into the private spaces of special accommodations (such as Muslim housing). At times, simply by expressing positive attitudes toward minorities, majority students can
insert themselves in and thus appropriate minority spaces, in addition to keeping the mainstream spaces they already enjoy. In these
private spaces they may then doubly minoritize minority students
and effectively neutralize policy accommodations, as Emma did for
Muslim housing. Under the rubric of pluralism and inclusiveness,
in regulating diverse student clubs and campus spaces, university
policies are often meticulously inclusive of *all* students, that is, not
just minorities but majority students as well; Muslim housing apartments (and minority student groups and spaces) are therefore required to be open to applicants of all faiths and none. However, the
core spaces of campus culture are in fact culturally exclusive and
not equally open to all groups. In the practice of even-handed im-
partiality, campus leaders must also actively attend to the interface
between sexualized youth culture and campus guidelines, and to the
majority cultural power that inundates specific policies.

In chapters 3 and 4, I showed that, in practices of social-cultural
style (e.g., extroversion, professional ambitions, attire), Muslim undergraduate women often countered pervasive stereotypes (Muslim
women are oppressed and different from *us*) with a corrective view
(Muslim women are normal, modern, and free). However, in the delicate field of sexual behavior, most—although not all—Muslim women
students tended to remain securely in a "middle ground" (Latifa) between "American" and "Muslim" identities, *not* inclined toward the
"American" side. Most Muslim women located themselves at a midpoint on the continuum between majority and Muslim sexual norms
though, contextually, they veered toward various points on the continuum and complied with *and* resisted both Muslim and mainstream
American expectations. "Enfolded" in a white, secularized "rubric" at
elite universities, my participants' gendered behavior took various
forms—"normal" American, "different," "normal-different" Muslim
American, conservative Muslim, liberal Muslim—and various combinations of the above.

In sexual behavior, far more than in other spheres, there was
much projection of idealized "Muslimness"—a carefully crafted
"strategic essentialism" (Spivak 1993). This essentialism often incorporated a degree of sex segregation in public spaces and a piety

that dramatically contrasted with an Occidentalist stereotype of promiscuous non-Muslims. This multifaceted identity mission had both personal and collective implications, and it subsumed political, religious, sexual, and social goals. Employing mainstream American as well as Islamicized gendered discourse, Muslim women were observed from twin towers of surveillance, or a double panopticon, of Muslims (families, kin, communities, future spouses, friends, etc.) and non-Muslims (the broader culture, law enforcement, campus authorities, "normal Americans," etc.). Majority American peers looked for the stereotypical "Muslim woman," and within the local or minority panopticon (which is no less intense), Muslim gatekeepers upheld the banner of "Muslim gendered behavior" to preserve the sexual and political honor of the community, at times only half meeting the majority gaze that cannot quite see whole, complex, and seamless identities in people of color. Muslim American women's complex gendered navigation of college spaces defied simple stereotypes. They maneuvered to remain safely suspended between "mainstream American normal" and "Muslim normal," feet planted in both worlds, shifting back and forth according to the demands of the situation.

6

Conclusion

"Covered" and Assertive Muslim Identities

YASMIN: Like, either I have to be completely assimilated, completely into this culture or either I have to become completely like, Muslim, and be separate instead of a part.

Muslim women felt the tension of binary identities on campus. Did it have to be a zero-sum game? Did you have to be socially divided from hedonistic campus culture or completely assimilated "into this culture"? Yes, actually, it seemed very *much* like a zero-sum game when Muslim identities were mauled not only by American military and intelligence actions but also in the social spaces of campus culture, when "that outcast . . . that really foreign belief about alcohol" and hijab, modest clothes, and not-dating clashed with the narrowly conceived "normal" American college student.

As my participants constructed Muslim American identities, they deployed as well as "covered" racial, cultural, and religious attributes contextually, and religionized identities were also inscribed on them. Increasingly perceived as outsiders, Muslim women made the camouflaging of religious identities an integral element of their response to encompassing cultural and political surveillance. As the boundaries of Americanness contracted, pushing out immigrants and people of color, Roshan and Heather tacitly disavowed the stigma of Muslim identity, protected it from public exposure, and disguised their religiosity under the secular "uniform" of "normal" behavior. In invisibility lies safety. In liminality one may conduct one's identity work in relative security.

Yet when the individual regards his or her own attributes as "defiling" (Goffman 1963: 7), how genuine can such safety be?

Muslim American women treated Muslim modesty, courtship, and teetotalism like dirty secrets, contaminations that reduced their normalcy quotient in campus culture. Yasmin, for instance, toned down the visibility of her religious affiliation by strategically excluding Muslim referees from internship applications: "Can you really change things from outside the system?" she asked. "So I think it's much more likely you can change the system from the inside." A political and cultural sea change required long-term, low-key labor. The luxury of being true to oneself—whatever that meant for an individual—was not available until the cultural project of Muslim American indigenization was complete. So Yasmin disavowed and covered Muslim identity: if accepted by the dominant majority, if "inside" the system, she might become part of a cultural undercurrent that would eventually pull Muslims into the mainstream.

Sharmila and Amber rejected the passivity of Yasmin's silences: the critical political situation demanded "loud" identities, not covered ones.

> AMBER: Yes, now in every single thing I feel like I have to speak up [bitter laugh]. No one else is going to do it for us and we're just going to be stomped on. And yes, it's constant pressure, but if I don't do it then I'm not going to respect myself. . . . There's a handful [of Muslims on campus] who care. And the rest, . . . they don't do anything about it. . . . They'll be like, . . . "They [law enforcement and intelligence] are all going to take us all." . . . But they're not going to do anything. . . . It [apathy] is a way to protect themselves too. . . . Personally.

But Sharmila and Amber, as conservative hijabis, along with their friends and families, prominent Washington area religious Muslims, were already at risk in the war on terror. The apathetic Muslims were protecting themselves "personally," but the visible Muslims were constructed as primarily *Muslim*, and not as private *persons* with secular interests and identities to protect. Her plans for the future in jeopardy, Amber became *more* visibly and vocally Muslim, rather than *less* visibly like Yasmin. For overtly religious Muslims like Amber, who had never been a vocal person, assertive identities were inescapable, rather than a choice.

Conservative Muslims like Amber could not benefit from the "diversity showcase" of college. When it is a subdued ingredient blended into a medley of flavors, differentness is "interesting" and "fun," but when bold and noticeable, differentness is seen as menacing and alien. Muslim women quickly learned that, to belong in campus social and leisure cultures, it was better to "cover" their religious Muslim identities, implement (or pretend to implement) the hedonistic hidden curriculum, and transcend religious and ethnic commitments. Visible Muslims, however, had no choice but to "speak out."

Whether in the form of Yasmin's covered identities or Sharmila's loud identities, the heart of campus culture—like the heart of American culture—remains populated by half-real minority individuals, or rather half-real members of homogeneous essentialized groups. The bodies inhabiting multicultural student clubs and the drama of veils and turbans pictured in glitzy brochures remain framed by the majority gaze.

Social Integration in Campus Culture

Amber's conspicuously Muslim identity did not mix well with dominant majority culture, true, but visible Muslims, because they were not socially well integrated into core campus culture, were *not* under undue pressure to cover their religious identities. Once you were out, you were out, after all. Muslims whose identities seemed outwardly "ambiguous or unformed" (Yoshino 2007: 44) masked their Muslim identities to earn the privilege (?) of peripheral social participation in campus culture.

Like mainstream campus culture, Muslim enclaves were fraught with difficulty. Muslims constructed religionized Muslim identities and shaped religionized Muslim spaces, in which Amira and Yasmin felt alienated. Amira objected to the MSA enclaves that were Sharmila's "enfolding rubric" and her safe space for visible religiosity. The muted religious identities that worked for Yasmin did not suit Sharmila. Minority enclaves were unseemly, Haseena said, because "it's having to do with being in America. You know what I'm saying. Because you can't close yourself off to like—because you have to deal with everyone. You can't just be like, I'm going to only deal with people that are like me. Like, that's not how it works." Amira agreed, even as she attacked the Patriot Act.

AMIRA: Become—it's like becoming a citizen. There's a lot that's attached to it. It's not just, oh I'm going to live in a country and enjoy the prosperity and not really become a part of it, not really contribute to it. And I think that's the difference between assimilation and—just living separately. . . . Yes, there's a social disadvantage but also, it can make it easy for you to live in an insulated world, where everyone you know doesn't drink. You become cushioned, and I think that's a very bad [thing].

Muslims became excessively "cushioned" in community enclaves, unprepared for the "real world," Amira contended. Yet the real world already pervaded these college students' lives, relegating to the margins any signs of difference, however skillfully disguised. Amber and Sharmila sought an "insulated world" because they were marked with the visible stigma of loud Muslim identities. Muslim American undergraduate women were already in the "real world," making the same costly choices of conformity and resistance.

While it does not seem appropriate that students should spend all their college years in protective enclaves—"like, that's not how it works," as Haseena said—it also does not seem FAIR to ask minority freshmen to plunge themselves into mainstream campus culture without the buffer of minority communities (if desired). White Christian American students can be immersed in a predominantly white Christian social world for the four years of college (and for their lives, if they wish), but minority students' search for camaraderie and community is typically pathologized as ghettoization or balkanization. My research findings challenge "the university and its observers to imagine segregated spaces that nobody has to worry about or apologize for, or for that matter to label as self-segregated. Instead, these ethnic spaces can be understood as inevitable features of a country and a university still gripped by the realities of race, even as the university makes its own noteworthy efforts to forge new ties and spaces" (Abelmann 2009: 166).

In chapter 5, I alluded to "unspoiled" or "healthy" Muslim American identities constructed in relative freedom from the constraining effect of stereotypes. By highlighting the symbolic violence Muslims experience in mainstream campus culture, I do not mean to suggest that they should be forever divided from their majority peers to construct religionized identities in Muslim enclaves. In this book,

I follow the trail of essentialized, religionized stereotypes inscribed on and adopted for public consumption by Muslims. The individual's authenticity is threatened by the imperative to perform stereotypically minority identities (such as Islamicized conduct) as it is by the imperative to "pass" as majority persons (such as non-Muslims) (Yoshino 2007: 23). In a "healthy" campus culture hospitable to Muslim students' religious *and* American identities, Muslim women would possess the freedom, flexibility, and vocabulary to construct their American, Muslim, ethnic, gendered, and youthful identities, to "emphasize [their] multiple subject positions," and to decide how Muslim, mainstream American, or ethnic to be, how much to "mute or flaunt [their] identities" (Yoshino 2007: 79). This means that I must recognize myself (and be recognized) as a woman, a double immigrant from Pakistani as well as the United Kingdom and culturally both Western and Pakistani, a heterosexual, a Muslim feminist, a cancer survivor, an anthropologist, an academic, and a resident of the United States for much of my life now—rather than merely as "Muslim" or "Pakistani." To treat our identities as complex, simultaneous, and seamless not only opens up multiple possibilities of identity for us but also "rupture[s] the boundaries between groups" and connects us to multiple communities of interest (Carlson 1994: 6, 22).

Campus Culture and Policy

Despite the efforts of higher education leaders, the vacuum of effective, authorized campus policy on religious minority students enhances the unauthorized power of mainstream leisure culture. Mainstream campus leisure culture is engaged in policy formation by appropriation (Levinson and Sutton 2001: 3) in the student union, the dorm, the local bar, and the nightclub, where diverse identities are most vulnerable to homogenization. Even moderately determined students can break the constraints of a "dry" campus, and campus housing habitually bends the rules on overnight opposite sex guests. Students who refuse to join in such culturally authorized bending of policies are uncool, marginal sticklers who must learn to disavow their identities in order to belong.

Campus policies related to leisure matters that affect religious Muslims are weak, shallow, inconsistent, and selectively applied. Campus policy in many such areas (e.g., drinking and overnight dorm visitors) also fails to reflect meaningful acknowledgment of campus demographics. "Limp endorsement and bland acceptance of principles such as 'nondiscrimination,' 'diversity,' and 'openness' in the abstract" not only enable "the Right's ruthless appropriation of the vision and language of multiculturalism" but also protects the hegemony of the dominant group (S. Giroux 2005: 315). More-over, "religion-blind" policy is incomplete in its religion-blindness, as even accommodations for minority students (such as Georgetown's Muslim housing) are majority-referenced and uphold dominant group hegemony. Policy accommodations for minorities often fail to achieve their goals because majority students, accommodated across the length and breadth of campus culture, must be equally accommodated within such special minority provisions such as Muslim housing.

Campus Culture, Assimilation, and Pluralism

Students have a "seismographic" quality (Dahrendorf 1974). They sense, record, and make manifest the tremors and fissures underly-ing the cultural day-to-day. College students do not by themselves *invent* Islamophobic anxieties, Orientalist essentialism, and Muslim women's hypervisibility on campus: they co-construct campus cul-ture and make these problems visible in ways that we can scrutinize and address. Rich in the possibilities of cultural interrogation and creative chaos, campus leisure culture brings out in sharp relief the problems that plague American pluralism. In campus social spaces, where symbolic violence occurred on an excruciatingly intimate scale, the potential for symbolic violence was garbed not in force and incivility but in "good times," sociability, and romance (Holland and Eisenhart 1990). In the leisure rituals of drinking, clubbing, fash-ion, and dating—"integral to social life, . . . unspectacular, repetitive, and predictive" (Magolda 2000: 34)—"the real work of creating com-munity (or of resisting it) occurs" (Quantz and Magolda 1997: 222). At the heart of campus social culture, despite diversity policy, minority youth are most vulnerable.

Campus culture at Georgetown University and George Washington University offered students the liberty to select from a variety of so-cial options. But these options ranged between the (normal) majority cultural core and the (not normal, weird, stigmatized) periphery, so in reality, the "closed openness" (Asher 2007: 69) of campus pluralism accepted but a limited range of difference. Muslim religiosity was decidedly located at the periphery of campus culture, and if anything could make religious Muslims normal, it was concealed religiosity. Like gays, blacks, and women in the United States, Muslim Americans feel "increasing pressure to pledge an allegiance—to fade gratefully into the mainstream or to resist in the name of persisting difference" (Yoshino 2007: 78). Those who refuse to cover marginalized identities are perceived as having "somehow forfeited social protection against all kinds of micro- and macro-aggressions. They are, effectively, 'asking for it'" (Galman 2013: 125). Assimilation is proffered as an escape route from discrimination: if a Muslim woman can *hide* her Muslim identity, she can be normal. But when young Muslim American women drink, dress "like everyone else," and start dating simply to fit in, this is an occasion not to celebrate the possibilities of American pluralism but to examine its inflexibility.

Today, university communities make public commitments to inclusion, integration, and diversity. Yet a right-wing backlash against liberal multiculturalism has been turning campuses into ideological battlegrounds that frame diversity as particularism. Conservatives and neoliberals complain vociferously about diversity, about the "silencing" of conservative politics in classrooms, about the demands for "political correctness," and about the alleged lack of immigrant acculturation. Though cultural assimilation has had a face-lift, the expectation that "newcomers" and Others should bury their angular differences in an Anglo facade is not just alive and well: we have experienced a "renaissance of assimilation" (Yoshino 2007: 3).

Intensely mindful of the scrutiny that read them as static texts and half persons, Muslim women spoke to the gaze in its language. They varied their social roles, masterfully playing them out in different situations, now stretching the possibilities of identity and now adapting to its constraints, and simultaneously negotiating multiple expectations emanating from the non-Muslim majority, from conservative and liberal Muslims, and from the self.

Will the Real Muslim People Please Stand Up?

I was as nervous as a freshman that Friday evening in August when I arrived at the Copley Hall musalla for the Georgetown MSA open meeting for all members. I had been "screened" by MSA officers and was to deliver my research recruitment spiel as the meeting concluded. It had taken me a good few weeks to make it this far. I was diligently trying to fit in, wearing a studiously friendly manner and a conservative fitted hijab I *never* wore otherwise. At thirty-four, I felt staid and *old* as I glanced around the musalla. The room was filled to capacity with fresh-faced Georgetown students, a few of whom I now knew, a large group of young, attractive, stylish men and women stealing chaste glances at each other as they brainstormed MSA events for the year. They all sat on the carpet—men on the left side, women on the right—in a rather cramped basement room, where muffled laughter from the Copley dorm residents trickled in, as Heather and Nikhat talked about religion and community. Meanwhile, on that mild fall evening much of the campus community was already whiling away the hours at trendy Georgetown nightclubs. Some of the demure attendees at the MSA meeting would probably join their non-Muslim friends after the meeting. Some would drink, some would not, some would dance, some would not. And on Monday morning, they would go to class and listen to white people talk about Islam and terrorism, and Islam and women.

Yasmin did not sign up for research participation that evening. A few weeks later, after a few interviews, she revealed that her reluctance had stemmed from a sentiment that she "shouldn't really be the one representing Islam." She had thought that I, as a researcher of "*Muslim* American college students" was "looking for *real Muslim people* who like, live *the real Muslim lifestyle*" (emphasis added).

No one could singularly represent Muslims. But by participating in the discursive representation of Muslim Americans via my research, Yasmin came to consider the possibility that her voice counted. In the rugged and varied terrain of Muslim American identity, her navigation of identity borderlands (Anzaldúa 1987) made sense. Arguably, those borderlands made more sense than imaginary "real Muslim people" did.

> YASMIN: I think it's really made me understand, and made me think about the fact that—you know what—I am a Muslim and I have the right to represent Islam as much as anyone else does. . . . [I used to think], "it's not me; I'm trying to be Muslim; some of the time, I'm not really doing it." But I think it's

really made me—you kind of gave me—... I was like there's so many other Muslims out there like me, who are just like, "if I'm not always the one who's always organizing the protests, or doesn't do the [religious] study, or outwardly doesn't look immediately to someone as Muslim, then something's not right."

At the margins of the Muslim American community and with deep involvement in "normal American" culture, Yasmin staked her claim as a Muslim woman with a right to speak *as* a Muslim woman. As she did so, she contrasted her flexible, "some of the time," half-concealed ("covered," as Goffman would say) Muslim identities with those *real* Muslims who projected visible, forceful, representative identities in the political sphere ("always organizing the protests") and in the religious sphere ("doing the [religious] study"), who "outwardly look immediately to someone as Muslim."

People like Yasmin shrank when called on to "represent Islam," not because they were *not* Muslim, but because the terms of the discussion were all wrong. Who could claim to be the *real* Muslim people? More important, during the War on Terror, who would *want* to be those real Muslim people?

Those visible Muslims had the power and the glory of being representatives. It was to them that "heads turned" (Amber), and it was they who were perpetually interrogated about the Islamic standpoint on terrorism and polygamy. These representative Muslims were reduced to *just* Muslims. They were "the Muslim girls[s] who *don't* [drink/have sex/party]" (Sarah). Yasmin was free to be complex and American, and Tehzeeb to be "low-key and on the margins." But Amber's politicized and religionized identity was drained of its normal American youthfulness. Hijabis were not free to play basketball, and non-hijabis' temperance was endlessly shocking to their non-Muslim peers. Yasmin chafed against her invisibility as a Muslim representative, while Amber was trapped in the task of ineffectual Muslim representation, always apologizing, always defending, always in vain.

Muslim women asserted that majority peers really could not figure them out without abandoning previous assumptions about Muslims. To understand, they had to directly approach these fellow Americans without the use of discursive translations. As she constructed new modalities of Muslim and American youthful gendered codes, Intisar claimed fundamentally that her peers "really couldn't figure [her] out" until they came directly to her and "embraced that difference" (chap. 4). It was not enough that they tolerated her hijab: she demanded that her peers master a new vocabulary. But Intisar's challenge was stifled by America's existing vocabulary about Muslims. She was *not*, she explained, "your regular Muslim girl." And Latifa added, she was not "your typical, traditional Muslim female." Given a chance, my participants could remedy your "perception that all Muslim girls cover their heads, all Muslim girls don't talk to people that are not Muslim, all Muslim girls are very intolerant or uncomfortable" (Amira). They could demonstrate by their "normal American" comportment that they were "a little different" (Latifa), and then non-Muslim Americans could "approach [Amira] about it." (What was "it"? Muslim womanhood? The true nature of Islam? The normalcy of Muslim Americans?)

Intisar, Amira, and Latifa were compelled to begin with a negative statement, an apology, an explanation, a footnote. To reshape the terms of the discussion, they had to employ the Orientalist, essentialist American vocabulary about Muslims. In order to edit the stereotypical image of a subjugated, immobile, timid, xenophobic Muslim woman, Muslim American women were obliged to first adopt that image and to work with it. The stereotype was unavoidable.

As Muslim women revised stereotypical images, they in the process perpetuated these images. And as they adopted their peers' vocabulary and attempted to correct it, my participants found that they had become official representatives of "Islam." By its very nature, such representation was centered on static images, rather than on the constant flux of diverse lives and identities.

In this book, I have shown the play of multiple identity layers and the manner in which Muslim American women contextually emphasize and overemphasize particular identities. This kind of ethnographic scrutiny enables us to jettison such old and overused identity tropes as the oppressed Muslim woman, the angry hijabi, and the secularized non-hijabi Muslim. On encountering these tropes, we may also become aware of how they are forged. Today, in academic publications and popular diatribes, the notions of timeless, unchanging, angry, and essentially un-Western Muslim identities feed the right-wing frenzy for such civilizational conflict and spells danger for our very survival on this planet. In this climate, as we explore the dynamic, changing, and strategic nature of identity, we may come to see the Other as a complex work in progress, rather than as a finished product perpetually engaged in warfare against Us. We may also realize that *They* are really part of *Us*.

Glossary

ADHAN (Arabic): The call to Muslim prayer.

ALLAHU AKBAR (Arabic): God is the Greatest.

BALAAGH (Arabic): Delivering the message of Islam.

BURQA (Urdu, Hindi): An outer garment worn by some Muslim women to cover their bodies and usually their faces.

DAʿWAH (Arabic): Calling people to Islam.

DEEN (Arabic): Religion.

HADITH (Arabic): A saying or act ascribed to the Prophet Muhammad.

HARAAM (Arabic): Islamically forbidden or prohibited.

HIJAB: (Arabic) Literally, a curtain or barrier. In contemporary Islamic usage, the word is used to mean the headscarf.

HIJABI: The word "hijabi" is popularly used among Muslim North Americans in place of the Arabic term "muhajjiba," which denotes a woman who wears the headscarf.

IFTAR (Arabic): The evening meal when Muslims break their fast.

ISLAM AWARENESS WEEK: A week of events related to Islam held by Muslim student groups at university campuses in North America and the United Kingdom.

JUMʿAH (Arabic): Friday congregational prayer.

KHIMAR (Arabic): A Muslim woman's head covering that hangs to the waist.

KUFI (Arabic): Skullcap.

MUSALLA (Arabic): Prayer area or prayer room.

NON-HIJABI: A Muslim woman who does not wear hijab.

NOWRUZ (Farsi): The Iranian New Year.

QUR'AN (Arabic): Also transliterated as "Koran." The main scripture of Islam, believed by Muslims to have been revealed to Muhammad by God.

RAMADAN (Arabic): The Islamic month of fasting.

SALAAT (Arabic): The Muslim ritual prayer, observed five times daily.

SALAFI (Arabic): Also referred to as Salafist or Wahhabi. A religious movement within Islam that is often associated with strict reliance on Qur'an, Hadith, and the interpretations of the aforementioned that are reported from the Prophet's Companions and others in temporal proximity to them.

SATI (Sanskrit, Hindi): A Hindu custom in which the widow is burned to death on her husband's funeral pyre.

SHAIKH (Arabic): Muslim religious leader.

SHALWAR-KAMEEZ (Urdu, Hindi): South Asian outfit of tunic and baggy pants.

SHARI'AH (Arabic): The moral code and religious law of Islam.

SUHOOR (Arabic): The pre-dawn meal eaten by Muslims before a day of fasting.

TARAWIH (Arabic): The optional congregational prayers offered by Muslims during the nights of Ramadan.

'URF (Arabic): Custom, or customary law, an important source of Islamic law. Muslim jurists traditionally respected local customs that did not violate Islamic principles.

The Research Participants

The tables below provide a brief outline of the research participants and some of the main characteristics that are the focus of my study.

Key

Year: College academic year
Y→N: Eventually quit this behavior during fieldwork (e.g., was hijabi and became non-hijabi, or used to drink and quit drinking).
N→Y: Eventually adopted this behavior (e.g., was not hijabi and became hijabi).

Georgetown University Participants

NAME	ETHNIC BACKGROUND	YEAR	HIJAB	ALCOHOL	MSA ACTIVITY	RESIDENT/ COMMUTER
Amira	Pakistani	Sophomore	No	No	Moderate to none	Resident
Diya	Pakistani	Freshman	No	No	Moderate	Resident
Fatima	Indian	Sophomore	No	No	Moderate	Commuter
Haseena	Pakistani	Sophomore	No	No	Moderate	Resident
Heather	White	Senior	No	No	High	Resident
Latifa	Arab	Freshman	Yes	No	Moderate/ High	Resident
Mahnaz	Bangladeshi	Junior	No	Yes	Low	Resident
Nadira	Pakistani	Sophomore	No	No	High	Resident
Sharmila	Bangladeshi	Senior	Yes	No	High	Resident
Shireen	Iranian	Junior	No	No	Low	Resident
Tehzeeb	Bangladeshi	Senior	No	No	Low/ Moderate	Resident
Yasmin	Pakistani	Sophomore	No	Yes	Low	Resident
Sarah	Pakistani	Freshman	No	No	Moderate	Resident

George Washington University Participants

NAME	ETHNIC BACKGROUND	YEAR	HIJAB	ALCOHOL	MSA ACTIVITY	RESIDENT/ COMMUTER
Amber	Pakistani	Senior	Yes	No	High	Resident and Commuter
Elizabeth	Black	Senior	N→Y	No	Low/ Moderate	Resident
Faiyza	Pakistani	Junior	No	Y→N	None	Resident
Farah	Pakistani	Junior	No	No	Low/ Moderate	Resident
Intisar	Somali	Sophomore	Yes	No	Moderate/ High	Commuter
Leila	Pakistani	Sophomore	No	No	Low/ Moderate	Resident
Muna	Saudi/Iraqi	Sophomore	Yes	No	None	Commuter
Neelam	Bangladeshi	Freshman	No	Yes	None	Resident
Roshan	Bangladeshi	Sophomore	N→Y	No	High	Resident
Tehmina	Pakistani	Sophomore	No	Yes	Low/ Moderate	Resident
Teresa	White	Senior	Y→N	No	Low/ Moderate	Resident
Zeinab	Iranian/Pakistani	Sophomore	Yes	No	High	Commuter
Zoe	Black/Hispanic	Freshman	N→Y	No	Moderate	Commuter

References

Abelmann, N. 2009. *The Intimate University: Korean American Students and the Problems of Segregation*. Durham: Duke University Press.

Abowitz, Kathleen Knight, and Jason Harnish. 2006. "Contemporary Discourses of Citizenship." *Review of Educational Research* 76 (4): 653–90.

Abu el-Haj, Thea Renda. 2007. "'I Was Born Here, but My Home, It's Not Here'": Educating for Democratic Citizenship in an Era of Transnational Migration and Global Conflict." *Harvard Educational Review* 77 (3): 285–316.

Abu el-Haj, Thea Renda, and Sally Wesley Bonet. 2011. "Education, Citizenship, and the Politics of Belonging: Youth from Muslim Transnational Communities and the 'War on Terror.'" *Review of Research in Education* 35 (1): 29–59.

Abu-Laban, Yasmeen. 2002. "Liberalism, Multiculturalism, and the Problem of Essentialism." *Citizenship Studies* 6 (4): 459–82.

Abu-Lughod, Lila. 2002. "Do Muslim Women Really Need Saving? Anthropological Reflections on Cultural Relativism and Its Others." *American Anthropologist* 104 (3): 783–90.

Ackerman, S. 2011. "FBI Teaches Agents: 'Mainstream' Muslims Are 'Violent, Radical.'" *Wired*, September 14, http://www.wired.com/dangerroom/2011/09/fbi-muslims-radical/.

Ahmed, Leila. 1982. "Western Ethnocentrism and Perceptions of the Harem." *Feminist Studies* 8 (3): 521–34.

Ali, Kecia. 2002. "Rethinking Women's Issues in Muslim Communities." In *Taking Back Islam: American Muslims Reclaim Their Faith*, edited by Michael Wolfe and the producers of Beliefnet, 91–98. New York: Rodale Press.

———. 2003a. "'A Beautiful Example'? The Prophet Muhammad PBUH as a Model for Muslim Husbands." Paper presented at the Critical Islamic Reflections Conference, Yale University, April, http://www.yale.edu/cir/2003/alipaper.doc. Accessed December 28, 2012.

———. 2003b. "Progressive Muslims and Islamic Jurisprudence: The Necessity for Critical Engagement with Marriage and Divorce Law." In *Progressive Muslims: On Pluralism, Gender, and Justice*, edited by Omid Safi, 163–89. Oxford: Oneworld Publications.

Allied Media Corporation. 2004. "American Muslims: Demographic Facts," http://www.allied-media.com/AM. Accessed December 28, 2012.

American Civil Liberties Union. 2008. "Discrimination Against Muslim Women," http://www.aclu.org/pdfs/womensrights/discriminationagainstmuslim-women.pdf. Accessed April 15, 2013.

Anderson, Benedict. 1983. *Imagined Communities: Reflections on the Origin and Spread of Nationalism*. London: Verso.

Ansari, Kari. 2011. "A New Lowe for Anti-Muslim Bigotry." *Huffington Post Religion*, December 12, http://www.huffingtonpost.com/kari-ansari/a-new-lowe-for-antimuslim_b_1140734.html.

Anzaldúa, Gloria. 1987. *Borderlands*. San Francisco: Aunt Lute.

Asher, Nina. 2007. "Made in the (Multicultural) U.S.A.: Unpacking Tensions of Race, Culture, Gender, and Sexuality." *Educational Researcher* 36 (2): 65–73.

Associated Press. 2012. "NYPD Monitored Muslim Students All over Northeast." *USA Today*, February 18, http://www.ap.org/Content/AP-In-The-News/2012/NYPD-monitored-Muslim-students-all-over-Northeast.

Astin, Alexander W. 1997. *What Matters in College? Four Critical Years Revisited*. San Francisco: Jossey-Bass.

Aswad, Barbara C., and Barbara Bilge. 1996. Introduction to *Family and Gender among American Muslims: Issues Facing Middle Eastern Immigrants and Their Descendants*, edited by B. Bilge and B. Aswad, 1–13. Philadelphia: Temple University Press.

Barnett, Michael. 2003. "Muslims Request Zero Tolerance." *GW Hatchet Online*, March 27, http://www.gwhatchet.com/2003/03/27/muslims-request-zero-tolerance.

Bayoumi, Moustafa. 2008. *How Does It Feel to Be a Problem: Being Young and Arab in America*. New York: Penguin Press.

Beauvoir, Simone de. 1952. *The Second Sex*. Translated by H. M. Parshley. New York: Vintage.

Benton, Stephen L., Ronald G. Downey, Peggy J. Glider, and Sherry A. Benton. 2008. "College Students' Norm Perception Predicts Reported Use of Protective Behavioral Strategies for Alcohol Consumption." *Journal of Studies on Alcohol and Drugs* 69 (6): 859–65.

Berns McGown, Rima. 1990. *Muslims in the Diaspora: The Somali Communities of London and Toronto*. Toronto: University of Toronto Press.

Bhabha, Homi. 1994. *The Location of Culture*. London: Routledge.

Billig, Michael. 1995. *Banal Nationalism*. London: Sage.

Black, Dennis R. 2008. "A Clearer Picture of College Drinking." *Student Affairs Leader* 36 (6): 4–5.

Bogle, Kathleen A. 2008. *Hooking Up: Sex, Dating, and Relationships on Campus*. New York: New York University Press.

Bourdieu, Pierre. 1977. *Outline of a Theory of Practice*. Translated by Richard Nice. Cambridge: Cambridge University Press.

———. 1984. *Distinction: A Social Critique of the Judgement of Taste*. Translated by Richard Nice. Cambridge: Harvard University Press.

Brady, Joann. 2005. "Binge Drinking Entrenched in College Culture." *ABC News*, Good Morning America, September 7. http://abcnews.go.com/GMA/Health/story?id=1085909#.T7qekHlYuuE.

Butler, Judith. 1993. *Bodies That Matter: On the Discursive Limits of Sex*. London: Routledge.

Carlson, Dennis. 1994. "Gayness, Multicultural Education, and Community." *Educational Foundations* 8 (4): 5–25.

Center for Alcohol and Other Drug Education (CADE). 2012. "Alcoholic Beverage Consumption and Distribution Policy," George Washington University, http:// studentconduct.gwu.edu/abcd-policy. Accessed May 4, 2013.

Cesari, Jocelyn. 2004. *When Islam and Democracy Meet: Muslims in Europe and in the United States*. New York: Palgrave Macmillan.

Cherry, Conrad, Betty A. DeBerg, and Amanda Porterfield. 2001. *Religion on Campus*. Chapel Hill: University of North Carolina Press.

CoEd Staff. 2008. "The Real Campuses behind the Top Nineteen College Movies of All Time." 2008. *CoEd Magazine*, August 6, http://coedmagazine.com/2008/08/06/ the-real-campuses-behind-the-top-19-college-movie-of-all-time.

College Confidential. 2007. "Does Your College Roommate Have Overnight Guests?," http://talk.collegeconfidential.com/college-life/309581-does-your- college-roommate-have-overnight-guests.html. Accessed May 4, 2013.

Cooley, Charles Horton. 1922. *Human Nature and the Social Order*. New York: Charles Scribner's Sons.

Council on American-Islamic Relations (CAIR). 2005. "The Status of Muslim Civil Rights in the United States 2005: Unequal Protection." Washington, D.C.: CAIR. At http://cdn1-cair.netdna-ssl.com/images/pdf/CAIR-2005-Civil-Rights-Report. pdf. Accessed May 4, 2013.

Craig, Steve. 1998. "Feminism, Femininity, and the 'Beauty' Dilemma: How Advertising Co-opted the Women's Movement." Paper Presented at the Southwest/ Texas Popular Culture/American Culture Association Conference, Lubbock, Tex., January 1998, http://www.feministezine.com/feminist/fashion/The- Beauty-Dilemma.html. Accessed May 4, 2013.

Critical Islamic Reflections Group (CIR). 2011. "Critical Islamic Reflections Conference," http://www.yale.edu/cir/about. Accessed May 4, 2013.

Dahrendorf, Ralf. 1974. "Lecture 2, The Liberal Option: Reith Lectures 1974; The New Liberty." Radio 4, November 20, http://downloads.bbc.co.uk/rmhttp/ radio4/transcripts/1974_reith2.pdf

Dasgupta, Shamita Das. 1998. "Gender Roles and Cultural Continuity in the Asian Indian Immigrant Community in the U.S." *Sex Roles: A Journal of Research* 38 (11–12): 953–74.

Denson, Nida, and Nicholas Bowman. 2013. "University Diversity and Preparation for a Global Society: The Role of Diversity in Shaping Intergroup Attitudes and Civic Outcomes." *Studies in Higher Education* 38 (4), 555–70.

DeSimone, J. S. 2010. "Binge Drinking and Risky Sex among College Students." NBER Working Paper No. 15953. Cambridge, Mass.: The National Bureau of Economic Research. At http://www.nber.org/papers/w15953. Accessed May 4, 2013.

Dowd-Galley, J. 2004. "Islamism's Campus Club: The Muslim Students' Association." *Middle East Quarterly* 11 (2), http://www.meforum.org/603/islamisms- campus-club-the-muslim-students. Accessed May 4, 2013.

Du Bois, W. E. B. (1903) 1995. *The Souls of Black Folk*. New York: Signet/Penguin Books.

Dunn, Brad. 2006. *When They Were 22: 100 Famous People at the Turning Point in Their Lives*. Kansas City, Kans.: Andrews McMeel Publishing.

Edensor, Tim. 2002. *National Identity, Popular Culture, and Everyday Life*. Oxford: Berg.

———. 2006. "Reconsidering National Temporalities: Institutional Times, Everyday Routines, Serial Spaces, and Synchronicities." *European Journal of Social Theory* 9 (4): 525–45.

El Guindi, Fadwa. 1999. *Veil: Modesty, Privacy, and Resistance*. Oxford: Berg.

El-Or, Tamar. 1997. "Visibility and Possibilities: Ultraorthodox Jewish Women between the Domestic and Public Spheres." *Women's Studies International Forum* 20 (5–6): 665–73.

Emerson, Steven. 2003. *American Jihad: The Terrorists Living among Us*. New York: W. W. Norton.

Erickson, Frederick. 1973. "What Makes School Ethnography 'Ethnographic'?" *Council on Anthropology and Education Newsletter* 4 (2): 10–19.

Fairness and Accuracy in Reporting (FAIR). 2008. "Smearcasting: How Islamophobes Spread Fear, Bigotry, and Misinformation." October, http://www.smearcasting.us/FAIR_Smearcasting_Final.pdf. Accessed November 18, 2012.

Fanon, Frantz. (1952) 2008. *Black Skin, White Masks*. Translated by Richard Philcox. New York: Grove Press.

Federal Trade Commission. 1999. *Self-Regulation in the Alcohol Industry: A Review of Industry Efforts to Avoid Promoting Alcohol to Underage Consumers*. Washington, D.C.: Federal Trade Commission. At http://www.ftc.gov/reports/alcohol/alcoholreport.shtm. Accessed May 4, 2013.

———. 2008. *Self-Regulation in the Alcohol Industry: Report of the Federal Trade Commission*. Washington, D.C.: Federal Trade Commission. At http://www.ftc.gov/os/2008/06/080626alcoholreport.pdf. Accessed May 4, 2013.

Foucault, Michel. 1979. *Discipline and Punish: The Birth of the Prison*. Translated by Alan Sheridan. New York: Vintage.

———. 1980. *Power/Knowledge: Selected Interviews and Other Writings, 1972–1977*. Edited by Colin Gordon. Translated by Colin Gordon et al. Brighton, U.K.: Harvester Press.

Fox, Jon E., and Cynthia Miller-Idriss. 2008. "Everyday Nationhood." *Ethnicities* 8 (4): 536–76.

Gallup. 2009. *Muslim Americans: A National Portrait; An In-Depth Analysis of America's Most Diverse Religious Community*. Washington, D.C.: Gallup.

Galman, Sally C. 2013. "Un/Covering: Female Religious Converts Learning the Problems and Pragmatics of Physical Observance in the Secular World." *Anthropology and Education Quarterly* 44 (4) (in press).

Geller, Pamela. 2011. *Stop the Islamization of America: A Practical Guide to the Resistance*. Washington, D.C.: WND Books.

George Washington University Office of University Relations. 2005. "Guide to GWU," http://www.gwu.edu/explore/aboutgw. Accessed May 4, 2013.

Ghaffar-Kucher, Ameena. 2009. "Citizenship and Belonging in an Age of Insecurity: Pakistani Immigrant Youth in New York City." In *Critical Approaches to Comparative Education: Vertical Case Studies from Africa, Europe, the Middle East, and the Americas*, edited by Frances Vavrus and Lesley Bartlett, 163–80. New York: Palgrave Macmillan.

Ghumman, Sonia, and Linda Jackson. 2010. "The Downside of Religious Attire: The Muslim Headscarf and Expectations of Obtaining Employment." *Journal of Organizational Behavior* 31 (1): 4–23.

Gibson, Margaret A. 1988. *Accommodation without Assimilation: Sikh Immigrants in an American High School*. Ithaca: Cornell University Press.

Giroux, Henry A. 2005. "Translating the Future and the Promise of Democracy: Address to Convocation," http://www.henryagiroux.com/awards/convocation_address.htm. Accessed May 4, 2013.

Giroux, Susan Searls. 2005. "From the 'Culture Wars' to the Conservative Campaign for Campus Diversity; Or, How Inclusion Became the New Exclusion." *Policy Futures in Education* 3 (4): 314–26.

Glassman, Tavis. 2002. "The Failure of Higher Education to Reduce the Binge Drinking Rate." *Journal of American College Health* 51 (3): 143–44.

Goffman, Erving. 1959. *The Presentation of Self in Everyday Life*. New York: Anchor Books.

———. 1961. *Asylums: Essays on the Social Situation of Mental Patients and Other Inmates*. Harmondsworth, U.K.: Penguin.

———. 1963. *Stigma: Notes on the Management of Spoiled Identity*. Englewood Cliffs, N.J.: Prentice Hall.

Greenberg, Blu. 1996. "Ultra-Orthodox Women Confront Feminism." *Moment* 21 (3): 36–37, 63.

Grewal, Zareena A. 2013. *Islam Is a Foreign Country: American Muslims and the Global Crisis of Authority*. New York: New York University Press.

Grossman, Michael, and Sara Markowitz. 2005. "I Did What Last Night?! Adolescent Risky Sexual Behaviors and Substance Use." *Eastern Economic Journal* 31 (3): 383–405.

Haddad, Yvonne Y., Farid Senzai, and Jane I. Smith, eds. 2009. *Educating the Muslims of America*. Oxford: Oxford University Press.

Haddad, Yvonne Yazbeck, Jane I. Smith, and Kathleen M. Moore. 2006. *Muslim Women in America: The Challenge of Islamic Identity Today*. Oxford: Oxford University Press.

Hall, Kathleen D. 2002. *Lives in Translation: Sikh Youth as British Citizens*. Philadelphia: University of Pennsylvania Press.

Hall, Stuart. 1993. "What Is This 'Black' in Black Popular Culture?" *Social Justice* 20 (1–2): 104–14.

Halstead, Mark. 1991. "Radical Feminism, Islam, and the Single-Sex School Debate." *Gender and Education* 3 (3): 263–78.

Hammer, Juliane. 2012. *American Muslim Women, Religious Authority, and Activism: More Than a Prayer*. Austin: University of Texas Press.

Hermansen, Marcia K. 2003. "How to Put the Genie Back in the Bottle: Identity Islam and Muslim Youth Cultures in the United States." In *Progressive Muslims: On Justice, Gender, and Pluralism*, edited by Omid Safi, 303–19. Oxford: Oneworld Publications.

———. 2004. "Muslims in the Performative Mode: A Reflection on Muslim-Christian Dialogue." *Muslim World* 94 (3): 387–96.

Herzfeld, Michael. 1997. *Cultural Intimacy: Social Poetics in the Nation-State*. New York: Routledge.

Hingson, Ralph, T. Heeren, M. Winter, and H. Wechsler. 2005. "Magnitude of Alcohol-Related Mortality and Morbidity among U.S. College Students Ages Eighteen to Twenty-Four: Changes from 1998 to 2001." *Annual Review of Public Health* 26:259–79.

Hingson, Ralph W., Timothy Heeren, Ronda C. Zakocs, Andrea Kopstein, Henry Wechsler. 2002. "Magnitude of Alcohol-Related Mortality and Morbidity among U.S. College Students Ages Eighteen to Twenty-Four." *Journal of Studies on Alcohol* 63: 136–44.

Hingson, Ralph W., Wenxing Zha, and Elissa. R. Weitzman. 2009. "Magnitude of and Trends in Alcohol-Related Mortality and Morbidity among U.S. College Students Ages Eighteen to Twenty-Four, 1998–2005." Supplement to *Journal of Studies on Alcohol and Drugs* 16: 12–20.

Hirschkind, Charles, and Saba Mahmood. 2002. "Feminism, the Taliban, and Politics of Counter-insurgency." *Anthropological Quarterly* 75 (2): 339–54.

Hoffman, Diane M. 1999. "Turning Power Inside Out: Reflections on Resistance from the (Anthropological) Field." *Qualitative Studies in Education* 12 (6): 671–87.

Holland, Dorothy C., and Margaret A. Eisenhart. 1990. *Educated in Romance: Women, Achievement, and College Culture*. Chicago: University of Chicago Press.

Holland, Dorothy, William Lachicotte Jr., Debra Skinner, and Carole Cain. 1998. *Identity and Agency in Cultural Worlds*. Cambridge: President and Fellows of Harvard College.

hooks, bell. 1990a. "Marginality as a Site of Resistance." In *Out There: Marginalization and Contemporary Cultures*, edited by Russell Ferguson, M. Gever, Trinh T. Minh-ha, and Cornel West, 341–47. New York: The New Museum of Contemporary Art.

———. 1990b. *Yearning: Race, Gender, and Cultural Politics*. Boston: South End Press.

Hudson, Kathleen, and John Stiles. 1998. "Single-Sex Classes: A Plus for Preadolescent Girls." *Principal* 78 (2): 57–58.

Human Rights Watch. 2003. "Human Rights after September 11," http://www.hrw.org/legacy/campaigns/september11/#Domestic. Accessed May 4, 2013.

Huntington, Samuel P. 1997. *The Clash of Civilizations and the Remaking of World Order*. New York: Touchstone.

Jackson, Sherman A. 2005. *Islam and the Blackamerican: Looking toward the Third Resurrection*. Oxford: Oxford University Press.

Kahani-Hopkins, Vered, and Nick Hopkins. 2002. "'Representing' British Muslims: The Strategic Dimension to Identity Construction." *Ethnic and Racial Studies* 25 (2): 288–309.

Kahf, Mohja. 2003. *E-mails from Scheherazad*. Gainesville: University Press of Florida.

Kandiyoti, Deniz. 1991. "Introduction," *Women, Islam, and the State*, 1–21. Philadelphia: Temple University Press.

———, ed. 1991. *Women, Islam, and the State*. Philadelphia: Temple University Press.

Kapoor, Ilan. 2003. "Acting in a Tight Spot: Homi Bhabha's Postcolonial Politics." *New Political Science* 25 (4): 561–77.

Khan, Shahnaz. 2002. *Aversion and Desire: Negotiating Muslim Female Identity in the Diaspora*. Toronto: Women's Press.

Kluckhohn, Clyde. 1949. *Mirror for Man*. New York: McGraw-Hill.

Lesko, Nancy. 1986. "Individualism and Community: Ritual Discourse in a Parochial High School." *Anthropology and Education Quarterly* 17 (1): 25–39.

Levinson, Bradley A., and Margaret Sutton. 2001. "Introduction: Policy as/in Practice—A Sociocultural Approach to the Study of Educational Policy." *Policy as Practice: Toward a Comparative Sociocultural Analysis of Educational Policy*, 1–22. Westport, Conn.: Greenwood Press.

Levinson, Bradley A., Margaret Sutton, and Teresa Winstead. 2009. "Education Policy as a Practice of Power: Theoretical Tools, Ethnographic Methods, Democratic Options." *Educational Policy* 23 (6): 767–95.

Levinson, Bradley A. and Dorothy Holland. 1996. "The Cultural Production of the Educated Person: An Introduction." *The Cultural Production of the Educated Person: Critical Ethnographies of Schooling and Local Practice*, edited by Bradley A. Levinson, Douglas E. Foley, and Dorothy C. Holland, 1–54. Albany, N.Y.: SUNY Press.

Lorde, Audre. 1984. *Sister Outsider*. Freedom, Calif.: Crossing.

Mack, Phyllis. 2003. "Religion, Feminism, and the Problem of Agency: Reflections on Eighteenth-Century Quakerism." *Signs* 29 (1): 149–77.

Magolda, Peter M. 2000. "The Campus Tour: Ritual and Community in Higher Education." *Anthropology and Education Quarterly* 31 (1): 24–46.

Magolda, Peter, and Kelsey Ebben Gross. 2009. *It's All about Jesus! Faith as an Oppositional Collegiate Subculture*. Sterling, Va.: Stylus Publishing.

Mahmood, Saba. 2001. "Feminist Theory, Embodiment, and the Docile Agent: Some Reflections on the Egyptian Islamic Revival." *Cultural Anthropology* 16 (2): 202–35.

Maira, Sunaina Marr. 2009. *Missing: Youth, Citizenship, and Empire after 9/11*. Durham: Duke University Press.

Mamdani, Mahmood. 2004. *Good Muslim, Bad Muslim: America, the Cold War, and the Roots of Terror*. New York: Doubleday.

Martín-Muñoz, Gema. 2002. "Islam's Women under Western Eyes." Open Democracy, October 8, http://www.opendemocracy.net/faith-europe_islam/article_498.jsp.

Mathews, Jay. 2007. "25 Hottest Schools." *Newsweek*, August 20–27, 53.

McCloud, Aminah Beverly. 1995. *African-American Islam*. New York: Routledge.

Mead, George Herbert. 1934. *Mind, Self, and Society*, edited by Charles W. Morris. Chicago: University of Chicago Press.

Miles, M., and M. Huberman. 1994. *Qualitative Data Analysis: An Expanded Source-book*. Thousand Oaks, Calif.: Sage Publications.

Miller, Margaret A. 2006. "Religion on Campus." *Change*, March-April, 6–7.

Mir, Shabana. 2003. "'You Can't Really Look Normal and Dress Modestly': The Problem of Dress and American Muslim Women College Students." Pluralism Project, Harvard University. http://www.pluralism.org/affiliates/student/mir/.

———. 2005. "Sania Mirza's Clothes: What's Really Going on Here?" *Altmuslim: Global Perspectives on Muslim Life, Politics, and Culture*, September 29, http://www.patheos.com/blogs/altmuslim/2005/09/sania_mirzas_clothes_whats_really_going_on_here/.

———. 2007a. "American Muslim Women on Campus." *Anthropology News*, May, 16–17.

———. 2007b. "'Where You Stand on Dating Defines You': American Muslim Women Students and Cross-gender Interaction on Campus." *American Journal of Islamic Social Sciences* 24 (3): 69–91.

———. 2008a. "17 Reasons Why Women Wear Headscarves." *Religion Dispatches Magazine*, March 27, http://www.religiondispatches.org/archive/sexandgender/152/17_reasons_why_women_wear_headscarves/. Accessed May 4, 2013.

———. 2008b. "It's Not Raining Eligible Muslim Men." *Religion Dispatches Magazine*, June 16, http://www.religiondispatches.org/archive/sexandgender/299/it_s_not_raining_eligible_muslim_men.

———. 2009a. "Diversity, Self, Faith, and Friends: Muslim Undergraduates on Campus." In *Muslim Voices in School: Narratives of Identity and Pluralism*, edited by Ozlem Sensoy and Christopher Darius Stonebanks, 117–34. Rotterdam, The Netherlands: Sense Publishers.

———. 2009b. "'I Didn't Want to Have That Outcast Belief about Alcohol': Muslim Women Encounter Drinking Cultures on Campus." In *Educating the Muslims of America*, edited by Yvonne Y. Haddad, Farid Senzai, and Jane I. Smith, 209–30. Oxford: Oxford University Press.

———. 2009c. "'Not Too College-Like, Not Too Normal': American Muslim Undergraduate Women's Gendered Discourses." *Anthropology and Education Quarterly* 40 (3): 237–56.

———. 2010. "In Conversation." *Material Religion* 6 (1): 115–16.

———. 2011. "'Just to Make Sure People Know I Was Born Here': American Muslim Undergraduate Women's Construction of Americanness." *Discourse: Studies in the Cultural Politics of Education* 32 (4): 547–63.

———. 2011. "Irony of the Iranian Women's Burqa Ban." *Religion Dispatches Magazine*, June 16, http://www.religiondispatches.org/dispatches/guest_bloggers/4762/irony_of_the_iranian_women_s_burqa_ban_/.

Moffat, Michael. 1991. "College Life: Undergraduate Culture and Higher Education." *Journal of Higher Education* 62 (1): 44–61.

Mohanty, Chandra Talpade. 1991. "Under Western Eyes: Feminist Scholarship and Colonial Discourses." In *Third World Women and the Politics of Feminism*, edited by Chandra Talpade Mohanty, Ann Russo, and Lourdes Torres, 51–80. Bloomington: Indiana University Press.

Muslim Students Association of George Washington University. 2012. "Muslim Students Association, George Washington University," http://www.gwu.edu/~msa. Accessed May 15, 2013.

Muslim Students Association of the U.S. and Canada. 2012. "MSA of the U.S. and Canada," http://www.msanational.org. Accessed May 15, 2013.

Narayan, Uma. 1998. "Essence of Culture and a Sense of History: A Feminist Critique of Cultural Essentialism." *Hypatia* 13 (2): 86–106.

New York City Police Department. 2006. "Weekly MSA Report," November 22, http://hosted.ap.org/specials/interactives/documents/nypd-msa-report.pdf.

NIAA (National Institute on Alcohol Abuse and Alcoholism). 2002. *A Call to Action: Changing the Culture of Drinking at U.S. Colleges*, http://www.collegedrinkingprevention.gov/media/TaskForceReport.pdf. Accessed May 15, 2013.

———. 2012. "College Drinking," http://pubs.niaaa.nih.gov/publications/CollegeFactSheet/CollegeFactSheet.pdf. Accessed May 15, 2013.

NPR. 2011. "Childish Gambino is Trying to Be a Grown-Up," November 15. http://m.npr.org/story/142317100?url=/2011/11/15/142317100/childish-gambino-is-trying-to-be-a-grown-up.

Nussbaum, Martha C. 2012. *The New Religious Intolerance: Overcoming the Politics of Fear in an Anxious Age*. Cambridge: Harvard University Press.

Patel, Eboo. 2010. *Acts of Faith: The Story of an American Muslim, the Struggle for the Soul of a Generation*. Boston: Beacon Press.

Pedersen, Eric R., and Joseph W. LaBrie. 2008. "Normative Misperceptions of Drinking among College Students: A Look at the Specific Contexts of Prepartying and Drinking Games." *Journal of Studies on Alcohol and Drugs* 69 (3): 406–11.

Peshkin, Alan. 1986. *God's Choice: The Total World of a Fundamentalist Christian School*. Chicago: University of Chicago Press.

Pew Research Center. 2011. "The Future of the Global Muslim Population: Projections for 2010–2030," http://pewforum.org/The-Future-of-the-Global-Muslim-Population.aspx. Accessed May 15, 2013.

Purkayastha, Bandana. 2005. *Negotiating Ethnicity: Second-Generation South Asian Americans Traverse a Transnational World*. New Brunswick: Rutgers University Press.

Quantz, Richard A., and Peter M. Magolda. 1997. "Nonrational Classroom Performance: Ritual as an Aspect of Action." *Urban Review* 29 (4): 221–38.

Read, Jen'nan Ghazal. 2008. "Muslims in America." *Contexts* 7 (4): 39–43.

Renn, Kristen A. 2000. "Patterns of Situational Identity among Biracial and Multiracial College Students." *Review of Higher Education* 23 (4): 399–420.

Renn, Kristen A., and Karen D. Arnold. 2003. "Reconceptualizing Research on College Student Peer Culture." *Journal of Higher Education* 74 (3): 261–91.

Rodinson, Maxime. 2006. *Europe and the Mystique of Islam*. Translated by Roger Veinus. London: I. B. Tauris.

Rymes, Betsy, and Diana Pash. 2001. "Questioning Identity: The Case of One Second-Language Learner." *Anthropology and Education Quarterly* 32 (3): 276–300.

Sacks, Harvey. 1984. "On Doing 'Being Ordinary.'" In *Structures of Social Action: Studies in Conversation Analysis*, edited by J. Maxwell Atkinson and John Heritage, 413–29. Cambridge: Cambridge University Press.

Safi, Omid, ed. 2003. *Progressive Muslims: On Justice, Gender, and Pluralism*. Oxford: Oneworld Publications.

Said, Edward. 1978. *Orientalism: Western Conceptions of the Orient*. New York: Vintage.

———. 1993. *Culture and Imperialism*. New York: Alfred E. Knopf.

Sarroub, L. K. 2005. *All-American Yemeni Girls: Being Muslim in a Public School*. Philadelphia: University of Pennsylvania Press.

Schmidt, Garbi. 2004. *Islam in Urban America: Sunni Muslims in Chicago*. Philadelphia: Temple University Press.

Scott, Joan Wallach. 2007. *The Politics of the Veil*. Princeton: Princeton University Press.

Shachtman, N., and S. Ackerman. 2012. "U.S. Military Taught Officers: Use 'Hiroshima' Tactics for 'Total War' on Islam." *Wired*, May 10, http://www.wired.com/dangerroom/2012/05/total-war-islam/all/.

Shankar, Shalini. 2008. *Desi Land: Teen Culture, Class, and Success in Silicon Valley*. Durham: Duke University Press.

Sirin, Selcuk R., and Michelle Fine. 2008. *Muslim American Youth: Understanding Hyphenated Identities through Multiple Methods*. New York: New York University Press.

Skolnik, Sam, Daikha Dridi, and Paul Shukovsky. 2002. "Inquiry Targets Muslim Charities: WSU and U. of Idaho Groups Investigated." *Seattle Post-Intelligencer*, August 2, http://www.highbeam.com/doc/1G1-90049855.html

Smith-Hefner, Nancy J. 1999. *Khmer American: Identity and Moral Education in a Diasporic Community*. Berkeley: University of California Press.

Spencer, Robert. 2008. *Stealth Jihad: How Radical Islam Is Subverting America without Guns or Bombs*. Washington, D.C.: Regnery Publishing.

Spivak, Gayatri Chakravorty. 1993. *Outside in the Teaching Machine*. New York: Routledge.

Steinback, Robert. 2011. "Jihad against Islam." *Intelligence Report* 142, http://www.splcenter.org/get-informed/intelligence-report/browse-all-issues/2011/summer/jihad-against-islam#.UYXf5yvwJ6k. Montgomery, Ala.: Southern Poverty Law Center.

Stepan, Kate. 2003. "SJT Addresses Muslim Concerns." *GW Hatchet Online* April 24, http://www.gwhatchet.com/2003/04/24/sjt-addresses-muslim-concerns.

Stephens, Julie. 1990. "Feminist Fictions: A Critique of the Category 'Non-Western Woman' in Feminist Writings on India." *Subaltern Studies* 6: 141–61.

Sutton, Margaret, and Bradley A. Levinson, eds. 2001. *Policy as Practice: Toward a Comparative Sociocultural Analysis of Educational Policy*. Westport, Conn.: Greenwood Press.

Tatum, Beverly Daniel. 2003. *Why Are All The Black Kids Sitting Together in the Cafeteria? And Other Conversations about Race*. New York: Basic Books.

Turner, Janice. 2008. "Islam and the Great Cover-Up." *Times* (London), July 18.

Wadud, Amina. 2006. *Inside the Gender Jihad: Women's Reform in Islam*. Oxford: Oneworld Publications.

Walsh, J. 1991. "A Different Kind of Liberation: White Women Who Choose Islam Smashing the Stereotype of Oppressed Muslim Women." *San Francisco Chronicle*, November 3.

Waters, Mary C. 1990. *Ethnic Options: Choosing Ethnic Identities in America*. Berkeley: University of California Press.

Wechsler, Henry. 1996. "Alcohol and the American College Campus: A Report from the Harvard School of Public Health." *Change* 28 (4): 20–25, 60.

Wechsler, Henry, Toben F. Nelson, Jae Eun Lee, Mark Seibring, Catherine Lewis, and Richard P. Keeling. 2003. "Perception and Reality: A National Evaluation of Social Norms Marketing Interventions to Reduce College Students' Heavy Alcohol Use." *Journal of Studies on Alcohol* 64: 484–94.

Wechsler, Henry, and Bernice Wuethrich. 2002. *Dying to Drink: Confronting Binge Drinking on College Campuses*. Emmaus, Pa.: Rodale Press.

Weitzman, Elissa R., and Toben F. Nelson. 2004. "College Student Binge Drinking and the 'Prevention Paradox': Implications for Prevention and Harm Reduction." *Journal of Drug Education* 34 (3): 247–66.

Willis, Paul. 1981. *Learning to Labor: How Working Class Kids Get Working Class Jobs*. New York: Columbia University Press.

Wills, Emily R. 2011. "Political Discourse in Motion: Social and Political Contestation in Arab New York." Ph.D. diss., New School.

Wolfe, Alan. 2003. *The Transformation of American Religion: How We Actually Live Our Faith*. New York: Free Press.

Yoshino, Kenji. 2006. "The Pressure to Cover." *New York Times Magazine*, January 15, http://www.nytimes.com/2006/01/15/magazine/15gays.html?pagewanted=all.

———. 2007. *Covering: The Hidden Assault on Our Civil Rights*. New York: Random House.

Zine, Jasmin. 2000. "Redefining Resistance: Towards an Islamic Subculture in Schools." *Race, Ethnicity, and Education* 3 (3): 293–316.

———. 2004. "Staying on the 'Straight Path': A Critical Ethnography of Islamic Schooling in Ontario." Ph.D. diss., University of Toronto.

———. 2008. *Canadian Islamic Schools: Unraveling the Politics of Faith, Gender, Knowledge, and Identity*. Toronto: University of Toronto Press.

Index

Academics, 27; courses on the Middle East or Islam, 92, 101–2, 115–16

Agency, 9, 38–40, 111, 125

Alcohol culture, 23, 32–33, 47–51, 79; and academic events, 70–71, 76; and Arabs, 84; and being "normal," 48, 58; and friendships, 49, 52–53, 63–64; related to injuries and crimes, 49; resistance to, 67–71, 73–74; and semi-peripheral participation, 55–56, 59, 63, 85; and sexual activity, 62, 73–75; and South Asians, 82–84; and visibility of Muslims, 56, 60, 73, 86

All-American Muslim, 13

Amber, 4–5, 15–16, 61, 93, 114–15, 118, 166, 174

American identity of Muslims, 4–6, 13, 30, 157–58

Amira, 58, 61–62, 134, 146–47, 154, 176

Anti-Western identities, 41

Appropriation, 39–40, 72, 177–78

Authenticity of Muslims, 42, 148–50, 161–62, 180–81

Bend it Like Beckham, 2

Black Muslim women, 54, 118–20, 122, 124

Burqa, 95, 111

Chastity, 152–53; religious belief, 127; stereotype, 38, 155

Christian majority cultural practices, 25, 37, 44, 60, 176

Clothes, 12–13, 23–24; and othering, 103–7

College, 44, 126, 147, 179; "diversity showcase," 59, 61, 106, 170, 175; in loco parentis, 32; leisure culture, 19, 32–33, 49–50, 54, 67–68, 79, 81, 132, 151, 175, 177–78; peer culture, 23–24, 31–34, 90; and pluralism, 3–4, 14, 31, 45, 86, 116, 125, 170–71, 178–79

Conformity, 14, 25, 36–37, 59, 63, 86, 88, 100, 106, 127, 156, 176

Conservative Muslim, 20, 39, 66, 85, 137–39, 141–42, 145, 149–54, 160–64, 171, 175–76, 179

"Cool," 32, 61, 101, 106

Cultural accommodation, 4, 37, 58–59

Cultural assimilation, 4, 15, 39, 45, 48, 58, 96, 110, 116, 148, 151, 165, 173, 175, 178–79

Data analysis, 23–24

Dating culture, semi-peripheral participation in, 131–32

Da'wah, 97–98, 114, 138

Deculturalization, 40

Diya, 91, 93–94, 99

Dorms, 32, 134

Double consciousness, 15, 35

Drinking. See Alcohol culture

Elizabeth, 54, 63, 73–74, 79, 89, 113, 118–22, 151–52, 169

Essentialism, 15, 34, 40–42, 69, 85, 110, 170–72

Ethnography, 21–22, 34, 37, 42, 44, 104, 159, 182; and fieldwork, 8, 16, 25–27

Faiyza, 51, 59–60, 80, 142
Fatima, 47–48, 54–55, 64–65, 69, 117, 138–44
FBI, 13, 16
Femininity, 34–35, 123, 153, 170
Feminism, 10, 12, 23, 88, 94, 110–12, 114–15, 118, 168–69
"Fitting in," 1, 59, 75, 116
Foucault, Michel, 34, 35, 39, 167
Freedom, 28, 31, 39, 50–51
Friendship: with Muslims, 56, 59, 65, 79–81, 116–17; with non-Muslims, 54, 79, 84, 90–91, 108, 112, 118–20
Fun. See College: leisure culture

"Gatekeepers," 20–21, 108, 159, 162–64
Gaze: response to, 97, 100, 150–53, 179; and stereotypes, 34–35, 40, 88, 91, 110, 125–26, 156, 158
Gendered behavior: and alcohol culture, 73–74; and comfort with other sex, 165; and immigrants, 156–58; and limits, 135, 160; and location, 166; and Muslim Student Association (MSA), 159–64, 168; and non-Muslims, 147–49; public and private aspects of, 151–52, 156, 168; and risks to reputation, 134–36; and "talking," 140
Gender segregation and "mixing," 20, 151, 153, 157, 160–62, 164–67, 169–71
Georgetown University (Washington, D.C.), 15–17, 160, 162
George Washington University (Washington, D.C.), 1, 15–17, 160
Goffman, Erving, 15, 30, 36–37, 40, 42, 45, 48, 64, 68, 92, 99, 147, 152–53, 156, 163, 173, 181

Hadith, 120, 122–23
"Halal hedonism," 105
Haseena, 53, 66, 82–83, 96, 129, 145, 167

Heather, 51, 54–56, 69–70, 73, 93–95, 102–7, 118–19, 131–32, 138–39, 141–42, 149, 161, 166
Hedonism, 28, 31–32, 49, 68, 70, 101, 131, 133–34, 159, 173, 175
Hidden curriculum, 37–38, 175
Higher education. See College
Hijab, 2, 73–74, 78–80, 104–5; bans on, 111; decision about wearing, 110, 115–16, 121–22; and gender oppression, 87–91; and ideological change, 109–10; and marginalization, 90; and non-hijabis, 116–17; and non-Muslims, 94–97, 104–6; and religiosity, 93–94, 112; and visibility as Muslim, 7–8, 16, 92–93, 113–14, 124
Hindu American identities, 135
Hooking up, 131–32

Idealizations: of Muslim identities, 125, 153, 160, 163, 171; of Muslim image, 138, 151, 154–55; of "West," 35
Identity: ambivalence, 37, 75–77, 80; "covering," 36–37, 70, 86, 107, 139, 148, 175; integrating, 51, 80–81; playing down, 36, 83; "spoiled," 7, 38, 153, 176; "toning down," 36, 116
Iftar meal, 17–18
Immigrants, 9–10, 108, 119, 122–23, 128, 135, 141, 149, 152, 156; demographic shift, 17, 44–45
Indigenous American Muslims, 6, 10–11, 27
International students, 17–18, 47–48, 84
Intisar, 1, 99–100, 107, 150–55
Islamic identity, 160–61
Islamic Society of North America (ISNA), 10
Islamism, 10, 158, 161
Islamophobia, 7, 13–14, 178

Latifa, 31, 56, 70, 91, 99–102, 115, 125, 136, 160, 162
Leila, 95, 136, 143, 147, 158
Liberal Muslim, 66, 77–79

Loneliness, 74–75, 81

Mahnaz, 50, 77, 137
Marginality, 32, 45, 47–48, 50, 64–65, 84, 103, 132, 170
Marriage: arranged, 127, 141–44; early, 144–46; fear, 144–45; mate-seeking strategies, 124, 139–41; parents not wanting to set up, 143–44; prospects, 74–75, 128
Modesty, 11–12, 89, 105, 122–23, 127; ceremonious, 151
Musalla (Muslim prayer room), 19–20, 155, 168, 180
Muslim enclaves, 56, 78, 82, 85, 175–76
Muslim Interest Living Community (MILC), 19, 135
Muslim "middle ground," 137, 149–50, 160, 171
Muslims: acceptance by non-Muslims, 9–10, 57; collective public image, 114–15, 151–52, 155, 166–67; expectations of, 103–4, 116–17, 125; "extremes," 153–54; as homogenous, 115; as insular, 86, 175–76; and public unity, 114, 117–18
Muslim Student Association (MSA), 10, 17, 81–82, 119, 151, 164–65; conservative and liberal elements of, 20, 159–60, 162–64; influence by non-campus community, 20, 138

Nadira, 80–81, 135, 137
Neelam, 76–78, 144
Neo-fundamentalist Muslim identities, 41–42
Nightclubs, 14, 48, 66–67, 83–84, 96, 154, 162, 177
Non-Muslim Americans: assumptions about Muslims, 34, 94, 103–4, 165 (*see also* Stereotypes); ignorance of Muslim gender norms, 148; knowledge of Islam, 9–12
"Normal" identities, 37–38, 100, 105, 128, 150–51, 154

Orientalism, 6, 11–12, 27, 34–35, 38–39, 41, 110–11, 153, 182
"Outcast," 68, 85, 90, 154, 170
Outsider status, 36, 55, 63, 65, 67

Panopticon, 172
Parents, 77–78, 142, 145–47, 157, 166
Passing, 15, 37–38, 48, 90, 97, 103, 147
Policy: accommodation, 133, 171; informal, 33–34; university, 133–34, 177–78
Premarital sex, 128–29, 132, 167
Progressive Muslim, 42, 110, 114–16, 128

Qur'an, 95, 113, 115, 120, 122, 127

Race and ethnicity, and alcohol culture, 83–84
Racializing of Muslims, 6, 95
Racism, 3, 14, 169
Ramadan fasting, 17
"Religion-blind" attitudes, 45
Religious identities, 60; majority, 45; minorities, 45, 73; scholarship on, 43–44
Resistance, 39, 48, 61, 69, 70, 82, 100, 110–11, 127, 168
Romantic relationships, 131–32
Roshan, 67, 69, 81, 90, 97, 163

Sacks, Jonathan, 11
Said, Edward, 11, 35, 170
Salwa, 134–35, 154
Sarah, 48, 50, 59, 62, 66, 80–81, 113, 129–30, 150–51, 157
September 11, 2001, 7, 11–12, 14–16; post–September 11, 2001, 5, 7, 16, 30, 45, 58, 92, 127, 153
Sex. *See* Chastity; Gendered behavior
Sexual continuum, 128
Sharmila, 16, 71, 115, 123, 145, 161
Shyness, 34, 38, 98–99, 152
Sikh American identities, 45, 135
Sociability, 31–32, 48–49, 52–55, 59–61, 65, 68, 79, 178; shallow, 63–67

Social class status, 18–19, 43, 55, 104, 127, 156–57
South Asian American, 78, 82, 142, 152
Sports, 1–2, 108
Stereotypes: dodging, 99–100, 103, 108; of Muslims, 2, 7, 15, 34–35, 40, 58–59, 153, 163–64; Muslim appropriation of, 40, 150; of non-Muslims, 172; resisting, 57–58, 98, 100, 103–4, 156, 165, 182
Stigma, 1, 11, 14, 19, 30, 37, 59–60, 66, 73, 76, 80, 91, 107, 118, 144, 173, 176
Strategic essentialism, 168–69
Student academic concerns, 24–25
Sufism, 10
Suhoor meal, 17–18
Surveillance, 8, 13, 15, 35; self-surveillance, 35–36

Teaching non-Muslims about Muslims, 97–98, 103–4, 109
Tehzeeb, 66, 109–12, 154, 181
Teresa, 112, 140, 165, 168
Terrorism, 11–12, 15, 16
Third space, 6, 11, 41, 47, 51, 62, 66, 77, 100–101, 125, 127, 142

United States, and Christianity, 43
University. See College
ʿUrf, 116

The West, 6, 34–35, 42, 95, 110
White Muslim women, 70–71, 94–96, 103–4, 118, 140

Yasmin, 48, 52–54, 62, 75–76, 129, 173, 180

Zeinab, 12–13, 84–85, 91, 105, 156, 169